CREATIVE MOTION GRAPHIC TITLING FOR FILM, VIDEO, AND THE WEB

CREATIVE MOTION GRAPHIC TITLING FOR FILM, VIDEO, AND THE WEB

YAEL BRAHA
BILL BYRNE

AMSTERDAM • BOSTON • HEIDELBERG • LONDON • NEW YORK • OXFORD
PARIS • SAN DIEGO • SAN FRANCISCO • SINGAPORE • SYDNEY • TOKYO

Focal Press is an imprint of Elsevier

Focal Press is an imprint of Elsevier
30 Corporate Drive, Suite 400, Burlington, MA 01803, USA
The Boulevard, Langford Lane, Kidlington, Oxford, OX5 1GB, UK

Notices

Knowledge and best practice in this field are constantly changing. As new research and experience broaden our understanding, changes in research methods, professional practices, or medical treatment may become necessary.

Practitioners and researchers must always rely on their own experience and knowledge in evaluating and using any information, methods, compounds, or experiments described herein. In using such information or methods they should be mindful of their own safety and the safety of others, including parties for whom they have a professional responsibility.

To the fullest extent of the law, neither the Publisher nor the authors, contributors, or editors, assume any liability for any injury and/or damage to persons or property as a matter of products liability, negligence or otherwise, or from any use or operation of any methods, products, instructions, or ideas contained in the material herein.

Library of Congress Cataloging-in-Publication Data
Application submitted

British Library Cataloguing-in-Publication Data
A catalogue record for this book is available from the British Library.

ISBN: 978-0-240-81419-3

For information on all Focal Press publications
visit our website at www.elsevierdirect.com

10   11   12   13   14   5   4   3   2   1

Printed in China

Working together to grow
libraries in developing countries

www.elsevier.com | www.bookaid.org | www.sabre.org

ELSEVIER   BOOK AID
             International   Sabre Foundation

Dedication

Bill Byrne:

To my wife

Suzanne, for her love and support that makes everything I do possible.

To my brand-new daughter

Elinor, for being the most wonderful gift anyone could ever receive.

Yael Braha:

To all my friends, family, and colleagues that encouraged me throughout the writing and editing of this book. To the surrounding nature and animals that kept providing balance and a source of inspiration. In particular, I dedicate this book to Deny and Shannon, who enrich my life with creativity, love, strength, and courage.

CONTENTS

ACKNOWLEDGMENTS

Yael Braha:

Thank you

Jennifer Arvai

Jonathan Bardelline

David Bolt

Jackie Brady

Michael Braha

Jesse Brodkey

Eva Camarena

Heidi Goldstein

Steve Holmes

Jay Lamm

Dan Levinson

Terry Minkler

Spencer Nielsen

Stacy Nimmo

Synderela Peng

Ben Radatz

Sarah Reiwitch

Rock Ross

Rich Simon

Jacob Trollbäck

Bill Byrne:

My parents, Tom and Marie Byrne

My closest friends, Larry Caldwell, Jonah Goldstein, and Bryan Wetzel, for their advice and council

The Art Institute of Austin's Dean Carol Kelley and President Newton Myvett. The students in the Media Arts and Animation and Graphic Design departments, whose creativity and questions inspired many of the elements this book.

My colleagues at AI Austin, including Barry Underhill, who offered council and advice at the beginning of this process, and Luke Dimick, for allowing me healthy distraction time from this project by playing countless games of Words With Friends.

My co-author, Yael Braha, for a positive working experience despite the distance and breadth of this project.

Focal Press, Dennis McGonangle, and Carlin Reagan, who made all of this possible.

TITLE SEQUENCES: FUNCTION WITH FORM

You sit in a movie theater. The lights go down. The music and picture start. The opening titles fade in, and you know you're in for a journey! On the surface level, the primary purpose of title sequences is to accurately credit the cast and crew, or even more simply, to give the film's title. But if we dig a bit deeper, title sequences offer much more than that. In some ways, the function of a title sequence is very similar to the cover of a book. It not only gives the title and relevant authorship information; it also attracts the curiosity of the audience, encouraging them to open it up and start reading.

The music of title sequences could be compared to the concert overture of a classical musical performance or opera. A typical overture precedes the main performance by introducing the main musical themes. It is like a musical call for attention, as if to say, "Everyone! We are starting now! So hold onto your seats!"

Title sequences are a powerful expression of motion graphics. They are a prelude to the movie. They engage the audience by hinting at what is about to start, whether it's a movie, TV show, or Web animation.

The Purpose and Functions of a Title Sequence

One of the primary functions of a title sequence is to **set the tone** of the movie you are about to see. Even if you didn't know anything about the movie—and whether you are watching at a movie theater, at a TV in your living room, or at your computer— you get a sense of the **genre** and **pacing** of the movie simply by experiencing the first few seconds of an opening title sequence.

Imagine watching the opening title sequence of a horror film such as Zach Snider's **Dawn of the Dead** (1994), created by Prologue, versus a comedy-drama such as Jason Reitman's **Juno** (2007), with a title sequence created by Shadowplay Studios. Or imagine watching the fast-paced sequence made by Jay Johnson for David Lynch's **Lost Highway** (1997) as opposed to the calmer and dreamier pacing of the title sequence made by yU+co for Kevin Lima's **Enchanted** (2007). Even if you stumbled into any available room at a multiplex without checking the show title first, at the end of the title sequence you should know what genre you are about to experience.

Effective title sequences **engage and excite the audience** by hinting at some of the topics, themes, and, in some cases, the challenges that characters will be facing. The intention is to build anticipation, sometimes revealing some of the main character's traits and possibly setting the stage for questions that will be answered later in the movie. Successful title sequences create an emotional reaction from the audience, leaving them glued to their seats, waiting for more.

Effective title sequences **foreshadow** themes of the movie without overshadowing the movie itself: They anticipate what will come later in the movie but do not give away key plot points. Title sequences shouldn't summarize the plot of the movie or give away a perpetrator's identity that is supposed to be revealed only at the ending.

Sometimes a title sequence can be designed so ingeniously that it adds additional meaning, or, even better, exposes some details that are missing from the movie or could go unnoticed. Maybe the scenes that contained the specific details got cut; maybe the script wasn't developed enough, so the title sequences need to clarify a confusing detail; maybe the movie was taken in a different direction in the editing room; or maybe details were intentionally omitted in order to let them thrive in the titles.

At times, the most interesting and enduring title sequences offer the audience details whose significance will be revealed by the end of the movie or after a second viewing, such as the one created by Kyle Cooper for David Fincher's **Se7en** (1995).

While fulfilling these functions, the author(s) of a title sequence must visually capture the essence of the movie. You have an arsenal of **elements** at your disposal to accomplish this task. The following are some elements that as a designer and animator you will have to keep in mind while beginning to work on a title sequence:

- Typography
- Color palette
- Textures
- Lighting
- Camera/movement style
- Editing

Functions of title sequences:

- Set the tone, pacing, and genre of the movie
- Build anticipation
- Create an emotional response; engage and excite the audience
- Foreshadow without overshadowing the plot

- Imagery (video footage, still images, 2D or 3D animation)
- Styles/techniques (cell animation, CG animation, stop motion, video, match moving, etc.)

By carefully picking these elements, you are making a statement about the look and feel of your work and carefully directing the audience's emotional response toward the desired result. Before we dive into all these topics, we'll explore title sequence processes and their history.

Creative Process Overview

There is no set formula on how to create an effective and successful title sequence. Success depends on a variety of factors, including objective, strategy, and the target audience of a movie.

A common tool that will help you navigate through the myriad options, keep the project on target, and avoid pitfalls is to compile a **creative brief** after the initial meeting with the client. This necessary document will help maintain the focus of your work and identify the best possible creative solution for a given client or project.

Every designer should compile this document at the inception of a title sequence project and have it signed by the client. In larger agencies this document is generally prepared by a creative director and then given to the creative team, so that each member can keep the big picture of the project close by.

A typical creative brief might include all or some of the following sections: client and company/designer contact information, overview/background, objective, target audience, timeline, deliverables, and budget.

When working on larger projects that require large production teams, creative briefs could be quite elaborate and as long as 20 or 30 pages. For smaller projects, a creative brief of two or three pages is often sufficient.

To compile a creative brief, you'll want to meet with the client first, learn about the project, and then do as much research as possible. Part of this research includes:

- Watching the movie, TV pilot, or series (at least once!)
- Reading the treatment
- Reading the script
- Researching the themes and topics covered in the movie (this includes thorough audio/visual research)

Doing your homework will greatly affect your creative brief and the successful completion of your project.

Creative Brief in Depth

Here is a closer look at the common sections of a creative brief:

- **Client contact information.** Insert the client's name, phone number, and email address. Include the main contact person for this project; if there are multiple contact people, indicate the ultimate decision maker, the person who will sign off on your final project.
- **Project name.** Assign a name to your project (e.g., "*The Matrix* opening and closing title sequence").
- **Prepared by.** Insert your name, role, company name, date, and contact information.
- **Overview/background.** Provide a short overview of and background on the project.
- **Objective.** What is/are the main objective(s) you are trying to achieve? What strategies will you utilize to achieve these objectives?
- **Target audience.** Describe the primary and secondary target audience. Include any relevant information regarding demographics.
- **Timeline.** Insert your project's milestones. These are due dates that need to be established at the start of the project. Generally these dates are built forward in the calendar, from the actual date to the project's desired delivery date.

  However, if there is already a set due date because of a fundraising event, theatrical release date, or other reason, an easy solution to determine your milestones is to work your way back rather than forward. For example, if your delivery date is April 16 and today's date is February 1, you'll need to build all the milestones backward from April to February. That will give you a rough idea of how many days or weeks you'll have to work on each of your design phases. Besides giving you more negotiating power before starting a project, having a detailed timeline at hand will help you by forcing you to create a realistic plan of what can or cannot be done.

  Make sure that you reserve enough time for yourself or your team to complete the designated tasks. Most important, set deadlines for the client to provide feedback. A designer can do everything in her power to maintain her deliverables (e.g., three concepts for an opening title sequence by a set date), but if the client doesn't provide feedback (such as which one of the three concepts is the best) in a reasonable or designated timeframe, the designer is prevented from completing the next deliverable by its deadline.
- Another important step is to identify the client's deadline to deliver you a digital file with all the credits for the title sequence. More often than not, especially in smaller-scale projects, this is a task that is overlooked or left until the last minute, which could cause delays, especially when your project files require a long render time.
- **Deliverables.** Insert details on the exact deliverables that need to be delivered to the client, including file format, frame size, frame rate, color information, and video codec. Indicate whether there are any technical special instructions (such as alpha channels) or any practical instructions (for example, final deliverables must be sent to the film lab for a film-out).
- **Additional remarks.** Include any relevant information or special instructions received from the client that don't fit in the other categories. For example, you could list elements that the client wants or doesn't want to see in this project, such as specific fonts or color palettes.
- **Budget.** Indicate your compensation. This could be a flat fee, an hourly rate, or by accomplished task. When working for an hourly rate, indicate your estimated work hours per each milestone. It would be wise to also indicate the payment plan(s). Is there an advance? Will the payment happen after the deliverable of the final project? Or will there be multiple payments based on what's completed?

Typical Workflow Overview

Now that you are familiar with what should be included in a creative brief, and before moving forward, let's have a quick overview of a typical workflow. While creating a title sequence, a designer (or a creative team) will have to go through three major phases: preproduction, production, and postproduction. Each phase includes a variety of steps. These might be slightly different, depending on whether you are working for a company that has its own workflow in place or if you are working on a smaller-scale project on your own.

Typical steps in preproduction are:

- **Research.** Perform any necessary research prior to compiling a creative brief. Research can be carried out throughout the project, especially when researching reference images or while performing a fact or scientific check.
- **Creative brief** *(see above)*. After the creative brief is completed and approved by the client, the creative team can proceed in developing ideas, which will be consolidated into concepts to pitch to the client. A typical pitch might include a minimum of three different concepts. Each concept is generally presented to the client with (1) a treatment, (2) a storyboard, (3) style frames, and, optionally, (4) preliminary tests.
- **Treatment.** This is a paragraph describing the story and the look and feel of the concept. It is a good rule of thumb to summarize the action as it will be seen on-screen with one sentence per scene. After the description of the action is complete, you can spend a few lines talking about the look and feel of the title sequence: the color palette, textures, characters, sound effects, music, typography, camera movement, editing, and lighting.
- **Storyboarding.** A storyboard is a visual summary of the presented concept. Storyboards consist of rough visuals (generally hand-drawn) of key frames of the title sequence that summarize the story and the flow of the concept being presented. By pointing at their progression, the designer can talk through the key elements of the title sequence: how the story unfolds, the main action of any characters or talent type movement, camera movement, cuts, and so on.
- **Style frames.** A style frame is a still frame that is 80–90% identical to how the final title sequence will look. It could be created in a two-dimensional software (such as Illustrator or Photoshop) or in a two-and-a-half- or three-dimensional one (such as Cinema 4D or After Effects) and then saved as a still frame. Still frames are a necessary complement to the storyboard. Because the storyboards are generally hand-drawn, clients will have a better idea of the look and feel of the title sequence being pitched if they can see frame samples. A good number of style frames

ranges between 6 and 10, and ideally the frames should be picked throughout the title sequence, especially to visually represent a turning point or a change in the story visuals.

- **Preliminary testing (optional).** If time allows, it is definitely impressive to present a preliminary test in support of one or all concepts. A few animated seconds are sufficient to give the client an idea of the direction in which the concept is going. If time allows for only one preliminary test, I'd recommend picking the idea that the designer (or team) feels the strongest about and creating a test for it.

- **Pitch.** Once the concepts are completed with storyboards, treatment, and style frames, they are pitched to the client. By the end of the meeting, a client should be instructed to pick one concept. Often a client likes elements from Concept #1 and others from Concept #2. The task and challenge of a title designer is to satisfy the client's request while still maintaining the original creative vision.

- **Revised storyboards.** Once one idea has been picked, the creative team works on further developing the storyboard. A complete storyboard should include a frame for each cut, character or talent screen direction, visual cues to camera movements (including pan, tilt, dolly, ped, and zoom), title card numbering, dialogue, voice over, or any audio cues.

- **Preliminary testing.** Prior to devoting precious hours in producing the title sequence, any appropriate preliminary testing must be done to guarantee a smooth production and post and to avoid any unexpected roadblocks. This could include testing greenscreen live action keyed and composited onto animated backgrounds, any transitions that could be problematic, verifying the production and render time of particular shots, and so on.

- **Animatics.** Animatics are a preliminary motion animation that give a precise idea of the timing of the animation and type on-screen. The animatics could be presented to the client for approval and can be used as a guideline during the production phase to shoot or animate shots of the desired length. It is also a great way to test the animation with a soundtrack or voiceover in place, so that you can make sure that everything falls into the desired place. The animatics could be presented in the form of animated storyboards or, even better, an animation that could include preliminary testing and rough animation of the title sequence assets. If the title sequence requires live-action performances, you should consider shooting them (even with a low-resolution camera, without the high production value of a full crew) using substitutes for the talent you intend to cast in your actual shoot.

- **Live-action shoot preproduction.** Any location scouting, casting, permissions, and logistics must be dealt with around this phase of the project. Depending on the scope and budget of the project, this is a step that ideally requires a full film or video camera crew. The shoot's organization and logistics can be delegated to a producer or outsourced to a production company so that the title designer can keep focusing on the testing and preproduction of the title sequence.

Production:

- **Additional testing.** While getting ready for production, any testing that hasn't been performed must be done by now. Any unanswered questions should be dealt before beginning the title sequence production.
- **Live-action shoot (if applicable).** You should begin to film live action if your title sequence requires it. The title designer (or the art director or creative director of a motion design company) could act as director or even as on-set visual effects supervisor. It's a good idea to bring the animatics on set; a title designer could be involved to monitor the talent's performance and make sure it adheres to the action and timing of the animatics. Additionally, the cinematographer should have a deep understanding of the nature of the project so that he can frame, light, and compose the shots appropriately.
- **Creating and animating assets.** You should begin to create assets through illustration, modeling, and/or animation, if your title sequence requires it. If the workload is divided among various animators, modelers, or illustrators, an art director or creative director will make sure that all crew follow consistent style guides and guidelines so that the look and feel will be consistent throughout.

Postproduction:

- **Rough cut (offline editing).** In this step everything begins to come together. Live action, animation, title cards—all should be combined in a rough cut. A rough cut is a rough preliminary assembly of all assets of your title sequence, including sound.
- **Fine cut (online editing).** A fine cut is a refined version of a rough cut. Both editing and animation are tightened, and any placeholder assets need to be replaced with the final assets at full or "online" resolution.
- **Final deliverable.** This final step involves creating the final deliverable of your title sequence for your client. It could involve delivering a digital file—a QuickTime file, for example—or creating an edit decision list to conform the video to film, or even delivering an image sequence to create a film-out. You should make sure that the final project not only is delivered but also is received correctly; everything should be working, displayed, and playing back properly. Only then is your job over and you can begin working on your next one!

Title Sequence Positioning

You now have a client. You have a movie or animation to create a title sequence for. You have a creative brief and have started brainstorming or even storyboarding. Let's spend a moment thinking about how your title sequence could weave into the movie. The positioning of a title sequence within a movie or animation is an important factor to keep in mind and will affect the execution of your title sequence. A title sequence could be positioned:

- At the beginning of the movie (an opening title sequence)
- In the middle of the movie (generally after the first scene)
- At the end of the movie (a closing title sequence)
- At the beginning and at the end of the movie (an opening and closing title sequence)

1. **At the beginning of the movie.** This is a situation in which the movie or animation is short and does not include many credits, so the end credits are omitted and opening titles are created. Typically this is the case for early silent films, independent short films, and homemade movies. Other mainstream directors, such as Italian filmmaker Giuseppe Tornatore, also prefer adopting this approach; right after the main title card, they prefer to jump-start to the feature film instead of entertaining the audience with an opening title sequence.

2. **In the middle of the movie.** At times the opening title sequence could be placed in the middle of the movie, generally after the first scene. When the scene reaches its conclusion, that's generally when the opening titles begin. This is the case for the title sequence made by Big Film Design for **Intolerable Cruelty** (2003), directed by Joel and Ethan Coen, and the title sequence of **Delicatessen** (1991), directed by Marc Caro and Jean-Pierre Jeunet.

   This approach creates an unusual, unexpected, and direct beginning. The audience is not eased into the movie but is instead presented with a stark beginning. Only after the first scene has accomplished its goal of setting up the premise of the movie or introducing the main character can the audience relax, take a breather, and enjoy the title sequence.

3. **At the end of the movie: the main-on-end titles.** In the absence of an opening title sequence, the closing title sequence, also called the *main-on-end titles*, has a slightly different set of functions. In this case, the designer/animator will have to create such an engaging end title sequence that it will encourage the audience to keep watching instead of leaving the theater or turning their TVs off. The imagery and sound are not intended to introduce the movie but rather to create a closing statement. An effective main-on-end title sequence pulls the threads

of the movie together and offers the audience a moment of reflection while keeping them engaged and entertained. This is the case of the title sequence for **Iron Man** (2008), designed by Prologue.

4. **At the beginning and end of the movie.** This is the most common format. The opening sequence generally includes the main title and the names of the director, director of photography, various producers, and lead actors. The lengths of these titles vary depending on the movie; they could be as long three-and-a-half minutes, as in the opening title sequence made by Pic Agency for Peter Berg's **The Kingdom** (2007), or as short as the 30-second opening titles for Paul Thomas Anderson's **Magnolia** (1999). Opening title sequences for TV shows are generally shorter, catering to a shorter-attention-span audience and the tight limitations of airtime. The end title sequence generally includes all the credits from the opening titles plus the names of the rest of the cast and crew.

Title Sequence Style, Integration, and Transitions

How do you transition from the opening titles to the movie, and from the movie to the closing titles? This could appear to be a simple question with a simple answer, but it is indeed more complex. The most intuitive answer is to fade out the opening titles, then fade in the end titles. Although this is definitely a viable option, you should think outside the box and explore other options that could better facilitate the transition between titles to movie.

The options and eventual decision making for transitions are defined by the following factors:

• **How early in the production process the designer is involved.** Title designers who are involved at the very beginning of the project will have more creative options than those who start to work on the project when the movie is already completed and the picture locked. They will have a chance to discuss with the director the possibility of shooting extra footage to use in the title sequence. For example, simply shooting additional shots during principal photography, or even with a second camera crew, will provide additional footage for the designers to work with and guarantee that the look and feel decided on by the director of photography will carry through to the footage used in the title sequence.

• **How much rough material is available to work with.** This could be production still pictures, backstage footage, stills, footage from deleted scenes, or B-roll footage.

This approach can be very elegant and effective in its simplicity. A few issues to keep in mind are **readability, title placement** (in two-dimensional space but also in temporal space), and the **nature and quality of the footage**.

- **Readability.** The quality of the footage beneath a title card can affect its readability (for more details, see Chapter 3). For example, do the luminosity or color values change dramatically within one shot? To solve this issue, you can explore a variety of solutions that might enhance the titles' readability. Some effective and quick solutions are as simple as adding a subtle drop shadow, an outline, or even a faint glow to your text (see Chapter 4).

- **Title placement.** The placement of title cards over footage is quite important and deserves adequate time and attention to detail. You should examine the edited footage and determine whether there are any elements in the frame that are key pieces of information or other visual clues that need to come across to the audience. This could be as simple as an object or even the action of a person in the background. If that's the case, plan on placing your title cards so that they don't obscure any relevant visual information.

  On the other hand, if a focal point is already established in the footage, you'll need to decide how the type articulates on the screen. Is it complementing or contradicting it? If a title complements the focal point, most likely it can be placed close to it. If it is intended to create a tension with the focal point, it can be placed far away from it, so that the audience will have to work a bit harder and longer to decipher all the elements in the shot.

  How long a title is in place is important to consider as well. If you place a title card over a picture cut, it can be both visually jarring and can distract the audience from the title card, so the title card might require additional screen time. That can also make that picture edit more evident and therefore less invisible and powerful. A good rule of thumb is to keep a title card over a picture shot without overlapping its editing point. It can be shorter than or the same length as a shot but ideally not longer.

- **Nature and quality of the footage.** When you're examining the footage of an opening title sequence, you should pay particular attention to the nature and quality of the footage. Is the footage static, jittery, or a handheld shot? Are there any major camera movements (pan, tilt, boom, dolly, track), or are there any movements in the screen (a person or a car entering or exiting the frame)? If so, you might want to explore embedding the titles in the footage so that they appear to be in sync with the picture. If the footage is jittery, the titles will be jittery as well. To achieve this effect you could use a technical technique called *two-dimensional motion tracking*. You might also separate the titles from the footage, so if the footage is jittery, the titles stay still and the footage shakes. If there are any major camera movements or talent movements, you could attach a title to a particular movement (see **motion tracking** for a two-dimensional match, or **match moving** for a three-dimensional match)…or not! These are all possibilities to explore when you're creating titles.

Whatever the case, you might need to work on each title card individually to determine the best *placement* (without obscuring any relevant visual information), its best *typographical form* (to enhance its readability, depending on the background luminosity levels, color shifts, or content of the imagery and story), and its *duration and movement* (to offer an easy read to the audience by avoiding keeping a title card over a picture cut, and considering embedding or molding the title into the picture when appropriate).

Alternating Title Cards and Footage

Another viable solution is to alternate title cards with the edited picture. In this case the title sequence alternates a live-action shot, then a cut to a title card, then back to live action, and so on. This approach leaves the footage pristine and unaltered by any design or animation the title designer conceives. Each title card has a blank canvas and its own start and end time in which it can manifest as simple as static white type on black background or as elaborate typographic animations moving in and out of frame. This approach is particularly effective when a musical score is already in place, so the edits can be synced to music.

In **Requiem for a Dream** (2000), the transitions from the opening scene to the main title card and subsequent editing between shots of the movie and the title cards are particularly successful, especially with the amazing soundtrack composed by Kronos Quartet.

This is a solution that allows minimal manipulation of the edited picture. In a scenario in which the footage has been shot on film, the titles can be printed directly on the film (in a process called *film-out*), and once processed, the negative cutter can splice its negative together with the original film negative. When a digital intermediate is used, the titles can be provided digitally to the post-house, which will edit them with the entire sequence and then create a film-out.

Video-Based Title Sequence

If shooting an additional live-action sequence is a possibility, you might as well have a party. Joking aside, this is probably the most desirable situation. This option gives you complete freedom to brainstorm and sketch out a variety of design concepts to propose to your client: footage with superimposed titles, footage and motion graphics…the possibilities seem to be endless.

In Park Chan Wook's **Sympathy for Lady Vengeance** (2005), yU+co directs a wonderful title sequence. After she has spent 13 years in prison for the murder of a boy, the heroine of the movie, Geum-ja Lee, is able to find herself a bakery job and reunite with her daughter while plotting her revenge on the man who is really responsible for the boy's murder.

The title sequence visuals alternate shots of growing rose stems and thorns animated onto beautifully photographed white hands, extreme close-ups of serrated knife blades, and close-up shots of baking. While the title cards are composed with elegant text in both Korean and English, the main title card is created on-screen out of a light stream of blood superimposed over an extreme close-up of a hand's palm. The entire title sequence is dominated by white, minimal blacks, and red accents. The reds play a prominent role as the red of the rose flowers, droplets of blood, and red food coloring. The last shot is a close-up of a rose leaf that dissolves into an eye; the eye blinks, revealing red makeup on the eyelid, and the camera pulls out to reveal the close-up of a woman with a stark white face shedding a black tear, which generates the last title card crediting the director. The entire sequence is delightfully complemented by a harpsichord musical theme that is later coupled with a string orchestra.

The title sequence creates a dynamic tension between dark and light themes: The first shots that portray images of thorns, red droplets, and knives immediately evoke the feelings of danger and murder that the movie later explores. But these shots are later contradicted by editing shots of a knife blade cutting a soft sponge cake, and the red—once believed to be blood—is revealed to be food coloring. The juxtaposition of the same imagery used in different contexts to evoke different meaning and emotion creates a fantastic dynamic tension—the same one that is later developed in the film itself.

For this title sequence, Art Director Synderela Peng of yU+co went as far as creating hand casts of the chosen talents, filming them, and then animating the typography and rose stems in postproduction as well as directing her own baking shoot to obtain the footage needed for her title sequence.

Case Study: *Sympathy for Lady Vengeance*

Motion Graphics Studio: yU+co
Art Director: Synderela Peng
www.yuco.com

Preproduction. When we began the storyboarding process, I was very drawn to this image of a rose on a vine tattoo drawn onto the palm of the hand. During our phone call with the director Park Chan Wook (which required a Korean-to-English translator), he mentioned that he wanted to use the colors red and white. So we went forward with that simple design directive and presented two ideas. Director Park liked the vines a lot and asked for us to marry a few of the visuals from the other idea into it. The entire sequence was boarded out in detail, and once approved, we prepared for the shoot. The storyboarding phase was about two weeks (including revisions). Once the idea was signed off on, we had three weeks to shoot, composite, and deliver final. It was a quick turnaround.

Production. Sixty percent of the sequence comprised shots of the female body, painted bleach white, with these CG vines crawling and spreading. We had to go through a casting process to find a woman with a delicate hand and (per the director's request) a woman with eyes that matched the lead actress's. We ended up with two actresses. We brought in Scott Tebeau, a friend who won an Emmy for make-up in **Six Feet Under**, to create the casts and rigs that were needed to support the actor's bodies so they could hold these long poses without trembling and twitching.

Since we had to track the CG vines onto the bodies, it was important that there was minimal movement. Obviously, with the knowledge and the technology available to us now, it would have been fine if the bodies moved. But back then we were very restricted by our 10-day postproduction schedule and had to sacrifice some of that fluidity so as to get the job completed. The rigs and casts were crucial for that.

The supporting visual for the vines on the body was the cake. Since the movie narrative greatly revolved around the lead's experience out of jail as a pastry chef, the director wanted us to use a white cake as a metaphor for purity and introduce red for passion and vengeance. We asked another baker friend for a favor to help bake the cakes and create the white icing. There were a total of six cakes baked, followed by a lot of icing … the trick was to make sure they were heavy enough that they wouldn't melt under the lights. So none of the baked goods were edible.

We did run into a minor challenge with the shooting of the last scene. We asked (a very tall order) our eye model to cry on camera. Most of that footage looked too messy and too natural compared to our highly stylized sequence, so we opted for a clean plate and tracked a digital tear to run down her cheek. I am satisfied with the result we got but still wished we had more time to make that scene work better.

Postproduction. Once the shoot was completed, we began doing animation tests on the red vines. We used the paint effects module in Maya to generate the flowers and the crawling vines. While that was going on, the digitized footage (shot in HD with the Sony 900) was given to an editor to cut, to a Baroque trombone piece by Vivaldi. Meanwhile we started creating vine animation in Maya, followed by compositing of the vines in Shake.

I still hold this project very close to my heart because it was a labor of love. We had a small budget to work with but managed to make it work. Ultimately, anything that involves creative prop making (cakes, for example) will make for good stories.

Animation-Based Title Sequence

In **Cirque du Freak** (Paul Weitz, 2009) we enter a journey in perpetual movement. A spider web holds letters by a thread; they transform into a face whose mouth leads us into a graveyard, which reveals the spider that evolves into the hands of a puppeteer (Mr. Tiny, the bad vampire in the movie) controlling two shadow-puppet boys as they become part of a chase scene through circus settings and surreal landscapes sprinkled with ominous trees, bats, and vampires. A tree trunk that becomes a waist and teeth becoming stair steps should be transformations of no surprise. "The journey of the two boys gave us a way to interweave all the characters they pass along the way, such as the Bearded Lady, Octa the Spider, Monkey Girl, and Snake Boy. The features of these characters are used as transitional devices that cleverly transform into other images to keep the action moving along from scene to scene," says Garson Yu in an interview with Videography. Yu is the Creative Director and founder of yU+co, who directed this title sequence.

All along this title sequence the letters are hand-drawn as though they were engraved in wood. The film's credits are artfully woven into the animation of each title card; titles are engraved onto tombstones, they appear on the spider web threads, they are embedded in the marionettes' strings, and they interact with the boy puppets. Moreover, Yu says, "I also wanted to invent a new way of seeing how the credits behave. If you see the credits as actors on stage instead of just titles in the foreground, then we can imagine them to do anything that you want them to do as long as you direct them. They can dance and they can interact with the characters. In this case, they are truly the actor on stage with the puppets."

Black stylized graphics and characters inspired by German Expressionist woodcut prints and paintings dominate the frames, coupled with a color palette of muted blues, oranges, and green accents. Subtle organic textures such as ink splatters are orchestrated throughout the title sequence, while the camera flows fluidly from title card to title card.

The title sequence is accompanied by a thrilling orchestral soundtrack; minimal sound effects emphasize the tension, dark humor, and ominous mood of the title sequence and the film.

Other notable animation-based title sequences include those of **Monsoon Wedding** (Mira Nair, 2001), designed by Trollbäck+co; **Intolerable Cruelty** (Joel and Ethan Coen, 2003), created by Big Film Design; **Lemony Snicket's A Series of Unfortunate Events** (Brad Silberling, 2004), created by Jamie Caliri, and **The Kite Runner** (Mike Forster, 2007), created by MK12.

Text as Character

Panic Room (2002), directed by David Fincher, opens with shots of Manhattan and slowly moves through New York all the way through the Upper West Side of the city, where the movie unfolds. Embedded in the shots of the city's buildings appear the gigantic titles, floating in air. They hover ominously over the city while they match the adjacent building perspectives and lighting, giving the impression that they are not merely "guests" of the scenes; they have actually gained an important role in it. Not only do they look like they belong to the city's architecture, but their prominence and stance in the frame almost suggest that they are treated as talents on-screen. Computer Cafe artist Akira Orikasa explains: "The titles themselves are constructed and fit so that they appear to be real and near but not attached to building façades. It was important to light and composite them so that the light shining on each title matches the lighting in the scene."

Because most of the film takes place in a claustrophobic interior location—the house that gets broken into, and its panic room—this opening title sequence, which features these vast exterior cityscape shots coupled with menacing titles, not only creates an interesting contrast but visually introduces the themes of this impenetrable architectural structure where the movie will unfold, while emotionally introducing the tense mood the audience will experience in the film.

William Lebeda, Picture Mill's creative director, explains in an interview with DVD talk: "[Fincher's] main concern was to add some scope to the film. It starts outside in the middle of the day, but the bulk of movie takes place in the middle of the night over a short time inside the house. A lot of it takes place inside the panic room. He really wanted to have a sense that it's in New York. It ends outside as well, so he really wanted to bookend the film outside."

Picture Mill and Computer Cafe worked together to create this powerful and elegant title sequence. David Fincher had the idea to use type, maybe floating in air. So, Lebeda digitized some of the production stills, and after importing them into 3D software, he added type in a variety of perspectives and fonts while keeping Fincher's inspiration in mind throughout the process.

After the title sequence's concept was approved, Fincher's production crew left for New York to shoot the production plates, and they returned with a variety of high- and low-angle shots. The sequence was edited in a rough cut and the typographical elements had begun to be composited, but Fincher wanted to create some camera movements that didn't exist in the original footage, so the team realized that some of the shots needed to be reconstructed in 3D. Computer Cafe utilized IMAX still pictures of the building—which were shot as a reference for the building in the background, in case they needed to be recreated—in a technique called *photogrammetry*. This method allowed them to reconstruct the geometry of the buildings in 3D and then move the camera around them. The final title sequence resulted in a combination of original film footage and 3D textured objects.

After considering a number of typefaces, the chosen font for this title sequence was a modified version of Copperplate because "It looked more like New York. That font fit the buildings better and didn't take away from them. It looked important," explains David Ebner, president and digital effects supervisor of Computer Cafe.

Figure 1.1 Title Card from "Panic Room" (2002).

Combining Footage and Motion Graphics

Gareth Edwards directs a gorgeous title sequence for the BBC series **How We Built Britain** (2007). As far as the creative process, he proposed eight different concepts, which didn't quite win the client over. By the end of the meeting, with an increased understanding of the scope of the project, Gareth pitched the winning idea: designing the letters of the show's title as buildings spread across Britain's landscapes. The letters would showcase the architectural styles explored in the series that spanned a thousand years of British architecture: medieval castles and churches, Scotland's buildings, Georgian houses, Victorian buildings, and modern skyscrapers.

Gareth sifted through BBC's aerial video footage and selected some shots that would be appropriate for the concept. He tracked the footage using Boujou and composited on it the modeled and textured giant 3D letters he created with 3D Studio Max.

Figure 1.2a Title Cards from "How We Built Britain" (2007).

Figure 1.2b

Figure 1.2c

Figure 1.2d

Figure 1.2e

Figure 1.2f

Figure 1.2k

Figure 1.2l

Figure 1.2m

Figure 1.2n

Figure 1.2o

Figure 1.2p

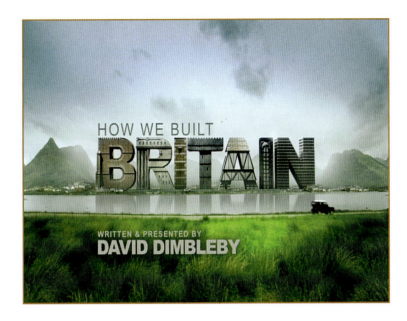

Figure 1.2q

The sequence begins with a view behind a Jeep starting a journey on a desolate road. As the orchestral score builds and the cuts begin to be synced to music, we see a wide shot of an odd castle. Just to clear any doubts, the camera cuts in to confirm that what we are seeing is indeed the letter B. All other letters, R-I-T-A-I-N, are slowly revealed across the landscape in a variety of architectural styles that increasingly become more modern.

Throughout the piece we do not lose touch with our Jeep, which, as a narrator, is guiding us to explore all these landscapes and buildings in first person. The use of point-of-view shots from inside the Jeep reinforces the feeling that it is indeed the viewer who is the hero conducting the journey; this technique projects the audience into the story—not as a spectator but as the story's hero.

The final shot reveals the entire title *BRITAIN*, composed of the individual letters/buildings arranged neatly in a British skyline, while our Jeep crosses the screen, revealing the director's credit.

Other notable title sequences that employ video and motion graphics include **Run, Lola, Run** (Tom Tykwer, 1998) and **Stranger Than Fiction** (Marc Forster, 2006), created by MK12.

Escamotage: Alternative Transitions

A clever example of a nontraditional transition between the title sequence and the movie is the one created by Imaginary Forces for the movie **Dead Man on Campus** (1998), directed by

Alan Cohn. This film is a dark comedy that centers on two students who, after learning about a college clause stating that if your college roommate commits suicide, you are awarded A's for the semester, decide to find the most suicidal student on campus to live with them.

This title sequence, led by creative director Peter Frankfurt and art director Karin Fong, revolves around a SAT (Suicide Aptitude Test), an exam in which the film's credits are embedded among the multiple-choice questions, diagrams, and illustrations, created by Wayne Coe. The visual imagery and text formatting are without doubt reminiscent of the college test iconography, and the sequence progresses fluidly from one title card to the next, reproducing typical suicidal scenarios coupled with multiple-choice questions, wrapped in a comical veil that preludes the dark comedy themes of the movie. Shots are tightly edited on the beat of a soundtrack by Marilyn Manson, whose lyrics hint at the irony of the title sequence. The color palette consists of the white background of the test paper, black type, and orange text accents and a blue background of the main title card.

One of the powerful aspects of this title sequence is its transition. By the end of the test—after the last title card dedicated to the film's director—we see a stop sign coming to full screen, we hear a camera-flash sound, the screen flashes to white, and we see the first shot of the movie, a close-up of a student whose picture is being taken for a library card. This transition has a strong audio and visual component that directly catapults the viewer from this animated title sequence into the live action of the movie, without a blink.

A Story Within a Story

In other situations, opening titles need to provide a bridge between the audience and the film. There is nothing more frustrating for an audience than to be distracted, especially during a documentary, because they don't know the background sufficiently to follow the story. Creating an opening sequence that offers the audience a basic historical or cultural background needed to properly enjoy the movie often bridges this gap.

Take a look at the title sequence of **The Kingdom** (2007). This Middle East action thriller directed by Peter Berg needed an opening title sequence to set up the movie and give it a political and historical context. Berg commissioned Pic Agency to handle the task. Creative director Jarik Van Sluijs, art director Stephan Burle, and producer Pamela Green created a 3-minute, 20-second opening title sequence presenting an audiovisual historical excursus of the controversy between Saudi Arabia and United States over oil during the last 80 years.

This sequence summarizes the political and historical events that unfolded from 1932 to 2001 by editing archival audio and video footage, by animating motion graphics summarizing key plot points, and by elegantly displaying simple typography on-screen. Nervous upbeat music underlines seamless transitions from video footage to three-dimensional graphic imagery, maps, graphics, timelines, charts, and pull quotes on-screen. The color palette of this title sequence focuses on desaturated reds, greens, and yellows; these muted colors help to not only achieve a historical look but to maintain a uniform look between all the different source video footage sizes and compressions, from VHS to 16 mm.

Producing this opening sequence took nine months. Pic Agency wrote their own script and dedicated countless hours to researching archival audio and video footage. Once the 128 shots were selected, it took another long effort to obtain their clearances, from CNN to the Saudi Arabia government. They even performed additional interviews for the sequence's voiceover.

It is clear that this opening title sequence contains the essence of motion graphics and filmmaking: storytelling, entertaining, information, and design. "Symbolize and summarize," as Saul Bass said. By the end, this opening sequence has offered the audience the necessary information in an exciting and compelling way. They are now ready for the film to begin.

Other notable "story within a story" title sequences include **Catch Me If You Can** (Steven Spielberg, 2002) and **Lord of War** (Andrew Niccol, 2005).

Pulling the Threads

The end titles for **An Inconvenient Truth** (2006) are one-of-a-kind. This powerful documentary, directed by Davis Guggenheim, deals with the issue of climate change and global warming. Al Gore plays a central character as he reveals necessary information through his traveling public presentations, interviews, and reflection on his life and politics.

After watching this emotionally compelling film, most viewers might ask themselves the question: "Yes, but what can *I* do?" And the answer is provided by the end titles. Elegantly designed by yU+co, the end titles provide practical tips on what to do to start positively affecting climate change on an individual and community level. Suggestions such as "When you can, walk or ride a bicycle" are interspersed with the film's credits, to a soundtrack of Melissa Etheridge singing "I Need to Wake Up." Transitions from one title card to the next are elegantly executed by leaving a few letters on-screen a bit longer so that they become part of the next title card.

Depending on the type of movie you are working with (home movie, independent flick, Hollywood movie, or something else), the order in which the credits in opening and closing titles appear on-screen and their font size, especially in large-budget productions, are greatly determined by the talent's contracts, union contracts, and industry conventions. The designer will have very little (if any) say in that. For example, a clause in a talent's contract might dictate that his credit shouldn't be in a smaller font size than the one of the main title card. A different clause in another talent's contract might dictate that her title card be the first one, regardless of who else acts in the film.

Also, depending on the film's domestic and international distribution, you might have to composite different studio logos at the head of your title sequence. Or you might even have to deliver a version of your title sequence without any text so that English titles can be replaced by titles in another language.

As you're approaching designing a title sequence, you should obtain any pertinent information about the talent or distribution contracts that might affect the title cards' order or text size.

Avoiding Typos

Typos are the one mistake you want to avoid while working on a title sequence. After you worked long and hard on a film or a TV show, would **you** want your name to be spelled wrong? I don't think so. The following are a series of tips that will help you avoid a number of headaches and keep your clients happy.

- Ask the client to give you a digital file containing the typed credits of the movie, with numbered title cards. For example:
  1. XYZ logo
  2. ABC logo
  3. DFG production presents
  4. A film by First Name Last Name
  5. With First Name Last Name
  6. And First Name Last Name
  … and so on.
- Avoid typing anything else; use only the typed information with which you've been provided.
- Copy and paste the names from the file the client provided you with into the software you're using to create the title cards.
- Check the titles often for accidental letters you might have inserted from using common keyboard shortcuts (for example, in Illustrator, watch out for extra *t*s from using the Type tool or *v*s from using the Selection tool). When you are pasting your title card text in your software and then pressing a keyboard shortcut, it's possible that instead of changing to a different tool you are actually typing an unwanted letter in the text box.
- When you're ready to show your title cards to your client, send the actual stills of your project file for review. Don't send an early version or alternate versions; simply send the stills taken from the latest version of the actual project you are working on. There are a number of quick ways to accomplish this task. You could take a snapshot of the title cards directly from the software interface or from your rendered QuickTime file, or you could even export a digital still frame from your software and then email or fax it to your client for approval.

The Video and Film Workflow

Depending on whether your movie has been shot on film, video, or CG animation, there are a number of possible workflows though which you will be able to deliver an accurate, foolproof title sequence that will match the client's desired specifications. To make an informed decision on the right workflow, when you're beginning to work on a title sequence you must ask your client these simple questions, the answers to which will better guide you in the creative process:

1. **What is the source format?** If your title sequence requires the use of previously shot video or film footage, you must find out its source format.
2. **What is the deliverable format?** Knowing the destination and platform of your title sequence at the inception of your project will determine a variety of factors, including the size and resolution of your project, aspect ratio, and frame rate, to mention a few.

   If your direct client or contact person doesn't know the answers to these questions, find people working on this project who do. Here are a few tips that will help you through your project:

1. **Any assets produced for the title sequence must be created at the adequate frame size.** If you need to hire a photographer or videographer to shoot additional assets, you need to communicate to them the resolution at which they need to be shot. If you are planning to do some work that requires **panning and scanning** in postproduction, you'll need to shoot at a higher frame size than the final output size.

Table 1.1 Common Frame Sizes

Width (Pixels)	Height (Pixels)	Screen Aspect Ratio	Description
640	480	4:3	An early standard for analog-to-digital video editing
720	480	4:3	NTSC DV and DVD image dimensions
720	486	4:3	NTSC SD video dimensions used for professional digital formats such as Digital Betacam, D-1, and D-5
720	576	4:3	PAL SD video dimensions used for digital formats such as Digital Betacam, D-1, and D-5 as well as DVD and DV
1280	720	16:9	HD video format
1920	1080	16:9	Higher-resolution HD video format
1828	1332	1.37	Cineon half resolution
3656	2664	1.37	Cineon full resolution
2048	1556	1.32	Film 2K resolution, used when printing half resolution onto 35 mm film with a film-out recorder; it offers a more affordable price than 4K resolution
4096	3112	1.32	Film 4K resolution, used when printing high resolution onto 35 mm film with a film-out recorder

If so, you will need to clarify with your client whether you need to create two different title sequence versions (one for HD, the other for SD) or if you need to create only one title sequence that will work for both the HD and SD versions; in this case the titles will be designed a bit more centered on-screen, not reaching the right and left margins to avoid being cut off during the HD-to-SD format conversion.

Film Process and Transfer: The Digital Intermediate Process

Digital intermediate (DI) is a process that might be necessary while working on your title sequence if your project requires transposing your source footage from one medium to another—from digital video to film, for example, or from film to video and from film to digital, then back to film.

A typical digital intermediate workflow consists of three steps:

1. **A film scanner scans the original film negative frame by frame.** A typical scanner, such as the Arriscan, flashes each frame with a red, green, and blue light, and each frame is captured on a sensor as a "raw" file that is uncorrected. Based on an EDL (edit decision list) provided by the editor, the film scanner is capable of identifying and selecting each original roll of film to find the exact start and end frame of each needed shot. The scanning process varies from facility to facility and might offer a variety of image resolutions (2K, 4K, 6K; the higher the value, the sharper the image) and color bit depths (such as 10 bits per color channel). Each scanned frame is then recorded onto a hard drive and is numbered sequentially.

2. **The image sequence is conformed and manipulated.** The scanned film frames are delivered to the title designer as an image sequence so that titles can be composited over the footage. This is also the appropriate time to perform any necessary special effects or color corrections. Look-up tables (LUTs) are frequently used to make sure that the footage will match both the digital projector and the print film stock of choice. Once all the manipulation is completed, the image sequence needs to be prepared and exported so that it can be printed back onto film.

3. **The image sequence is printed back onto film (film-out).** This step involves the use of a film printer, which reads the information of each digital frame and uses a laser to engrave it frame by frame onto a film roll.

Depending on the project you are working on, there might be slight variables to this workflow. For example, if you are working on an opening title sequence that requires titles superimposed over the picture, a film lab will be requested to scan only the opening sequence (rather than the entire film!) so that once you complete your job, the sequence can be printed back onto film and spliced with the rest of the original negative.

Also, depending on the project, the digital intermediate could be performed only through its first part (film scanner scans the original film) or its latter one (film printer prints onto film).

Table 1.2 will help you understand the general video and film workflows while working on your titles.

Table 1.2 General Video and Film Workflows

Source	Working Format/Process	Final Deliverable
1. Digital video	Digital video	Digital video
2. Film	Digital intermediate	Digital video
3. Film	Digital intermediate or film	Film
4. Digital video	Digital video	Film

1. **If your source is digital video and your final deliverable is digital video,** your best bet is to work in digital video as well. Before you begin working on your title sequence, you should make sure that the source footage is of equal or higher image resolution than your final deliverable. If your source footage is lower resolution, you must immediately notify your client that higher image resolution footage is needed to avoid the final deliverable being blurry or pixilated—unless your creative plan is to heavily manipulate the source footage so that the low quality of the footage will be unnoticed.

2. **If your source footage is film and your final deliverable is digital video,** you must go through the first half of the typical digital intermediate workflow. The film will need to be digitized and delivered to you so that you will be able to start working on it at your workstation. When the titles are completed, you can export the final digital deliverable using the requested frame size and codec.

3. **If both your source footage and your final deliverable are film,** you could either remain in film or go through a digital intermediate workflow. If your client decides to continue to work in film, two options are to (a) create titles with an animation stand, shoot them on film, and then splice them onto the film's

to see, what works really well, when someone overdoes it, when it wears out its welcome, and when it's just right. When that works—when it's just right—it's sublime and transcendent. That's what remains with me—the good stuff.

Can you talk about your creative process when working on titles—from the early inspiration through development and to the final deliverable?

Usually filmmakers have a pretty good idea of what they want. Very often they direct you, or they will have an art director who will direct you, and I just follow the directions they give me or use the artwork they give me. When they have the artwork for the titles all done, ready to go, they might simply email it to me and tell me: "I want this seven seconds, no fades." I want them to give me a log, the order they want me to shoot them in, how big they want the titles in the frame, if they want a colored gel, if they want white type on black or red on black, for example.

Sometimes some people say, "I just want simple titles, white on black, here they are. Easy to read. I want them to be TV safe." And that's it. They won't tell me what their film is about; they'll say, "Shoot each title 10 seconds long and I'll cut them and I'll do the fades, and I'll decide how long they are going to be." Sometimes I don't even meet the filmmaker; it will be over the phone or email. They'll just email the file, their credits and titles, and I get to pick out the typeface, the typesetting, and shoot the titles.

But sometimes people give me a lot more creative freedom. They might say: "This is what I want, help me realize it. Here's the theme, here's the mood, here's the music I want for the main titles. You can be creative and make something dynamic, and make something subtle." And that's always fun to do. For example, I could do multiple passes, like having titles burn in on top of objects that are from the film: a leather jacket, or a bowl of onions, a wall, a knife or a gun, or a tire.

That's fun, laying an object down on the animation stand, like a leather jacket, and lighting it creatively with gels, and leaving a spot for the title to burn in and out of.

Or to go and shoot something that you know is going to be used for the titles. You go and shoot it with a precise plan in mind, then come back to the studio, and without processing it, you back up the film and burn in the titles on top of the live action that you've shot: that can be incredibly inexpensive and really satisfying. It's great to make something that looks good and satisfying to the filmmaker.

Figure 1.7 Rock Ross examining a 16mm film at his light table.

Can you elaborate on your creative process when you are given total creative freedom?

If a filmmaker wants me to do the creative part of the titles, I'll ask them a lot of questions. I want to see their film's work in progress, so I can study the colors and the mood of the film and try to accentuate that mood, or complement it, expand the mood of the music or of the opening scene. I need to get a feeling for the film, so I can pick a typeface and make the titles look right. Also, I pay attention to the pacing of the film—if it's moody or if it's peppy.

If someone is thoughtful, they can save themselves lots and lots of money by giving me a perfect log saying exactly how long the screen should be black, when the titles should pop on, how long they should be up, how long fades should be.

If they can give me a log like that, they've saved themselves many hundreds of dollars, instead of saying, "Shoot each one 10 seconds." They should just ask me to edit the titles in camera and then they're done. And for the end title crawl they should know how long they need them to run.

Can you talk about readability when you are working with your title sequences?

As a screen time guideline for readability, I generally calculate about a second per word, not including articles—the *a*'s or *the*'s or *is*'s.

The most important thing is that the titles can be read. Why have information up there if you can't read it or if it's gone too quick or if it's too tiny to read or if, when they transfer it to video or digital, it starts falling apart?

I like simple, clean fonts that are easy to read and big and bold when they are up there on-screen. If they are going to burn through objects, they must burn through well, nothing too delicate or stylized that is hard to read. They shouldn't have elements that are too fragile. If you expose the film stock for the fragile elements of the titles, the big ones become bold and hot, and if you expose for the bold elements, the fragile ones fade out and they are almost indecipherable. Titles have to be clean and neat, I think—nothing too stylized.

For the titles of my own films, very often I use a tip and I scratch them directly into the film's emulsion, so they appear to be panning across the frame. I like that look. And it's easy to read, too, it's like scanning down a sentence.

Do you work on your titles with the score/ soundtrack already in place? If so, how does that affect your work?

If the filmmaker has the music in mind that sets up the mood of the film, I can listen to that music and try to shoot the titles so that they are a complement or a juxtaposition of the music.

If there's peppy, wild music, sometimes it's nice to have slow, atmospheric titles. Sometimes it's nice to have a surprise, to have it be a different look. They seem to complement each other if they are different looking.

Figure 1.8 A film strip from "Thoughtless", a 16mm film by Rock Ross made with press-type and hand painted.

And sometimes the opposite can be very effective, too. Sometimes it's nice to have peppy titles and peppy music. You can do all kinds of nice stuff—popping titles on with a slow fade-off, and you can cut right to the beat.

Do you do any preliminary tests before you shoot your titles?

I've been designing titles for so long, I don't have to shoot preliminary tests anymore unless it's something I've never done before. I've got tests for all types of situations, both in 35 mm and 16 mm film: top lit and bottom lit, and any combination of top lit and bottom lit titles, burn-throughs, titles on top of all kinds of things.

Since I've got all kinds of tests, I can usually get the titles right the first time I shoot them. And almost every time I shoot a job, I shoot a test at the end of the setup, a wedge, half stops all the way through. When I have the finished film titles, I usually get a mid-light workprint, and if it doesn't look right, then at least I'll have a reference to do it again if I have to.

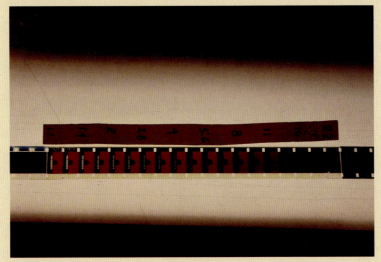

Figure 1.9 Wedge test.

Usually, color negative has a wide enough latitude that you can get it right the first time. There's some wiggle room for exposures in color negative. Hi-con film, which a lot of titles are shot in, has pretty much one or two f-stops [of latitude] and that's it. It has to be really hot [in terms of exposure] in order for the black to be rich and dark and the whites to burn though crisp and clean.

I did something recently with a bunch of broken windshield glass. A client brought in a big box of windshield glass—they wanted it bottom lit with other little pieces of glass in there, and they wanted the titles to burn through on top of that; top lit and bottom lit. So I had to do a test for that. They came out looking pretty nice.

Do you have any recommendation is regard to font size when working with 16 mm or 35 mm film?

I'd say nothing smaller than 12 points. And, you know, it could be enormous if the title of the film is *Yo*, or *M* ... so you can fill a frame. Sometimes people want their titles to look so big that they are going out of the frame but you can still read it, just so it looks kind of ridiculously huge.

What's a typical length of a project?

Usually the turnaround is one day to shoot the titles. Once I get the name credits, I'll take them to a typesetter, and they'll output them to film negative the same or next day. Then I can bring them back here and do all the artwork, prepare it to make it camera-ready, and shoot it. If the client brings me the film negatives, the codaliths, then I can do it that same day. I cut them out; if they are bottom lit I mount them on paper animation cells with black tape, put them on the stand, add colored gels. I can do it in a day, unless it's a subtitled project or a longer and more elaborate project.

Then the film will be processed at a film lab. Wait for it to come back—about a week sometimes—and then you can look at it and call the client and tell them to come and get them.

The client needs to proofread it because very often I'll shoot something and they'll go: "Oh my God, I misspelled my mother's name! She gave me the money [to do the film]," so I'll have to do it again, and if it's a crawl, I'll have to do the whole thing again.

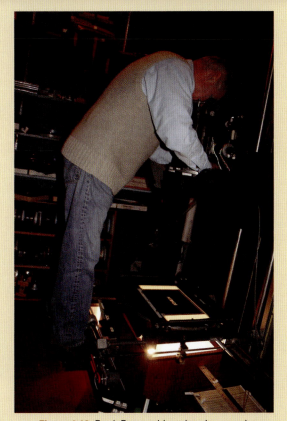

Figure 1.10 Rock Ross at his animation stand.

How do you control the kerning and leading of your titles?

It used to be, when I was using press-type—Letraset—you'd have to do it all yourself by eye, but now you don't have to do that much work anymore. Very often the typesetting equipment does a good enough job that doesn't need adjusting too much.

Sometimes, though, I will still do some kerning myself. If the main title doesn't look right—if it looks crowded, for example—I'll just cut it up and space the letters using black tape and make it look a little better, not so crammed. Or separate lines a little, just so that looks more balanced and fits in the frame neatly.

What are the most challenging aspects of your work?

My experience has been that by the time independent filmmakers get to do their titles, they are frustrated, stressed out, broke, and very impatient. So you've got to be patient with them, and you've got to work with a tiny budget. You try to give a great production value for very little money. And that requires putting on your thinking cap and using a lot of elbow grease, and making it look as good as you can.

It's always a challenge, and it's going to be satisfying if you can take all these discomforts and still come out with a good job. It's more satisfaction if it's a hard job, and you do it anyway and quickly deliver those good-looking titles. And then, of course, the tough part after that is getting paid.

Figure 1.11 Rock Ross at his animation stand.

What are the most rewarding parts of your job?

Well, if you go to a film's premiere and they have a great reception, they have a good audience, if the film was great and titles look great, that's satisfying.

How many movies do you think you have worked on, as a filmmaker and as a title designer?

Thousands. I've kept all the invoices that I've sent people, and I thought that maybe one day I'd get all the client's names and put them all together in a title sequence.

2

A BRIEF HISTORY OF TITLE SEQUENCES

Early Titles

The first examples of title sequences can be found in silent films. These consisted of simple, nonanimated title cards that informed the audience of the main film title, crew credits, and talent credits; they were usually placed at the very beginning of a movie.

Early title cards—often created by lettering artists employed by major studios—typically presented white type on a black background, but they soon included some minor decorations such as lines, outlines, or small drawings. Some title cards worth mentioning are the ones created by pioneer director D. W. Griffith. These title cards could be considered one of the first examples of branded title cards in that Griffith included his name as a signature at the edges of each card.

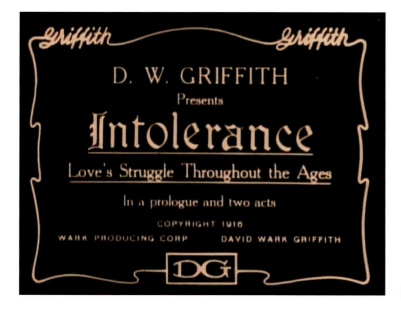

Figure 2.1 Intolerance.

doi: 10.1016/B978-0-240-81419-3.00002-7

Because the early movies were silent, the title cards often had an additional function: They displayed dialogue that was essential to comprehending the story, and they set the time and place for individual scenes. These title cards were first photographed and then edited into the main movie.

After synchronized-sound motion pictures, known as *talkies*, were introduced in the 1920s and color motion pictures were introduced in the 1930s, title sequences began to articulate and develop.

Marcel Duchamp (1887–1968) created particularly unique titles. He filmed **Anemic Cinema** (1926) in collaboration with American Dada artist Man Ray and cinematographer Marc Allegret. On the screen we see alternating spiral designs that rotate, creating the optical illusion of three-dimensionality, the spirals moving toward and away from the viewer. Sentences are written on a spiral, so they become readable while slowly spinning. The letters were pasted one by one on round black discs, which were then glued to phonograph records and changed after each shot.

Perfectly in sync with the style of the artist and the styles of the times (Dada, Surrealism, Avant Garde), Duchamp's fascination with language clearly emerges in this seven-minute experimental film, which presents a variety of visual and typographical play from beginning to end. First, the title. *Anemic* is an anagram for *cinema*, and *Anemic Cinema* becomes almost a palindrome. Second, the verbal puns appearing on the title cards are credited to Rose Sélavy, Duchamp's female alter ego. Third, the French sentences present plenty of puns, playful rhymes, and alliterations.

In **City Lights** (1931), Charlie Chaplin opens the film with a number of static title cards. The first one displays the film title and his name, the second one is almost a tagline for the movie and presents his name again ("A comedy romance in pantomime written and directed by Charlie Chaplin"), and the third and fourth title cards display the names of the crew and main cast before fading to black. At this point a night shot of the city fades in with cars rolling back and forth, lights on in the buildings at each side of the street, and a square in the background. After a few seconds, accompanied by music composed by Chaplin, the main title comes onto the screen, superimposed over the street night shot. It consists of the name of the movie (*City Lights*) in capital letters, which are all created by white circles, reminiscent of Broadway lights or light bulbs.

These titles are an impressive demonstration of superimposing techniques done at the film laboratory through an optical process—obviously, due to the time period, done without the aid of a computer—but most important, it is one of the first examples in history in which a particular amount time and effort was applied to create a main title card that presents a level of symbolism in its simplicity, a unique act at the time.

In **The Women** (1939), directed by George Cukor, we start seeing how title cards became more articulated and detailed. We see, displayed in white type with a drop shadow over a wood texture, the studio credits (Metro Goldwyn Mayer), a triple title card with the main talent credits, then the main movie title card, then a number of multiple title cards displaying crew and secondary cast roles. As soon as this sequence ends with the director credit, we enter into a secondary title sequence, almost as a preamble to the movie. Title cards for the same main talent credited earlier are shown again, but this time they have one title card dedicated to each of them. In addition to their names, we see a shot of an animal, which then dissolves into a shot of the actual talent (Norma Shearer as a baby deer, Joan Crawford as a leopard, Rosalind Russell as a cat, Mary Boland as a monkey, Paulette Goddard as a fox, Joan Fontaine as a sheep, Lucile Watson as an owl, Phyllis Povah as a cow, Marjorie Main as a horse). These talent/animal comparisons intend to give the audience a glimpse of the character or behavioral traits that they will experience watching the movie. Whether successful or not, it was definitely a step forward in the history of movie titles.

In addition to film titles for live-action motion pictures, it's worth mentioning an outstanding example in film titles for animation. In **Spook Sport** (1940), created by Mary Ellen Bute and animated by Norman McLaren, we see an interesting approach. This animated film features the *Danse Macabre*, composed by the French composer Camille Saint-Saëns, visually interpreted by scratches and painting done directly on the film by Norman McLaren.

After a number of intertitle cards display on-screen with green and red type on black background, introducing the type of work the audience is about to experience ("In the following short film novelty, color, music, movement combine to present a new type of Film-Ballet"), the main title cards show the two authors' credits and a "program note" sets the place, time, and mood of the movie ("The story suggested here is that at the bewitching hour of midnight, spooks and ghosts arise from their graves to cavort about and make merry"). We then see something quite unique: the cast of characters. This title card presents on one side the name of the characters (Spook, Ghost, Bat, Bell, Sun) and on the other the corresponding visual representation of that character (a red checkmark-looking *V*, a squiggly green *S*, an outline of a yellow bat, a green bell, and a red circular shape for the sun) which will animate in the film. At the end of the titles, the place ("a deserted graveyard") and the time ("midnight") are also indicated. Although this type of title card might not surprise us today, it must be analyzed within the context of its time. As a title sequence created in the 1940s, it is quite a remarkable one. It offers the general audience the visual keys—as though they were a map legend—to interpret a piece of abstract animation.

After the Second World War, film titles began a new phase. A Hollywood strike in 1946 led to the foundation of Scenic and Title Artist 816, a union for graphic artists and designers in the film industry; among its members were sign painters and advertising artists. Title sequences tended to become more artistic and personalized, as though the graphic design branding began to bleed over to the motion picture identity. More time, resources, and budgets were dedicated to the creation of original sequences that better integrated with the subject matter and genre of the movies.

With **Forbidden Games (Jeux Interdits**, 1952), the first feature film made by René Clément, the history of title sequences took a turn. This movie follows main characters Paulette, beautifully played by five-year-old Brigitte Fossey, and Michel during the Nazi invasion of France in 1940. Paulette, completely in denial about the death of her parents (caused by an aerial attack at the beginning of the movie), becomes fascinated with death as she starts creating a cemetery for anything dead the children find on their way. This is a film that provokes a powerful reflection on how the atrocities of war and loss affect children.

In the original opening title sequence, each title card appears printed on pages of a book, which are masterfully turned one after another while being filmed in one take, giving the audience enough time to read the text. While the titles are on-screen, we hear a gentle and relaxing lute, setting the tone and atmosphere for a relaxing story about to be told. As soon as the last title card appears on-screen, the movie punches you in the stomach with a Nazi aerial attack on escaping Parisians.

What I found most interesting is an alternate version of the opening title sequence, which was not included in the commercially released version of the film. This version portrays the two main characters, Paulette and Michelle, approaching a river, getting comfortably seated on a tree trunk; Michel carries a book, both obviously getting ready for a nice afternoon read. "It's the story of a little girl," says Michel. "A little girl like who?" says Paulette. "A little girl like you, and a little boy like me." Then Michel opens the book and begins to flip through the pages, onto which title cards are printed. After the last title card, the title sequence dissolves into the aerial attack. What is particularly remarkable in this title sequence is the new role that it takes on. On one hand, it acts as a frame for the movie, introducing it as though it were a story—in my opinion, hinting at the fact that a story that stark could only be read as a "story" by children and

not as the atrocious reality of war. On the other hand, this particular opening title sequence creates a meta-movie, a movie within
a movie. The two children sitting by the river and beginning to
read the book are the same talents who play the protagonists of
the movie the audience is about to experience, as though they
were extrapolated from the movie itself and given the chance to
observe it from a different frame and share their own story with
the world.

Saul Bass: *North by Northwest* and *Psycho*

Saul Bass (1920–1996) was an outstanding graphic designer,
title designer, filmmaker, photographer, and illustrator. His exper-
tise masterfully ranged among static two-dimensional posters
(*Carmen Jones, Vertigo,* the 1984 Los Angeles Olympic Games),
corporate identities (Continental Airlines, Minolta, United
Airlines, AT&T, Girl Scouts of the USA), packaging (Quaker,
Wesson, Alcoa), sophisticated animated title sequences (*The Man
with the Golden Arm, Vertigo, Anatomy of a Murder, Cape Fear, The
Age of Innocence,* and *Casino,* just to mention a few), and directing short and feature films (*The Searching Eye, Why Man Creates*),
which respectively earned him a Lion of San Marco from the
Venice Film Festival and an Oscar.

His title sequences expand from the function of crediting
the cast and crew. They complement the movie by piquing the
audience's interest while entertaining them with visually stun-
ning motion graphics. In his title sequences, utilizing a variety
of techniques such as paper cut-outs, live action, animation,
type design, and montages, he exquisitely demonstrates a strong
sense of typography, design, rhythm, pace, composition, and
color theory.

It's not a surprise that his graphic design education was
imparted by the Hungarian-born designer, painter, and educa-
tor György Kepes, who worked with Lázló Moholy-Nagy in Berlin
in the 1930s and was deeply influenced by the Berlin-based
Gestalt psychologists, the Bauhaus design theory, and Russian
Constructivism typography.

Saul Bass created title sequences over more than 40 years for
directors such as Otto Preminger (whose film **Carmen Jones** is
the first film in which the designer Saul Bass earns an on-screen
credit), Alfred Hitchcock, and Martin Scorsese. Here's how Martin
Scorsese describes his work: "Bass was instrumental in redefining
the visual language of title sequences. His graphic compositions
in movement, coupled with the musical score, function as a prologue to the movie; setting the tone, establishing the mood, and
foreshadowing the action. His titles are not simply identification

tags but pieces that are integral to the work as a whole. When his work comes up on the screen, the movie truly begins" (Meggs, Philip B., ed., **6 Chapters in Design: Saul Bass, Ivan Chermayeff, Milton Glaser, Paul Rand, Ikko Tanaka, Henryk Tomaszewski**; San Francisco, California: Chronicle Books, 1997).

North by Northwest, directed by Alfred Hitchcock in 1959, follows advertising executive Roger Thornhill (played by Cary Grant) in a series of intricate adventures during which he is mistaken for a government agent who is supposedly trying to smuggle microfilm containing government information.

The film opens with Bernard Herrmann's score, the fandango. As the music builds, diagonal and vertical gray lines enter parallel to each other in the screen at an irregular rate. While intersecting, they form a grid over a pale green solid background color. Then type comes onto the screen from the top and bottom frame edges and its baseline comes to rest on one of the diagonal lines. After this first title card, a few more appear (three single title cards for the main talent, then the director's title card), and finally the type comes onto the screen from the top and bottom frame edges to create the main title card: *North by Northwest*. This sequence is a fantastic example of how a main title, if designed by a skilled hand, can become and be used as a logo.

Shortly after the main title card exits the screen and a multiple title card enters frame, the pale green background dissolves to reveal the glass façade of a New York office building. Both the diagonal and vertical lines introduced in the first title cards (and now dissolved into the building shot) exactly match the structural lines of the building that is framed at a slight angle. Its windows reflect the busy streetscape, and the shots that follow portray some of the details of these streets (people exiting buildings, entering the subway, crossing the streets, and one person missing the bus—Hitchcock's cameo!). If you look closely, even at the secondary title cards, you can notice the details of the hands of a skilled designer, such as one title card elegantly and subtly exiting the screen on the right while the camera pans left, giving the impression of the titles being embedded in the scene. Even Alfred Hitchcock's title card exits screen right when he enters screen left, as though his entrance pushes away his own title while he tries to catch the bus.

Psycho (1960) opens with a full string orchestra playing music composed yet again by Bernard Herrmann, the New York-born composer who overall in his career collaborated with Hitchcock on nine films. "I felt that I was able to complement the black-and-white photography of the film with a black-and-white sound. I believe this is the only time in films that a purely string orchestra has been used," Hermann said about that opening (Steiner, Fred,

"Herrmann's 'Black and White' Music for Hitchcock's Psycho," *Filmmusic Notebook*, Fall 1994).

On a solid gray background, horizontal black lines alternate their entrance in the frame from the right, creating a regular ruled pattern and bringing with them a couple of horizontal sections of a dissected type. With a surprising and subtle play on foreground/background visual illusion, the gray horizontal lines exit screen left, creating a black background and leaving the full stage of the first title card: "Alfred Hitchcock." Another set of gray lines enter screen right, then exit again to the right, bringing with them and leaving on-screen the dissected pieces of the main title card: *Psycho*. After a couple of perfectly synced movements of the main title that emphasize their cuts, the type leaves the screen and other lines are introduced, this time vertical. The title sequence further develops with alternating horizontal and vertical lines, first inviting the type on-screen and then pushing it away to clear the way for the next title card. The result is an increasingly elaborate articulation of these seemingly innocent, but at the same time very jittery and nervous, lines dominating the screen.

While the lines evoke prison bars, cityscapes, order, and structure, their onscreen behavior and movement suggest jitteriness, nervousness, and irregularity. The dissected type in three horizontal rows evokes how something considered one unique, solid, and immovable entity can indeed be split, shattered, and dissected. It seems to allude to the fact that appearances can be misleading; after taking a first look at the movie and going back to watch the title sequence once again, we see that the type is a magnificent symbolic interpretation of the psychological state of the main character, Norman Bates (played by Anthony Perkins): split, shattered, schizophrenic, and incoherent.

"In those days," Bass said about his work, "I liked strong, clear, structural forms against which to do things. I liked giving more zip to **Psycho** because it was not only the name of the picture but a word that **means** something. I was trying to make it more frenetic, and I liked the idea of images suggesting clues coming together" (Rebello, Stephen, *Alfred Hitchcock and the Making of Psycho*; New York: St Martin's Griffin, 1998).

For this title sequence, Bass worked with Harold Adler, a hand-lettering artist who worked for the National Screen Service and who also worked on the title sequences of **Vertigo** and **North by Northwest**; animation director William Hurtz; and cameraman/production man Paul Stoleroff. The lines we see in this title sequence were actually six-foot-long aluminum bars that were sprayed black and animated on a table at different speeds and positions. The camera was rigged on top of the table, looking down.

Adler described the process: "We worked on a large white painted plywood board with push-pins to guide the bars. The bars had to follow a straight line and couldn't wiggle. Paul [Stoleroff] and I manually pushed in each bar at predetermined distances and speeds. Each bar was precisely timed by numbers of frames per second, called 'counts.' Each bar had to be pushed in and shot separately. Once a bar had gone across the screen, it was tied down. There were lots of retakes because they'd come in crooked ..."

Bass utilized two sets of sans-serif fonts in this title sequence, Venus Bold Extended and News Gothic Bold, all in capital. Each title card was recreated on reverse (white type on black) photostats (early projector photocopier machines that photographed documents and reproduced them onto sensitized photographic paper), which were cut into three horizontal parts. To add motion, Adler said, "I moved the top section [of the title letters] in one direction and shot it at a certain speed, moved the bottom in another direction at another speed, and the middle part at another speed. So you were really getting three images, each one a third of the height of the lettering, coming in at different speeds. For the last frame, we popped on the word *Psycho*, which was the intact photostat by itself. For the other big titles, like 'Directed by Alfred Hitchcock,' I used News Gothic Bold typeface and we did the same three-cut technique as for the title of the movie."

Dr. Strangelove and *Delicatessen*

For **Dr. Strangelove or: How I Learned to Stop Worrying and Love the Bomb** (1964), directed by Stanley Kubrick, Pablo Ferro created an outstanding title sequence.

The movie opens with an aerial shot coupled with a voiceover giving the political context and setting of the film, followed by a scene of a U.S. Air Force plane being refueled in midair. While the scene's details unfold (with an admittedly oddly sexual hint pervading the scene), the white titles appear superimposed on the black-and-white footage. While this imagery and type unfold on-screen, we hear a very relaxing classical soundtrack.

The type is handwritten, with alternating thin and thick strokes, outlines, and a variety of font sizes. It resembles some of the fonts typically used in comic books, giving the title sequence a comedic appeal. It seems that there is no rule that governs the font size. The crew and cast last names are displayed 300% larger than the corresponding first names, or vice versa. Articles are much larger than the following names. Every title card keeps the audience on edge. Where are the names going to be placed? What is going to come next?

This juxtaposition of the military imagery of a plane being refueled, the airy white handwritten typography, and the classical music all perfectly match the style, content, and emotional reaction that the audience is about to experience on a larger scale when they watch the entire movie: a political dark comedy.

For **Repulsion** (1965), directed by Roman Polanski, the title sequence was created by Maurice Binder—well known not only for his opening title sequences for the James Bond movies such as **From Russia with Love**, **Goldfinger**, and **Live and Let Die** but also for the spectacular opening title sequences of **Charade** and **Arabesque**.

Accompanied by a minimalistic ominous soundtrack, **Repulsion's** title sequence opens with an extreme close-up of an eye. The titles appear coming into and out of frame, except that the frame is actually the eye. The titles are masked by the edge of the eye and they have a slight rounded distortion on the edges, as though they are actually scrolling over the surface of the eye's cornea. After the first few title cards, the camera slightly zooms out and the title cards become populated by multiple names. The type is no longer masked by the eye and enters the frame from the bottom, moving across the screen on different diagonal trajectories, and exiting the top of the frame. The interesting aspect of this part of the title sequence is that we start noticing the eye moving and looking in different directions. A careful look shows it is actually following the type moving across the screen. Considering the time (the 1960s), I believe that this title sequence offers an innovative approach in that it involved creating and orchestrating a variety of assets (video and animated type) that interacted with each other.

Fantastic Voyage (1966) is a spy sci-fi movie directed by Richard Fleischer. The movie opens with an airplane landing, and Jan Benes, a scientist vital to the scientific formula of miniaturization, is escorted away from it. When the escort is attacked, the scientist suffers a major head injury.

Following this opening scene we see the opening titles, created by Richard Kuhn; they present a quick montage of close-ups of Benes's brain, X-rays, numbers, electroencephalograms, jump cuts of the patient in a hospital bed surrounded by doctors, medical machinery, and rolling tape. We hear heartbeats and synthetic sound effects. Title cards are superimposed on the imagery, and they appear as though they were typed in real time on a typewriter. It is a surreal title sequence that gives the audience a taste of the mysterious fantastic adventure on which they are about to embark. As soon as the quick title sequence is over, it dissolves back into the movie with a more sedate pacing.

The movie evolves into revealing that an agent will be miniaturized and will lead a group of scientists onboard a nuclear-powered submarine on a fantastic scientific expedition into the bloodstream of the scientist to try to save his life.

Matte Titling

When title cards are required to be superimposed over film footage, title designers utilize a technique called **matte titling**. This technique, which was thriving before the titling process became dominated by a digital workflow, is still utilized today by independent filmmakers whose movies are shot on film and who would like to avoid a digital intermediate process by creating their titles directly on film.

This technique requires the creation of two identical title cards, which are used as mattes. The first one consists of a title card with black type on white background, the second with white (or colored) type on black background. Using an optical printer, the first title card is exposed against the background footage, creating a blank area that corresponds to the title card lettering. Subsequently, the film roll is rewound and the second matte is printed over the background footage. This last optical printing pass allows the lettering to be registered over the previously blank areas. The visual result is white (or colored) titles superimposed over the footage.

In **Fahrenheit 451** (1966), director Françoise Truffaut gives us an outstanding title sequence. The movie is based on the futuristic novel by Ray Bradbury, which takes place in a state that forbids reading. A fireman, Guy Montag, must find people who are hiding books and confiscate and burn the books. The opening title sequence consists of a montage of shots that zoom in from wide to a close-up of a variety of antennae on top of suburban houses, indicating that television has replaced reading in this society. The shots alternate monochromatic orange, blue, green, purple, and red antennae. Similarly to **The Magnificent Ambersons** (Orson Welles, 1942) and **M*A*S*H** (Robert Altman, 1970), rather than seeing and reading title cards, the audience actually doesn't get to see the type on-screen but rather hears the opening titles being recited by a voiceover: "An Enterprise Vineyard production. Oskar Werner, Julie Christie…in *Fahrenheit 451*. Co-starring…" The soundtrack we hear is another brilliant musical composition by Bernard Herrmann. It is indeed a surprising and unexpected opening, which, in a way, poses the question at the core of the movie: "What happens in a world where there is no writing to read?"

In the same year, another movie made its impression: **Uccellacci e Uccellini** (**Hawks and Sparrows**; 1966), directed by Pier Paolo Pasolini. In this stark opening title sequence, simply designed title cards appear superimposed over a locked-down shot of a cloudy sky, accompanied by music composed by Ennio Morricone. When the title cards appear onscreen, a cheerful Domenico Modugno actually sings them. But he doesn't limit himself to singing the names and titles of the cast and crew—he embellishes the reading with adjectives and fun facts, almost as though the narrator was the modern version of a troubadour who is singing and preparing the stage for a well-narrated story that's about to begin. This opening fits perfectly with the movie, which has a deep political theme (the Marxism crisis of the 1950s in Italy), wrapped around a sweet-and-sour fairy tale structure.

Broadcast title design began to catch up to the creativity demonstrated by the movie title sequences of the time and definitely made their own mark. A couple of notable title sequences are the ones for **ABC Movie of the Week** (1969) and **The Partridge Family** (1970).

In the **ABC Movie of the Week** opening, we see titles that animate toward the viewer three-dimensionally, with exaggerated perspective. The effect was achieved by an optical technique called **slit-scan.** The technique's look and feel is definitely a precursor of what would later be applied to numerous other applications, including cinematography (the "Star Gate" scene in Kubrick's **2001: A Space Odyssey**, 1968), title sequences (the 1973–1979 **Doctor Who** opening titles or the crawling text block that opens 1977's **Star Wars**), and computer motion graphics (a number of software plug-ins are called *slit-scan*).

Slit Scan

Originally utilized in still photography to create blurriness or deformity, the slit-scan technique was achieved through the use of an animation stand. The image or title to be photographed is placed on the glass plate and is generally backlit. A black matte is placed over the image, with a slit in the center. The camera is arranged on a vertical rig framing down on the glass plate and can be moved up and down. When the frame is exposed, the camera moves down, creating an effect similar to a still shot with long exposure, which records the light streaks of fire or car headlights; instead of the object (car) moving, the camera is moved. When the camera reaches its desired end position, the shutter is closed and the film advances to the next frame to be exposed.

The visual result is the illusion of one, two, or even four planes of infinite proportions, moving either toward or away from the viewer.

The Partridge Family (1970) was an American sitcom broadcast on ABC from 1970–1974; the story followed a mother and her five children on their quest to seek a musical career. The opening title sequence features the theme song by Wes Farrell, "When We're Singing," with lyrics by Dianne Hildebrand, and animation by graphic designer Sandy Dvore, who later in his career went on to design more title sequences like the ones for **Blacula** (1972) and **Lipstick** (1976). The animation opens with an egg cracking open, from which emerges the main title, then a "mama" partridge emerging from and getting rid of the shell. The title card comes up on-screen, consisting of a monochromatic rendition of a photo of the mother, played by Shirley Jones. Then five little partridges are introduced, with all five children represented similarly to the first title card. Then the entire family of partridges walks across the screen to reveal the Mondrian-esque pattern of the back of the school bus in which the family travels, and the title sequence dissolves into the sitcom.

In the 1970s and 1980s, partly influenced by video art, we began to see computer-assisted title sequences such as **Superman** (1978), created by Richard and Robert Greenberg.

In the early 1990s, Adobe After Effects was released, marking another turning point in the history of title design. Title designers were now able to design, animate, and composite title sequences directly on their computers.

Delicatessen (1991), directed by Marc Caro and Jean-Pierre Jeunet, is a dark comedy film set in a post-apocalyptic France in the 1950s, where the food is scarce, animals are quasi-extinct, and a butcher hires helpers that he then butchers and sells as a delicacy to his clientele.

The film opens, revealing a sinister building in a rural street. The camera slowly enters an empty butcher shop, revealing a butcher sharpening his knife. The camera enters and continues through an air duct to reveal a man wrapping himself with paper and trash. It's garbage day, and the man makes his way into the trash can. The escape plan seems to be going well, except that right when the trash can is about to be collected, the butcher throws his cigarette into it, burning the man and causing him to yelp, blowing his cover. The butcher opens the trash can and, with a delightful point of view shot from inside the can, we see him raise his knife in the air while smiling sadistically, and as the knife falls to slash the man, the movie cuts to the main title card, *Delicatessen*, coupled with a brilliant combination of sound effects and a swinging metal pig—the butcher's logo.

After the first scene sets the mood and gives a few hints of the dark humor of the film that is about to unfold, the title sequence can truly begin.

Lulled by the calm, almost sedate version of circus-like music, the camera gently moves around and pauses to frame title cards embedded in a set composed of broken records, pictures, dirt, a variety of paper (production logs, labels, menus, newspaper articles), a vintage camera, patches, photo booth pictures, and mirrors. The camera wanders as though it is simply moving around to explore the territory, but then it pauses to allow the viewer to read and make out the title cards embedded in the set, as though they were meant to be there all along. This title sequence was artistically and skillfully orchestrated in one take; the set is composed of real props, as opposed to a computer-generated set.

Some of the type is handwritten, some is presented in varying qualities; all appears on a variety of surfaces. What is most striking is that each title card has a specific place in the set and a particular way of manifesting itself with a meaningful style: a concise summary and symbolic representation of the key people behind the movie. For example, the title card that credits the director of photography, Darius Khondji, is engraved on a vintage camera. The music credit is printed on a vinyl label, the wardrobe credit is embroidered on a patch, and the editor credit is handwritten on a set of photo booth pictures that had been hand-ripped and taped back together.

Last but not least, the transition from the end of the title sequence back into the movie is truly remarkable. After the last title card that credits both directors, the opening title sequence fades to black. We hear a paper-crumpling noise and we see the hand of the butcher taking a sheet of butcher paper off the lens (as though it was on the shelf in front of him) to wrap some meat for waiting customers. The result is a brilliant transition that throws the audience back into the swing of the movie.

Se7en, Kyle Cooper, and the Modern Title Sequence

Named by *The New York Times Magazine* as "one of the most important innovations of the 1990s," the opening title sequence of **Se7en** (1995) presents, without any doubt, one major turning point in the history of title design.

Se7en is a psychological thriller directed by David Fincher. In an interview with Thunder Chunky, talking about title sequences, title designer Kyle Cooper states, "Each film is a different problem to solve, so each solution is different." For **Se7en**'s opening title sequence, Cooper shot some extremely close-up footage, which complements the type scratched directly onto film, a technique seen in early film animation done by people such as Len Lye, Stan Brakhage, and other experimental filmmakers. The edgy soundtrack by Nine Inch Nails perfectly complements, enhances, and interweaves with the imagery.

In these titles we see overhead extreme close-up shots of a diary, fingertips cutting and taping, pages filled with handwriting, erasing words and then writing new ones with thick and intense handwriting, collecting hair, erasing eyes from pictures, and sawing pages. The title sequence alternates cross-dissolves, hard cuts, flash frames, and distorted and handwritten type, complemented by one- to two-frame shots with borderline-subliminal imagery of a variety of words, letters, and numbers.

As an audience watching this for the first time, we definitely feel the intended emotions: what we are about to experience is a piercing, fast, dark movie. We see a lot in this engaging title sequence, but what we never see is a complete picture, a long or medium shot of the setting. The audience doesn't get the privilege of understanding where they are, what's going on, and most important, how this montage ties into the movie they are about to experience. In the perfect vein of a thriller, they will have to piece it together, especially after the first viewing of the movie.

In the very beginning, the audience is given an important clue about how the killer was able to get away with his actions. He removes the surface of his fingertips with a razor blade so that he won't leave any fingerprints. "David Fincher wanted to set up the film's relationship with evil in a very direct and uncomfortable way," Cooper notes in an interview with David Geffner. "I think we accomplished that. But in **Se7en** there's also a structural concern going on. You don't see the killer until nearly 40 minutes in, so the titles need to bridge that gap. You're inside his head straight off, making the tension that much more intense when he does finally show up."

Because of the aesthetical qualities of the title sequence, its superb use of content in the appropriate context and moment, and the trust given to the audience that they will put the pieces together—rather than telegraphing what they are supposed to feel and understand—this title sequence is a successful and timeless piece.

"That sequence for *Se7en* is only good because it is the film, because it came out of the film," Cooper says. "I wanted to get across the idea of the killer, to make something that he would have made. That's how you want it to be. The form should be born out of the content."

It's not a surprise that the style of **Se7en** has been admired, looked up to, and especially mimicked by a variety of designers. As Cooper mentioned, what is important to understand, what is absolutely relevant, is the concept of a title sequence. How a title sequence articulates itself visually and aurally should be a consequence, dictated by the content. That is why **Se7en** is such a successful piece. It was created for the movie, and it would not work for any other movie other than **Se7en**.

David Lynch directed 1997's **Lost Highway**, a film that follows the confusing happenings—in which the boundary between reality and hallucination is very thin—of the saxophonist Fred Madison, played by Bill Pullman, when he is accused of having murdered his wife. This title sequence seems to have borrowed from an earlier concept of the 1968 title sequence for the movie **Girl on a Motorcycle**, but inevitably it develops into its own well-crafted, effective titles for this film.

Lost Highway's opening title sequence, designed by Jay Johnson, consists of a driver's point of view of a car speeding on a road in complete darkness. The only point of reference in the darkness is the middle broken yellow line that prevents the speeding car from crashing. The titles, as yellow and broken as the road's middle line, are designed with a stencil-esque font reminiscent of the roadwork imagery. They emerge out of the darkness, they hold for a moment on-screen to allow them to be read, and then they move furiously forward as though they were crashing onto the windshield. The soundtrack of these opening titles consists of a song by David Bowie called "I'm Deranged," perfectly complementing the feeling of the scene and the emotional rollercoaster that the audience is about to experience watching this dark and surreal movie.

The title sequence for **Monsoon Wedding** (2001), directed by Mira Nair, was designed by Trollbäck+co. This opening title sequence features animated lines and circles over colorful backgrounds, while the title cards appear on-screen. The graphic elements are simple and effective, and they dance and animate in sync to the soundtrack of an upbeat Indian marching band. The lines and circles expand and contract in size, filling up the screen and transforming from a foreground element into a background one, creating seamless and effective transitions from one title card to the next. Right when we begin to expect the next abstract title card unfolding on-screen, we see two lines slowly curling around each other to create two intertwined faces that symbolize the arranged marriage that is at the fulcrum of the film.

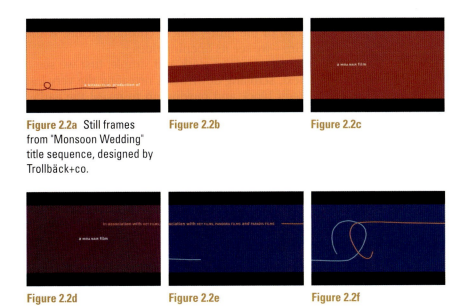

Figure 2.2a Still frames from "Monsoon Wedding" title sequence, designed by Trollbäck+co.

Figure 2.2b

Figure 2.2c

Figure 2.2d

Figure 2.2e

Figure 2.2f

Figure 2.4 MK12 creatives.

Through those conversations, we explored various conceptual and thematic elements derived from both *Quantum of Solace* and *Casino Royale*. We all liked that the title sequence could be looked at as a visual metaphor of Bond's current mental state, his feelings toward women, relationships, and his isolation in the world, given the death of his love interest, Vesper, at the end of *Casino Royale*.

So we went back to the studio and continued on with more tests, adding different elements, experimenting. We eventually landed on the sand motif, and through a series of test animations, everyone agreed this was the way to go.

We found that the desert theme served as a convenient metaphor for Bond's mental state while also referencing specific locations in the film—a perfect parallel that made for a great foundation. We liked how the sand itself worked perfectly as a centric object-element. Its ability to change form from a solid to a viscous substance was an interesting feature to us, which we explored both as a transitional element in the sequence and as a substance we could mold into whatever form we wanted. One moment it would act as an environment, the next, a field of stars.

The female forms—hidden within desert environments—could be looked at as a representation of Bond's current relationship toward women and love, after enduring the loss of Vesper. They act as the accelerant that jarringly alters the barren landscape, i.e., Bond's mind folding in on itself.

Other visual cues subtly parallel elements, moments, and visual motifs in *QoS*, finding a synergy with Marc's ideas and the beautiful cinematography of Roberto Schaffer.

There are also instances within the film that pay homage to past Bond title work by Binder, Brownjohn, and Kleinman.

For the majority of this previz [previsualization], everyone within the studio participated by means of animated tests, mood and style boards, and conceptual storylines and themes to adhere to the sequence. We shot various tests on our stage for the various pitches we created throughout the process. We had a small shoot with a model friend-of-a-friend and borrowed a small workshop in London that we shot in for an afternoon. We also built a sandbox on our own stage and shot multiple sand and environment tests over multiple test animations. All in all, we had a wealth of visual thought and experimentation that really helped us find a voice and a clear visual dialogue for the final product.

What was the length of this project?

From start to finish, our involvement with *Quantum of Solace* for both VFX and the direction and animation of the film titles was a little under a year's time.

How large was your production/postproduction team and what were their roles?

Our postproduction team consisted of our core studio artists, totaling nine at the time. We also worked with four freelance artists, three compositors, and one roto artist. We also had a senior producer working from NYC and a production manager that was with us in Kansas City. We also tracked down a particle animator in India who is literally one of the few people in the world who can do what he does.

For perspective, the live-action shoot team was at least 30+ people strong.

We work in a very organic way. Everyone wears different hats and can adapt pretty easily to whatever task is coming next down the pipeline. Of course, everybody has their strengths, which we play toward, but ultimately, we work as one giant brain, moving materials back and forth between artists within the studio.

Can you elaborate on the client dynamic?

The client dynamic, both in terms of our working relationship with the director Marc Forster and EON Productions, the owners of the Bond franchise, was a fantastic and an enjoyable experience. With Marc, it felt like any of the other projects we've collaborated on with him and his team in the past few years. We have a good time with those guys, and they're a group of brilliant minds that makes the creation process exciting and challenging.

EON was also fantastic to work with. They are a bunch of great people who are really dedicated to their jobs and really believe in the character and universe that Fleming has created. They have such a vast knowledge of the Bond world. It was definitely an educational experience, to say the least.

What was your involvement in the live-action footage for the opening sequence?

MK12 directed the live shoot. We secured one of the stages at Pinewood Studios in London and sent two of us to direct one day of sand FX, two days of sandboxes and our female talent, and the remaining day with Daniel Craig. Simon Chaudoir was our DP, and our crew were mostly holdovers from the feature Bond shoot, which had just wrapped. It was pretty fantastic; these are the guys and girls who had been living Bond for the past year and a half (many of them since the Roger Moore days), so their insights were very valuable to us franchise newbies. These were also the same folks who fabricated sienna in a warehouse, so it was always amusing to brainstorm some weird contraption and then see it built five minutes later, only better. Toby, who was in the props department on *QoS*, became one with the sand on set, to the point of obsession. By the end of the shoot, he'd be able to make it do exactly what you wanted it to do—again, only better. And he's just one in a long list of truly talented and dedicated crew. It was our biggest shoot by far, but those guys also made it our easiest.

We had a working animatic that incorporated the major shots that we'd be shooting passes of with the motion control rig: the Cyclops. We were using these scenes as foundational areas within the title sequence to build everything else around. It was imperative to use the motion control rig for this because of the complex scaling and speed issues that are inherent in taking a plate of a human—at human size—and compositing said plate into a world of human thighs, shoulders, faces, hips, and torsos that are meant to be viewed as mega-structures within a desert expanse. We never make it easy for ourselves.

On the female talent days, the motion control rig was situated in front of a 12 × 12 sandbox on one side of the stage. On the other side of the stage was a matching 12 × 12 sandbox. We had a jib arm on a dolly and track for nonmotion control shots. The Art Department would sculpt various environments that centered around one of our female talent half-

We weren't exactly sure what we were after at first, and we hadn't seen the film yet, so we made a lot of animated tests and mood boards solely as conversation starters with Marc [director Marc Forster]. We did a fair amount of homework before presenting ideas to him, but having already been invested in the project for several years, Marc was able to give us very constructive and informed feedback, which we'd then digest and work into our next round.

There was no specific message that needed to be conveyed in the titles. *The Kite Runner* had been a beloved book in many circles long before the film was greenlit, and the film itself is a very faithful adaptation of the source, so the titles themselves only needed to help set the tone of the film, not necessarily address the content. Knowing that, we first eliminated a list of things we knew the sequence **didn't** need to be: a micronarrative, a roller coaster ride, a backstory, and so on, and instead focused on what we believed it ought to be: a display of craftsmanship.

Craft is an interesting subtext in the film, from how Afghani kites are constructed to how they are competitively flown, to the intricacies in the relationships between the characters and their convictions in life. And specific to our influences for the titles themselves, Arabic calligraphy is an incredibly precise and symbolic craft; some argue that it can never actually be mastered. We had a deadline, but we were still very meticulous in our design of the sequence, giving special consideration to typeface development and animation, color interaction, and camera movement.

Some of the more expressionistic Arabic calligraphy uses unexpected colors and overlapping words and phrases to create new meanings and very intricate, dramatic compositions. We thought it would be interesting to take that a step further and introduce z-depth, so that the type compositions would change dynamically as the camera moved about.

Because we were working with delicate color combinations, we had to go through several rounds of film-outs (watching the sequence on film in a theater) and subsequent adjustments in order to get them right, but it really did pay off in the final piece.

Another consideration was the soundtrack. Alberto Iglesias composed a haunting piece using a traditional Arabic structure, with an aggressive drumbeat and notes that slid through the scales. We used that as our pacing cue as we moved from title card to title card, giving the camera a slight weight and drowsiness that really grabbed into the notes, as though tethered by a spring.

What was the length of this project, from the initial commission to the final deliverable?

From the time we got the call to delivery, just under six months.

How large was your production/postproduction team and what were their roles?

In total, there were seven of us on the creative side, but not always at the same time. The sequence called for a lot of specialization, i.e., understanding the basic rules behind Arabic script, animating that script, orchestrating the camera to compliment the layouts, etc., so we'd break off into smaller teams to tackle one issue at a time and come back together further down the pipe as "experts" in those areas. We'd then blend our efforts together to create the final.

Can you elaborate on the client dynamic?

We went through about a dozen rounds of internal design and revision before presenting anything to Marc. Of those, about half contained bits and pieces that we "Frankensteined" into our first official presentation; the others we mostly discarded. We formally presented only one direction, because we felt strongly about it and didn't feel the need to contextualize it. But after that we still went through another dozen or so rounds of tweaks to that core direction, only now with Marc's feedback.

One of Marc's strengths as a director is his ability to surround himself with the people he's able to trust with his vision. He has a knack for reading chemistry, so chances are if you're in his circle, you're already preapproved. With that said, presentations with Marc weren't an uphill battle because we didn't have to sell our work; we were able to focus on what we felt was the best direction, knowing that our discussions with him (even when he disagreed with us, which was often) would be a creative dialogue, not a one-way discussion.

Do you have any anecdotes related to this project that you would like to share?

If you're in Kansas City and insist on seeing a DreamWorks film in order to start work on it, 24 hours later a DreamWorks rep with a briefcase will be at your door. He will remove a screener from the briefcase and play it for you, never leaving the room. He won't talk much, but he'll apologize for the formality when he asks you disclose any hidden recording devices in the room, if any. He won't actually let you touch the disc and will insist on ejecting it himself (politely, of course). He will then thank you and immediately fly back to L.A. DreamWorks is way cooler than the CIA.

Stranger Than Fiction

What was the main concept and inspiration for the motion graphics and main-on-end title sequence in Stranger Than Fiction?

Initially, we were given a scrapbook, which was basically a personality guide to Harold Crick, Will Ferrell's character in the film. It was put together by Zach Helm, the screenwriter. From this, we knew we were working with an obsessive/compulsive type who is also an IRS agent and math aficionado. We also were given a basic knowledge of the premise of the film: that he is being followed around by an all-knowing voice, narrating and predicting his every move. He eventually discovers that the voice is that of a famous novelist, in which whose in-progress book he is a character and who plans to kill him off at the end of the book.

From this, we distilled two directions: exploiting the cluttered, disheveled stereotype of a writer, or the anal, antiseptic nature of an IRS agent with OCD. Like a schizophrenic, we started to play with both.

Can you talk about the creative process while working on the Stranger Than Fiction graphics and main-on-end titles, from early inspiration through development and final deliverable?

Our first pitch was based purely on some initial concepts and a general understanding of what Marc [director Marc Forster] was looking for. We didn't realize that the initial sequence had already been shot and was moving along in editorial, so we went out and filmed Timmy as Harold Crick and created this minute-long experimental short/pitch that was accompanied by a pile of style frames and mood boards. Marc and the team really liked what they saw. We were awarded the job and were passed a more or less final cut of the opening sequence.

From there, we created two concepts. The first concept was more of a collaged experimental animation style that was conceptually tied to the author character's perspective. It consisted of visual tropes that were related back to the author/narrator, such as calendars, notes, various kinds of paper, coffee stains, etc. The typography was a typewriter derivative, which we complemented with real-time typos, corrections, and notations. Little editorial notes would appear as the story progressed. We created another set of style boards as well as a minute-long animated sketch that incorporated moving footage from the opening sequence and was cut to the spoken narration by Emma Thompson.

The second concept came from the mind of Harold Crick, which we interpreted as a stark, white graphical world that played with all sorts of infographics, data tidbits, and formulas. We felt that a clean, stylized, very orderly visual language would parallel his personality and be a perfect visual expression to depict all these other ideas and thoughts in his mind. Style boards were created, and from those a test animation was completed, showcasing the early attempts at animating and compositing this infographical world into the live-action cut.

Originally, the titles were to be integrated into the opening, but Marc liked what we were doing with the graphical overlays, so he decided to have an entirely separate title sequence at the end of the film, which we realized as a moving photo album of sorts, mashing together B-roll footage of Chicago settings with kinetic title cards. The footage was shot by Marc and DOP Roberto Schaefer.

We worked on the title sequence concurrent with the opening sequence.

Was the opening sequence at a locked-picture stage when it reached you, or did you have any editing input?

The opening sequence was around 90% locked when we started to work with it. Some of the graphics had a hand in the storytelling, but ultimately, we worked within the cut given to us by Matt Chesse, the editor. The main input we had editorially was the implementation of a Fibonacci-like golden-spiral editing transitional device, which we employed several times in the sequence. This was a technique that we had developed early on, and we were happy that it made its way into the final. Conceptually, it speaks to the mathematical mind of Crick, and it's just a really neat visual storytelling device.

Can you elaborate on the motion graphics and film transfer workflow?

We were supplied with the opening sequence, and our other 30-ish shots were peppered throughout the film as 2K DPX file sequences. We did all the compositing ourselves, passing back full DPX sequences to the studio. We'd order film-outs consistently during the postproduction schedule, which we'd take over to a small, privately run theater in town for reviews. We were looking at graphic consistency, legibility, and overall color space compatibility.

For the main-on-end titles, we ultimately had to move into 4k plates because some of our graphic line work was just too thin for the emulsion. They would start to dance at 2K, and upping the resolution fixed the issue.

Can you elaborate on the rotoscoping and motion tracking work you did?

Oh, my God, we did so much rotoscoping during that project. It was insane. It ate up so much time but was well worth it for the final output. All roto work was done in After Effects. We did a bit of 3D tracking in Boujou but mostly utilized the built-in motion tracker in After Effects.

What was the length of this project?

We had about six months to complete the opening sequence and main-on-end titles. Half of that was conceptualizing, research, and development and the other half production.

How large was your production/postproduction team and what were their roles?

At the time, our studio was nine strong. We had seven creatives on the job and two producers on our side. The team had fluid roles, from graphical build and layout to rotoscoping and compositing.

Can you elaborate on the client dynamic?

The client dynamic was great. This was our first time working with Marc and his team. We immediately got along with everybody. There was great communication and they all were very patient and extremely helpful, as this was our first foray into the film world. It was quite educational, and they're really good teachers.

What about the type treatment?

We started with the Carson font **Thaitrade**, which is a very clean sans-serif. We felt it was the best typeface to parallel Crick's equally organized thought process. We then developed a "Swiss Army" animation technique in which all the type springs out from around him when called for. We extended this technique to the type treatments in the main-on-end sequence as well, though because they were superimposed over more ambient footage and disassociated with the character, we gave them some supporting graphic flourishes.

How about color and camera use in the main-on-end title sequence?

We thought of the sequence as a pile of photos, with an unseen hand sorting through them. Marc really wanted something energetic and bright to close the film out with, so we opted for a four-tone primary color palette and unpredictable, raw movement, both with the camera and with how the "photos" were tossed around. Instead of a front-lit light source, we chose to backlight the photos, creating interesting secondary/tertiary colors when they overlapped.

Interview: Synderela Peng on Designing Title Sequences

Motion Graphics Studio: yU+co
Art Director: Synderela Peng
www.yuco.com

Figure 2.5 Synderela Peng, Art Director, yU+co.

Can you talk about yourself and your background?

I was born in Indonesia and came to the U.S. to attend college in 1991. I went to Art Center for my undergraduate and received a degree in illustration in 1996. I then worked for a number of years, mostly in design-related jobs because work as an illustrator was hard to find and simply didn't pay a lot. In 1999 I applied for CalArts, for a masters in graphic design, with the idea that I could do more if I knew more. CalArts was great, opened my mind up to a lot of new ideas that didn't necessarily feed into the commercial endeavors but were invaluable nonetheless. And after I graduated in 2001 I started working at yU+co doing motion graphics and have been there since.

How did you get to specialize on motion graphics and, in particular, film titles? How does your life experience influence your work?

I knew Garson (yu) from my time working prior to CalArts. And when I got done with school I applied for work at yU+co. Much of the work produced at yU+co was film titles at the time, and I've always enjoyed the process of creating intros, like a mini story before the movie begins. If you are in a creative field of any kind, your life experience is inseparable from your work. I love to read, particularly short stories and nonfiction, and very often the literature in my life evokes a tone and a visual. Whenever it is possible I try to bring that into my commercial work. Not a lot of that makes it into the final product, but it's a great starting point to feed the imagination.

What are your guidelines and preferences in regard to font size and readability for theatrical releases, broadcast, and smaller screens?

Film is generally more forgiving than broadcast, for obvious reasons. So for film projects, type sizes can be a bit smaller. Occasionally we have to watch for typefaces that are too thin because as the reels get duplicated the quality deteriorates, and so will the thin type. Broadcast, general rule of thumb is to not have very thin serifs; they become muddled once pull-down is applied. Those nuances are lost.

What kind of guidelines do you usually receive from the client/studios in regard to title card order, font size, or size distinction between executives, main film title, main talent, and supporting roles?

Film companies usually send us a legal sheet that states the size relationship between the actors. Often we request waivers to unify the sizes between the actors; it makes our life as designers a little easier and gives a sense of visual unity.

Can you talk about the relevance of editing in the work you do?

Editing is integral to the process. In the case of film titles, we need the help of an editor to piece a story together. Having a good editor will make your life so much better! And in broadcast, an editor will determine the visual and audio rhythm, very important to our media-saturated world, since capturing that excitement and the eye of people with one-minute attentions spans is crucial.

Do you generally work on your titles while having the score already in place? If so, how does that affect your work?

Very often we work without the final score. About 40% of the time we get the final score when our design process begins. But the clients usually have a direction for where they want to take the piece. So we temp in music that simulates the rhythm and tone to help us along. It can be difficult to not have the music in place when you start production, but that never stops the process.

As an art director, can you elaborate on the dynamics of your team of designers, 3D artists, and illustrators?

I work with a team of rotating artists. There is a core staff of six or seven people, and we hire freelancers as required by the amount of projects. Most of the time the design process is very open and democratic. Garson puts everyone on board to contribute ideas. If the boards selected are not mine, I still get brought in to art direct, mainly to be a creative point person to interact with clients and to organize and manage.

Is there a typical length of time you are given (or a minimum amount of time you request) when you work on a title sequence project? What are the shortest and longest projects you have worked on?

Film titles, about two to three months. Shortest film title project: three weeks. Longest, I don't really remember. Those are hard for me to work on, so I must have shut them out of my memory.

Can you elaborate on the research you do in your projects and it affects your work?

I start with words, sentences. Which very often leads to visual explorations. Sometimes random pictures inform the concept. But lately, the instincts seem to have become more honed. So I am spending less time playing around with things that may not necessarily feed into the project. It may sound less spontaneous, but it really isn't. You just get better at narrowing your ideas down and finding fun things to explore within the constraints.

What are your main goals/objectives when you are working on a title sequence? What is your own measure of success?

First and foremost, how well we have complemented the film and how well it leads into the main body of the narrative. I don't perceive that statement to be driven by the Bauhaus modernist notion of problem solving but more by the idea of creating the appropriate context. Film titles are kind of unique in motion design in that stylistically they can be standalone pieces, but ultimately they have to contribute well to a larger narrative in order for them to work.

What are the most challenging aspects of your work?

Communication during crunch time! I find that my sentence structure becomes very short and reductive when deadlines are impending. Almost like your mind wants to work faster than your verbal motor skills can handle. It's a constant reminder to slow down and learn to explain things well. So, in essence I would say the communication component in production.

What are your favorite parts or aspects of the work you do?

My favorite is still design to start. And then the next high point is when you realize that the methodology you thought would work in your head actually is coming alive in previz.

How does technology affect your work?

Well, we have to embrace some of it in order to keep up. But ultimately it's still the creative process that holds the key. Every decade people talk about how cool it is that we are "going back to the analog process" in this or that other way. The truth is, we never lost that. That human element, the tacit way of understanding is integral to any creative process, and in that sense we never need to worry about losing ourselves in techy updates. But I am an optimist in that regard.

Throughout your career, approximately how many titles (or type-oriented motion graphics) have you worked on?

I actually don't remember … 30?

What are your favorite titles you worked on?

Sympathy for Lady Vengeance, W, Hulk, Enchanted.

What are your favorite titles (if different from the ones you worked on)? Favorite graphic designers, type designers, or motion designers? Favorite font?

I love the introduction to Goddard's _Contempt_, that long panning shot following the cinematographer. Imaginary Forces' _Donnie Darko_, that title sequence has such a strange hold over me that I cannot explain. Also the titles to Michael Haneke's _Funny Games_ (original German version), where the calming classical music is interjected by screaming death metal. Finally, _Zombieland_, ironic and dark, and visually so clever and good to look at.

I always enjoyed reading about Eric Gill, his was a colorful life. Big and flawed personalities are so fun.

There are too many designers I respect and love. One of the people on the top of my list is Karel Martens. And also my teacher Ed Fella; his work is so idiosyncratic.

I don't actually have a favorite font, I'm not so much of a type geek.

Who inspires you? What is your biggest influence?

I draw from the same pool that most of my friends get their inspiration from: artists, filmmakers, and writers. A lot of painters, not for any direct influences, but that visual exposure always puts me in the right state of mind to explore new ideas. And traveling does that too, it zaps me out of the jaded mode and puts a fresh spin on my perception of the world—an antidote to so many things.

What are you working on now?

Two title sequences: a main-on-end for _Shrek 4_ and another one for _Hot Tub Time Machine_, a total dude flick.

3

THE ESSENTIALS OF TYPOGRAPHY AND TIME

Typography allows designers and communicators to convey their ideas through the form of each letter. Each font has its own personality that manifests itself through weight, proportion, and detail. Furthermore, the way each font is articulated onscreen creates an additional "voice" and character.

There is no set rule about what is the "right" font. Using the appropriate font for the appropriate project is an acquired skill that comes with time and practice. Before we look into the kinds of type we utilize today, let's first dive into a bit of history.

Writing Systems and the Roman Capital

Writing is an organized symbolic system that can be:
1. **Logographic.** A system in which visual symbols represent words. This system includes **ideographic scripts** (graphemes are used as a graphic symbol to represent an idea or concept, such as Chinese characters) and **pictographic scripts** (each grapheme conveys its meaning through its visual resemblance to the physical object, such as Egyptians hieroglyphics).
2. **Syllabic.** A writing system that utilizes syllables. The sum of multiple adjacent syllables represents a word.
3. **Alphabetic.** A writing system that utilizes consonants and vowels—the alphabet. The sum of multiple adjacent letters represents a word.

The alphabet we use today is the **Latin alphabet**—different, of course, from the Latin language. The Latin alphabet is an alphabetic system originally derived from the Phoenicians that has reached us through a long process of geographical and linguistical transmutation.

One pioneer, the "mother" of all fonts used today, is called the **Roman Capital** (referred to as *Capitale Romana* in Italian). This font was historically used particularly in epigraphs. If you happen to take a walk in the center of Rome, you can see this font in epigraphs next to squares, buildings, or churches, and you can try to comprehend its meaning (unless you know Latin, it might

doi: 10.1016/B978-0-240-81419-3.00003-9

73

be quite a hard task!). Even better, you should take a walk in the Roman Forum and take a close look at Trajan's Column (built in 113 AD). The letters engraved in the epigraph by the column's base are considered a point of reference in typography because of their beauty and character.

The Roman Capital was primarily used as an official public communication form; it was engraved in stone, using a *V*-shaped chisel. The Ordinator (from Latin, meaning *the organizer*) was the graphic designer responsible for creating the layout of the text and hand-drawing the letters, which were then engraved with a hammer and chisel by the Lapicida. The Ordinator would use a brush to draw the letters, which explains the differences in the widths of letter strokes in the Roman Capital.

Form Follows Function: A Roman Exercise

Let's pretend for a moment that you are a designer who has been assigned the job of designing a font that, when engraved in stone, has to:

- Outlast time and weather conditions
- Be capable of being painted once the color fades, without re-engraving the stone
- Have depth

Put your thinking cap on and come up with a solution. Done? Now let's take a look at what the Romans did: By using a flat brush to draw the Roman Capital, they created thick and thin stroke weights. When these lines—used as guidelines—were engraved using a *V*-shaped chisel, they created enough depth that, when lit, they created the perception of depth (because of the shadows), and when the stone's surface was repainted, the letters remained readable so they didn't need to be re-engraved. This was a perfect solution that satisfied both function and form.

Types of Type: The Anatomy of a Typeface

Typefaces have different emotional qualities, depending on their form. Let's start by defining some of the common type styles:

- **Serif.** These generally include a little stroke at the edges of each letter. In *The Origin of the Serif: Brush Writing and Roman Letters* (Saint Ambrose University Catich Gallery, 1991), Edward Catich demonstrates how utilizing a brush gave birth to the serif. Even though their origin is still discussed today, the truth is that serifs facilitate the letters' alignment perception, and with it, the type's readability. Classic serifs include Times New Roman, Garamond, and Baskerville. Serifs can also be thin and straight (like Bodoni), or thicker, also called *slab serif* (Rockwell, Clarendon).

- **Sans serif.** These are typefaces without serifs, and the stroke weight is generally uniform. Typical sans-serif typefaces include Futura, Helvetica, and Gill Sans.
- **Script.** These typefaces resemble calligraphy made with a brush or quill. Their stroke weight varies from thin to thick.
- **Display.** These are typefaces that, for best appearance and readability, are better displayed at a larger point size. Nowadays **display** is used as a synonym for decorative or articulated fonts that are appropriate for a header or title.
- **Bitmap.** These are screen fonts; therefore they are at 72 dpi resolution and are designed to be used at a particular font size. Zooming in on or scaling up these fonts reveals that they are composed of pixels. These fonts are displayed correctly when used on Web sites or screen-based interface designs, but they are not appropriate for printing or motion-based work that requires a resolution output higher than 72 dpi (such as titles to be printed on film) unless you want their pixilation to be a conscious stylistic choice.
- **Monospaced or fixed-width.** These fonts are designed similarly to the way a typewriter works; each letter occupies the same exact amount of space, regardless of the adjacent letter.

A typeface could articulate itself in a variety of weights. When that happens, it is referred to as a *font family*. A font family can include some or all the following individual fonts, which range in weight from lighter to heavier:

- Ultra light
- Light
- Roman
- Italic
- Semi-bold
- Bold
- Extra bold
- Black
- Small caps

Each of these font weights might have additional variations: condensed, compressed, or wide.

The following terminology will help you obtain a better understanding of typeface properties so that you can better articulate your title sequence type:

- **X-height.** The height of the body of a lowercase letter such as *x* or *a*. Different typefaces are designed with different x-heights, depending on their use (newspaper fonts, for example, are designed with a taller x-height to make them easier to read). Keep in mind that different fonts displayed at the same size might actually look smaller or bigger, depending on their x-height.

Font Styles

Figure 3.1

Font Weights

Gill Sans

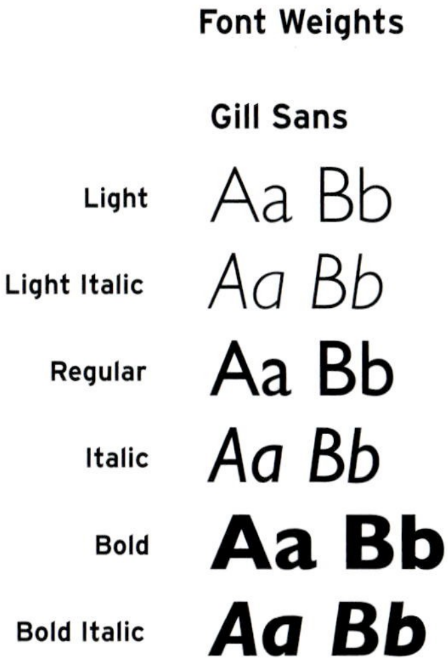

Figure 3.2 Font weights examples.

X-Height

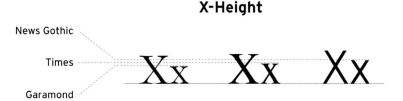

Figure 3.3 X-Height example. Notice the different x-height of these three fonts displayed at the same font size.

Understanding this small detail could help you argue with your client for the use of a particular font. Let's say that when working on your end titles, you have a problem with screen space, like the credit roles or names are longer than usual. In this situation you might opt for a font that has a taller x-height so that you can reduce the font size and still maintain legibility.

- **Stroke weight.** The variance between the thin and thick strokes of a font.
- **Type size.** The size of a font is measured in points, depending on their output and destination. A general rule of thumb in designing titles is to start at 24 points.
- **Uppercase.** Capital letters, also called *majuscules.*
- **Lowercase.** Smaller letters, also called *minuscule.*
- **Mixed case.** Words or sentences that alternate upper and lower case.
- **Small caps**. Smaller capital letters, generally designed to be as high as the x-height.
- **Ligatures.** Special characters that are combined to create a single glyph—the most common ligature being f+i or f+l.
- **Do's and don'ts.** If there is one set of rules you should follow from this very moment, it is the following:
  - **Smart quotes.** If you want to avoid being bashed by the design community, when you use quotation marks do not use the straight ones (also called the *prime symbol*) but instead use the *smart* (or *curly*) *quotes* that have been designed as part of the font you are using. A typical use of primes is in indicating values of length or time; for example, if you typed 5′10″, it could mean 5 feet 10 inches or 5 minutes and 10 seconds. Smart quotation marks generally are either open or closed and should be used at the opening and closing of the quotation, respectively; they are often curled toward the center of the quote. They can be single or double. Apostrophes fall into the category of smart quotes; when you're using apostrophes in your title cards, make sure that they display correctly, as though they were a single closed smart quote.
  - **Faux italic or bold.** Some software programs allow the user to create a faux (or fake) bold or italic. For example, if you

select your text and activate the faux bold option, your text instantly looks fat, but unhappy; the software created a Frankenstein's monster version of what your font should have looked like if you had actually used the correctly designed bold variant of your font. Sometimes the bold variant of a font doesn't exist or you don't have it available. In this case I'd simply recommend you either purchase that font weight or find another font to use.

- **Handwritten fonts.** Do not underestimate the character and uniqueness of handwritten fonts. Although hand-drawing each title card might seem like an enormous amount of work, the results can be spectacular. Take, for example, the titles created for **Where the Wild Things Are** or for **Juno**.

What does this all mean? Well, now you have an arsenal of options. You should never leave these options to chance. Never design your title cards with the default font settings of your software. Always make a conscious decision about font usage.

To get started, ask yourself the following questions:
- Are my title cards going to be uppercase, lowercase, or mixed case?
- Does the typeface offer the option of using ligatures?
- Which font weight should I use, Roman or bold?
- How am I planning to display the difference between the talent's names and their roles?

Every decision on how you shape and articulate your type on your title cards should be a conscious decision, motivated by the project, the audience, and your strategy.

Kerning, Tracking, and Leading

In addition to font families, there are additional parameters that allow you to personalize the text that you should take into consideration. Let's define a few more terms:
- **Baseline.** The invisible horizontal line that all letters rest on. This is the line across the bottom of the x-height. The curves of some letters, descenders, and punctuation marks often go below the boundaries of the baseline.
- **Kerning.** Kern is the measure of space between two characters. Kerning is the process of reducing or increasing the space between specific pairs of characters. Although it might seem appropriate to check the kerning throughout your titles, it could quickly become a time-consuming activity, especially when you're under a tight timeline. While you could be forgiven for not checking your end titles, you should absolutely check your main title card and single/double title cards for any necessary kerning adjustments. When doing so, pay attention to how each

KERN
KERN

Figure 3.4 Example of bad (top) and good (bottom) kerning.

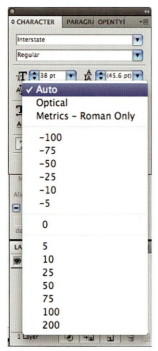

Figure 3.5 Selecting a kerning option.

letter looks adjacent to the previous or the following one and try to make spacing consistent between each letter. Depending on the letters, the space should be reduced or increased. Common characters that require some kerning adjustments include uppercase letters that have a diagonal shape followed by a curved one or another diagonal one. To get more accustomed to this thought process, consider looking at the negative (white) space between each letter and try the following:

- Manipulate it to make it of an equal mass within similarly shaped letters (e.g., straight/round, straight/straight, round/round letters).
- Once you've established your point of reference, keep the negative space consistent throughout your title cards.
- Avoid letting serifs touch each other.

Some typefaces require more attention than others. Generally, well-designed typefaces from a well-established font foundry require minimal kerning adjustments. Kerning requires practice, time, and attention to detail. Keep in mind that well-kerned type generally goes unnoticed, but to a trained graphic designer's eye, badly kerned type jumps off the screen immediately. Depending on the software you use to create your title cards—such as Adobe InDesign, Illustrator, or After Effects—you might be able to control your kerning via the following options:

- **Metric kerning (or auto kerning).** This adjusts the kerning based on settings originally designed by the type foundry. Metric kerning refers to the font's built-in kern pair tables and is generally the default setting.
- **Optical kerning.** This involves adjusting the kerning based on the actual shape of each letter. This option helps you save time while initially creating the layout of your text, but this should not be a substitute for your own judgment. You should still consider doing manual tweaks after you've applied optical kerning.
- **Manual kerning.** This involves adjusting the kerning manually, allowing you to choose a preset kern value or type in your preferred one.
- **Tracking (spacing).** The process of reducing or increasing the space between letters in words or blocks of text. Tracking can be tight or loose. Tightening or loosening the tracking decreases or increases the overall spacing throughout the selected words or block of text by the same proportional amount. When text is tracked too tightly, the words appear crowded and touch each other, and as a result it is difficult to read. On the other hand, when the text is tracked too loosely, it presents too much white space between the words, which makes it hard to read as well. Similarly to kerning, appropriate

tracking comes with practice and experience. Appropriately tracked text should go unnoticed by viewers. In tracking, follow these guidelines:

- Condensed or compressed typefaces generally require less tracking than wider typefaces.
- Smaller font sizes generally require more tracking than larger font sizes.

- **Ascender.** The part of a lowercase letter that stems up from its body, such as in the letters *l* or *b*.
- **Descender.** The part of a lowercase letter that stems down from its body, such as in the letters *p* or *q*.
- **Leading** (pronounced ledding). The distance between the baselines of a type that spans two or more lines of text. When you're setting the leading for your titles, especially when you're designing a double card or scrolling titles, pay particular attention to the ascenders and descenders and make sure they don't touch.

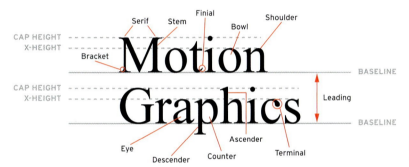

Figure 3.6 Examples of a typeface's properties.

and rearrange items to exceed above and below the grid lines to take advantage of their shapes and achieve a better design. Press **Control-;** (or **Command-;**) to hide and show your guides, and experiment by pushing design elements into and out of shapes.

Readability: Titles at the Movies, Online, and on Your Cell Phone

Now that we've explored some type flavors, we need to address a key component of successful typographical use: readability. Often overlooked and viewed as a secondary and less-relevant value compared to the coolness of a font or a particular layout, readability is an aspect of design that absolutely should not be overlooked. If the titles are unreadable, the information and messages don't come across, and that can obviously cause frustration for the viewer—or even cause you to lose a client.

Readability depends on a variety of factors. The audience is sitting still, but their head and eye movements, the type's animation, and the screen time often affect the way the audience identifies words and processes them.

For example, titles that face the viewer, displayed in 2D (as opposed to 3D) characters, allow for quick readability. In using 3D typefaces, especially if they are embedded in a 3D environment, give them slightly more screen time than 2D fonts.

What is important to understand is that there are no set-in-stone rules about readability. You will have to test each of your project's font sizes and screen times; use your common sense, experience, judgment, and client requirements; and know how your project will be distributed (online only, in theaters, or via some other method).

Cone of Vision and Screen Dimension

While designing title cards, designers should keep in mind the viewer's *cone of vision*. The screen's dimensions and the distance from the viewer to the screen are also relevant factors. A typical cone of vision for a spectator in a movie theater or screening room is between 30 and 60 degrees total view angle. In a 30-degree cone of vision, a viewer sees 15 degrees from the right eye and 15 degrees from the left eye, for a total of 30 degrees view angle. A viewer sitting in the front row will have to use a wider cone of vision to detect the entire surface of the screen; eye and head movements will be necessary to follow the action and type on the screen, and the close proximity to the screen will result in image distortion. A viewer sitting in the last row will have to employ a narrower cone of vision; head movements are minimal, giving the eyes the entire job of deciphering the information onscreen.

Font Size and Distance

Screen readability is determined by the font size, color, contrast between the font color and its background color, and the typeface. The United States Sign Council (USSC), through extensive research, has developed a Legibility Index (LI). In Table 3.2, you can find a reference for a sans-serif font (Helvetica) and a slab-serif font (Clarendon). A title card with an LI of 29 means that the font—when its capitals are 1-inch high—should be legible at a distance of 29 feet. For example, according to this chart, when we use black Helvetica on a white background, its capitals set at 1 inch, it should be legible from 29 feet (if it's uppercase and lowercase) or 25 feet (if it's all capitals). If the font is displayed at 10 inches, it will be visible from 290 feet and 250 feet, if uppercase and lowercase or all caps, respectively.

Table 3.2 Legibility Index Chart

Letter Style	Letter Color	Background Color	Legibility Index	
			Uppercase and Lowercase	*All Caps*
Helvetica	Black	White	29	25
Helvetica	Yellow	Green	26	22
Helvetica	White	Black	26	22
Clarendon	Black	White	28	24
Clarendon	Yellow	Green	31	26
Clarendon	White	Black	24	20

You might wonder why there is a difference between using uppercase and lowercase and using all caps when it comes to legibility. When using uppercase and lowercase, which use ascenders and descenders, the words' shapes are more distinctive and recognizable; therefore, this is considered more readable than using only capital letters.

Some research, though, contradicts this view. Research conducted by Tinker in 1963 found that even when a font with a great x-height was used, an uppercase font is more readable at greater distances than a mix of uppercase and lowercase. Further findings by Arditi and Cho in 2007 found that when text is very small, uppercase fonts are more legible in terms of reading speed, both for normally sighted readers and for readers with reduced sighting due to visual impairments.

What does this all mean to your titles? You don't necessarily need to use the 30-feet LI rule in your title sequence, but it is a good place to start.

In applying this information to title design, consider that signage is different from title design. Print design works with inches or a metric system; type is still measured in points, whether in print or digital format. Our main variable in working with a digital title sequence is the frame size.

Let's take, for example, a digital title sequence for a movie, which will be output to film at 2K resolution (2048 pixels wide by 1556 pixels high at 72 pixels/inch). Its correspondent dimensions in inches are 28.44 inches wide by 21.61 inches high. To create a font size that will be 1-inch high, you will have to set your font to approximately 100–104 points. This font will be legible from 30 feet away.

Table 3.3 shows how the USSC Legibility Index translates into our screen size world.

Table 3.3

Format	Frame Size	Point Size (Equivalent to 1 Inch Height and Legible from 30 Feet Away)
Film 4K	2048 × 1556	208 pts.
Film 2K	4096 × 3112	104 pts
HD/HDTV 720p	1280 × 720	65 pts.
DV NTSC	720 × 480	35 pts.

The Department of Computer Science and Communication of the University of Milan, Italy, has developed FontReader, a program that allows a user to calculate the dimension a typeface should be based on the minimum distance from which someone would see it, to guarantee its legibility. This application was created primarily for outdoor advertising (billboard, bus ads), but it could certainly apply to designing title cards that would be readable even by viewers sitting in the front rows of movie theaters.

Are Your Titles Safe?

To guarantee your titles' legibility—especially when you're working in broadcast title design—they should be placed within a title safe boundary box. With the exception of plasma and LCD screens, most television sets scale up the video signal received and cut off some of its content by the edge of the screen. Because this cropping, also called **overscan**, is not consistent among the various TV brands and models, titles should be placed within a title safe boundary box, and relevant live-action or animation content should be placed within an Action Safe boundary box. A title safe box is typically 80% of its frame size. An Action Safe grid is typically 90% of its frame size.

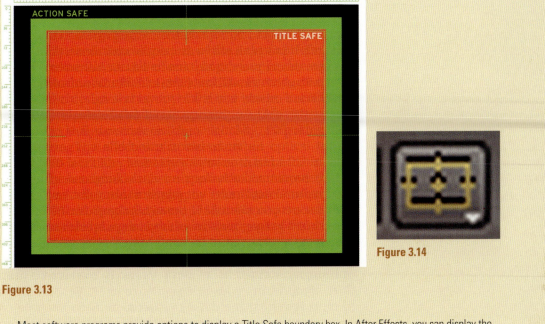

Figure 3.14

Figure 3.13

Most software programs provide options to display a Title Safe boundary box. In After Effects, you can display the Action and Title Safe boxes by clicking the **Choose grid and guide option** (Figure 3.14) icon on the bottom left of your Composition window. In Photoshop and Illustrator you can view the Action and Title Safe grids or overlay when you create a new file from one of the Video & Film presets.

Titles Online and On Your Cell Phone

How does a small screen compare to a large screen in a movie theater? For one thing, in a theater you are immersed in the dark, with nothing else to distract you. You empathize with the characters of your movie; the titles are readable, exciting, and entertaining. The size of the screen is wrapping around your perception, and the sound (whether stereo or Dolby 5.1 Surround Sound) is wrapping around you, immersing you in the reality of the movie. You are breathing, fighting, suffering, and loving with your characters. Compare that experience with viewing the same movie on an airplane, when you are interrupted by the passenger sitting in the window seat who needs to get up, or the hostess serving coffee, or even with looking at the same movie while in line or waiting for the next bus or train.

Regardless of the drastic dissimilarities in experiencing movies in various environments, the filmmakers' and designers' challenge is to create a product that will stand the technological limits and challenges posed by the new distribution channels.

There is relatively minimal concern when designing title sequences for the Web. As far as screen size, most Web sites are now designed for a screen size of 1280 × 1024 pixels, which allows movies to be embedded in the Web page at least at SD resolution. The one variable to keep an eye out for is the video codec. Depending on the film's compression, the typographical elements of a title sequence might become unpleasantly unreadable; the font's antialiasing could be deteriorated, and the serifs might become too thin or even disappear completely. Some Web sites might even require a maximum file weight for a video upload, and that's when the testing begins to try to find an appropriate compression that allows for quick video streaming while maintaining the title sequence's quality.

There are no set-in-stone rules; the compression depends on the nature and source quality of the title sequences—whether they include 3D elements, colors and textures, live action, heavy or light typographical elements, or the like. To determine the best video codec for your title sequence you should export a short segment using a variety of video codecs and then scrub through the video file to verify its result. To start off, you should try compressing your title sequence as H.264, Motion JPEG, or Apple ProRes. If you'd like to explore more compression flavors, you should import your title sequence into Apple Compressor and try a few of its presets.

When designing a title sequence for smaller screens such as mobile devices it is important to understand that there are a variety of screen sizes and resolutions, depending on the make and model. Although you are not expected to design for each and every one of these devices, at least one version of a title sequence, redesigned to be readable on smaller screens, might be required by your client.

Table 3.4 will help you understand the frame sizes and aspect ratios of common mobile devices.

When designing title sequences for smaller screens, you can still use the USSC Legibility Index as a guideline. A black Helvetica

Table 3.4 Screen aspect ratio of common mobile devices

Brand/Model	Aspect Ratio	Pixel Size	Inch Size (Diagonal)
LG, Samsung	1.67:1	400 × 240	3″
PSP Go	1.47:1	400 × 272	3.8″
Apple iPhone	3:2	480 × 320	3.5″
Nokia Tube	16:9	640 × 360	3.2″
Sony Ericsson Xperia	2:1	800 × 400	3″
iPad	4:3	1024 × 768	9.7″

displayed on white background at 0.1 inch high—equivalent to a 10-point typeface—will be readable from 2.9 feet (uppercase and lowercase) and 2.5 feet (all caps).

Tutorial: Modifying Text with Adobe Illustrator

One of the major strengths of Adobe's Illustrator software is its ability to apply an artist's touch to existing fonts. Illustrator allows users to "break" a font from the appearance it has and allow users to apply vector image editing tools to customize its appearance. This powerful feature alone often justifies a trip over to Illustrator.

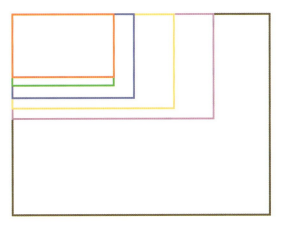

☐ LG, SAMSUNG 400x240 pixels
☐ PSP GO 400x272 pixels
☐ APPLE IPHONE 480x320 pixels
☐ NOKIA TUBE 640x360 pixels
☐ SONY ERICCSON EXPERIA 800x400 pixels
☐ APPLE IPAD 1024x768 pixels

Figure 3.15

Adobe Illustrator is the industry standard for vector image editing. It allows you to use Bezier tools to change the shapes of the objects you are editing by adjusting points. In the following tutorial we'll use Illustrator to bring a boring title to life.

Figure 3.16 The same letter in its normal presentation and after Create Outlines has been applied.

1 Before we start changing the shapes of the letters involved, we should resolve any issues we need to address while the material is still being treated as text layers by the software. Make sure you are happy with the font you've chosen as well as the leading and kerning. We can change the leading and kerning later, but it is more difficult.

2 When you are ready to proceed, with your text layer selected, select **Type | Create Outlines**. Now we can begin editing the shapes of the letters.

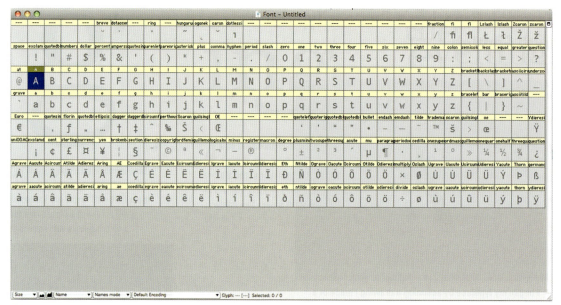

3 Launch Fontlab Studio and click **File | New**. This will open a new font window, which will show you a grid with all the **glyphs** in a font. Highlight the capital *A*. Go to the **Glyphs** menu and click **Create Glyphs If Empty**. Now double-click the capital **A** and its glyph window will open.

> A **glyph**, by definition, is any element of writing. In Fontlab Studio and most computer software, it simply means an individual character in a font.

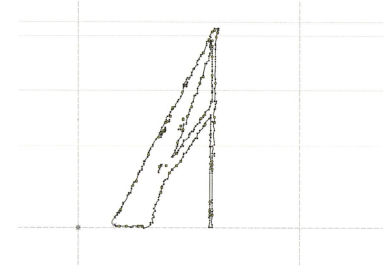

4 Go back to Illustrator and select the path and **Edit | Copy** it. Go back over to Fontlab and **Edit | Paste** it into the glyph window for the capital **A**. Now repeat this action for each letter. You don't have to individually scan each letter; you can draw them out on one page and Live Trace them as a group. I just demonstrated one letter for the purpose of clarity. In fact, you could build the other letters using Illustrator if you want, though that could take a while.

5 **Done** - When you have finished supplying the glyphs for all the characters, go to **File | Generate Font**. This will essentially export what you've done in Fontlab as a font that you can then install on your computer, like any other font.

Moving Type for the Web with Adobe Flash

It used to be that very few people watched video content on the Web, but those days are over. Title design has become an important part of new media content, and the new size issues and constraints are important issues to address. There's also been a significant boost for Flash's capability now that it's an Adobe application; it has some great features that make pairing it with After Effects a powerful suite of tools.

Considerations for Web Viewing and Mobile Devices

Watching something on the Web, or a mobile phone, is a much different experience than watching on TV or the big screen. It's not the comfortable, dedicated experience of home or theatrical viewing. Title designers must also take design considerations into account.

First, the standard size of Web video is different than TV or film. Obviously we are talking about smaller images. The problem is that the type size cannot be shrunk down relatively and still achieve maximum readability. We have to err on the side of displaying type at a larger relative size on the smaller Web/mobile device image.

In addition to the size concern, we also have to keep in mind that Web video displays the **entire** image. It's still a good idea to keep our titles within title safety so their distance from the edge is still comfortable for viewers to read. In case you've gotten into the bad habit of leaving elements in the image area just past the domestic cutoff edge, you can't do that when working on video for the Web.

Tutorial: Basic Type Animation in Adobe Flash

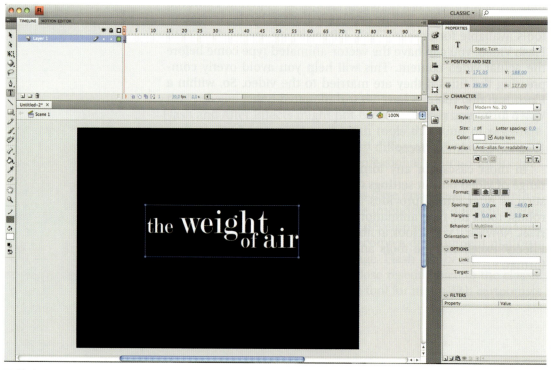

1 At the beginning of any Flash project, it is worth viewing the **Modify | Document** window and setting up your document accordingly. If it is your plan to add animated type to a Web site, it's important to match the dimensions of the final site or, if it's going to be a specified section of a page, to match the dimensions of the area that is already blocked out. If it's going to be added to a Flash Video presentation, it should match the setting of the Flash Video piece.

2 Typically when I am using Flash I will move the Tools panel to the left-hand side (call me a traditionalist if you want, but having a toolbar on the right feels wrong to me). Select the familiar **Type** tool and lay out your text.

3 Our next step is to go to the **Modify** menu and choose **Convert to Symbol** (or press **F8** on the keyboard). Select **Movie Clip** from **Type**. Name it **title**. In most cases you will need to use **Convert to Symbol** to create any animation.

4 Now, unlike After Effects, every frame in Flash is represented by an individual box. Highlight the box below the 10-frame mark. Now go to **Insert | Timeline | Keyframe** (or press **F6**).

2 **Cont'd** In Flash you adjust parameters to the elements you create with the **Properties** panel. Type controls are in the **Character** section. **Auto kern** has a switch. Tracking will be controlled by the oddly labeled **Letter spacing** number value. Also, you'll find leading below the **Paragraph** heading under **Spacing**.

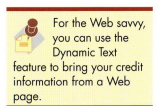

5 At the 10-frame mark, use the **Free Transform Tool** (or press **Q**) and scale up our text.

For the Web savvy, you can use the Dynamic Text feature to bring your credit information from a Web page.

Mac users will notice that Flash makes use of the F keys, which may interfere with OSX features such as Expose. You can change or turn off these keyboard commands for Expose by going to **System Preferences**, under **Expose and Spaces**.

6 **Done**-To execute any kind of animation in Flash, you have to tell Flash to *Tween*. Highlight the frames, and go to **Insert | Classic Tween**. Now an arrow will appear linking your first and last keyframes. Press **Enter** to view your animation.

Tutorial: Moving a Type Animation from After Effects to Flash with the XFL Format

Now that Flash and After Effects are both published by Adobe, we can take advantage of the strengths of both programs. In this tutorial, we'll see how to start a project with After Effects and then export it to Flash.

1 In After Effects I created a quick animation of a title, and I have applied the **Whirl In** preset to the type layer (**Effects and Presets | Animation Presets | Type Animation | Curves and Spins | Whirl In**).

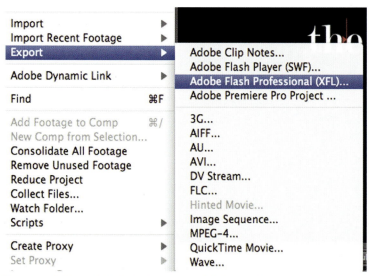

2 Choose **File | Export | Adobe Flash Professional (XFL)**. The XFL format works similarly to Flash's FLA files, so after we export, you can open the XFL file as though it were a FLA.

3 Flash's engine is vector-based and AE's is raster, so since they "speak different languages," we have to adjust our export settings so that we preserve the appearance of our timeline. After you choose **File | Export | Adobe Flash Professional (XFL)**, you will have to choose some export settings. Since the type animation work we are doing in After Effects would be an unsupported feature in Flash, under the heading **Layers with Unsupported Features**, turn on **Rasterize to:** and, from the pull-down menu, choose a **Format**. The FLV format will give you a compressed video layer in Flash, and PNG Sequence will give you a series of images. Either will support transparency.

4 **Done** - Grab the XFL file and open it with Flash. Now you can you use it as a part of your Flash project.

Case Study: *The Alphabet Conspiracy*

Motion Graphics Studio: MK12
Creative Directors: Ben Radatz, Tim Fisher
www.mk12.com

FOR IMMEDIATE RELEASE:

For millennia, the alphabet has been the building block of human communication and cultural understanding. The Greeks, the Romans, the Turks, the Celts—all were pioneers of our own modern-day writing, passing the linguistic torch down from their civilization to our own. You could say that the alphabet—and phonemes—are so pervasive in our everyday lives that we barely give them a second thought.

And that's what They're counting on.

In 1962, while conducting routine experiments at the Voice Research Laboratory (VRL), scientists discovered a curious mutation on the common phoneme **ɚr**: a faint, positively charged frequency that modified the implied meaning of the resulting sound. In ensuing tests conducted on primate subjects, it was observed that the modified **ɚr** phoneme, when amplified through a common telephone headset device, evoked strong feelings of confusion and anxiety in the primates.

Further experiments were conducted on human subjects using additional phonemes—**aʊ, ɔ**, and **ɔɚr** being the most common. These subjects also displayed increased confusion and disorientation and soon became detached and generally lethargic—most notably when the phonemes were arranged into distinct words and sentences, as with **ðɪ dɔg ɛt maɪˈsændwɪtʃ**.

There are opposing accounts of what happened next, but soon it was obvious that this subsonic Trojan horse wasn't a daughter of nature; indeed, the scientists at VRL had stumbled on a massive linguistic conspiracy, the depths of which are only now being excavated. It was an outright hijacking of our language from the inside out. But to what end? And by whom?

This colorful, geometric televideo is an accurate account of the known facts, including several minutes of never-before-seen footage accompanied by helpful diagrams and charts. It proposes new theories and offers supporting historical and scientific context and is two minutes and forty-nine seconds long. It is most likely both entertaining and informative.

Please discuss this film on completion.

///

Figure 3.21a Still frames from "The Alphabet Conspiracy" by MK12.

Figure 3.21b

Figure 3.21c

Figure 3.21d

Figure 3.21e

Figure 3.21f

Figure 3.21g

The Alphabet Conspiracy is a hybrid live-action/animated piece about the language working as a double agent, carrying a hidden meaning with it for reasons yet unknown.

The short came about after finding an educational film from the 1960s, also titled *The Alphabet Conspiracy* (we like to think of ours as a sequel of sorts). In the original, a young girl named Alice boycotts her homework and falls asleep, traveling to an enchanted world where she conspires with a Mad Hatter type to eliminate books and words (thus no homework). They're intercepted by a kind-hearted linguist who eventually convinces Alice that the alphabet really does matter. She then wakes up.

Figure 3.21h Still frames from "The Alphabet Conspiracy" by MK12, continued.

Figure 3.21i

Figure 3.21j

Figure 3.21k

Figure 3.21l

Figure 3.21m

We'd already been scripting a type-based short that was eerily close to this one, and so we figured that instead of reinventing the wheel, we'd simply add our own spin to the original. We cut up the soundtrack and remixed it into a slightly darker version of itself, and that became the foundation for the piece. From there we developed an animatic and began working in the key elements (though with nonnarrative pieces, we always treat the animatic as a general guide, since the tangents we follow while animating and designing usually end up becoming the piece).

The short takes other cues from the film as well as other educational films from days past, inspired by the awkward editing and absurd premises that often defined the genre. The color palette is simple and deliberate, and we worked with a technique in which all the elements were split out into their respective red, green, and blue channels, which usually remain superimposed to form a complete image but sometimes move independently of one another to create interesting transitional and graphic effects.

Figure 3.21n Still frames from "The Alphabet Conspiracy" by MK12, continued.

Figure 3.21o

Figure 3.21p

Figure 3.21q

Figure 3.21r

Figure 3.21s

We like to design custom typefaces for our film projects, and since this piece is about the alphabet from a scientific perspective, we spent a good deal of time developing a typeface that was theoretically perfect and balanced. We were less concerned with making an aesthetically pleasing font because we were ensuring that every measurement was a reciprocal of another. We also developed a pretty rigid set of rules for how the type was to be laid out and presented on-screen, making sure that exponents and weights were always considered. It's not something that's necessarily meant to be picked up on; it was more a starting point for our compositions, and it felt appropriate to the subject matter.

Figure 3.22

Interview: Stacy Nimmo on Title Design

Motion Graphics Studio: Gunshop
Creative Director: Stacy Nimmo
www.gunshop.tv

One of the wonderful things about broadcast design and kinetic typography is that there are so many different things that you can put into any piece you do. You have music, cinematography, 2D or 3D graphics, and typography, which stand on their own as a communication tool. Finding the right mixture of what to use for the message that you're sending is the real challenge. You have to find out what your client needs, what they need to communicate, and how it needs to be. Generally, on the emotional side you tend to have things that are much more ephemeral, and then on the very clear and concise side, you have "50% off" and giant "For Sale" signs. So, between those two extremes you need to find out what your client needs to communicate and what the consumer wants to hear.

Can you talk a little about yourself and your background in graphic design?

I studied design at the University of Florida in a very, very traditional sort of program, at a time just before computers became more popular. So, not to sound like a Luddite, but I think that there were some really positive things that can be learned in design before you get on a computer. And I think at some point, especially in the foundation time, it's actually helpful to stay away from a computer so that you deal with very basic compositions. You know, if you have After Effects or if you have Photoshop, you're immediately capable of layering 100 layers on there, and that's just not the case when you got a copy machine and you're blowing up some typography; you're physically limited to the number of things that you can do there. I think that that's really good because it helps you focus on saying the most with the fewest number of parts. And I think that is the essence of typography: say the most with the fewest number of parts.

I still urge schools and students coming into broadcast design for the first time to not do everything with the computer, to try to do things offline and in your head and in the sketchbook as much as possible. And one of the key pieces of that is learning to understand and work with typography, getting to know the cropping, and the scale, and the kerning, and the subtle sort of things that are really helpful to have. To look at it offline, as in printmaking and using stenciling, for example, where you have a physically engaging process and you have a feel for the physical weight and positioning of the letters.

It's almost the difference between reading a book on a computer and reading an actual book. It has a different feel and weight to it, and I think you become much more familiar with typography when it's reflective versus when it's on a computer screen.

Figure 3.23a Client: Symantec;
Project Title: Higher Level;
Duration: 00:30.

Figure 3.23b

Figure 3.23c

Figure 3.23d

Figure 32.23e

Figure 3.23f

Figure 3.23g

Figure 3.23h

Figure 3.23i

Figure 3.23j

Figure 3.23k

Figure 3.23l

Figure 3.23m

Figure 3.23n

From studying graphic design, how did you end up specializing in motion graphics?

I went from studying design, which was primarily print design in college, to working on movie posters for Miramax in New York City in the early 1990s, when they were starting. When you look at a movie poster you have the actors, and you have them composited usually in some vague world, and then you have the title.

And the title really speaks volumes about what it is that you're going to see; it especially has the capability of doing that, of setting the tone of the movie outside the particular image of the people. It's about the people and about the title design. In fact, the title is so relevant to these posters that it's actually written in contracts that certain people's names have to be a certain relative size compared to the title: "If a title is *X* size, my name has to be 20% of *X* size." And that's how movie posters end up with very skinny, very tall typography, because it is a legal requirement that people's names be the same size as the title.

I went back to film school to study traditional film production, and there's still a lot of things that I draw on from that experience that have nothing to do with being on a live-action set but have everything to do with the way a camera moves through a 3D scene or the way drama or motion is carried through camera movement. I think that that is a very important step in the progress in anybody's broadcast design growth.

When and how did you start Gunshop?

We started Gunshop in 2000. We're now 10 years old, which is pretty exciting, and pretty old in this business, too, but we have a lot of benefits of having that experience. The main reason we started Gunshop was because in the late '90s the main places that were doing sophisticated broadcast design had some very, very expensive equipment. We had started doing more and more work on the desktop with After Effects and realized that we didn't need all these expensive tape decks, we didn't need the Inferno, and just really began to produce jobs soup-to-nuts on the desktop. We opened up our shop as a sort of desktop solution for broadcast design. It was one of the first in the city, and it was very popular, and we ended up doing a lot of work with HBO and all their family of channels, like Cinemax, as well as Viacom and their family, like MTV and VH1.

How do your life experience, interests, and passions influence your work? And what are your interests and passions?

If someone asks me, I generally don't refer to myself as a commercial artist, though at essence that's what I am. I'm an artist who is working in a commercial atmosphere, in a commercial manner, basically creating commissioned works of art for the client.

So, for me, there's a lot of creativity that goes into all these pieces. It's very fulfilling to create, as I call them, tiny worlds. We create these tiny, very special, very specific, very branded worlds for our clients so that they can communicate whatever they need to about their product. And I think that as an artist it's very fulfilling, I think it's very challenging as well as it is very commercial, and you have a client that's paying for it, so there's a lot of negotiation, sacrifice, and changes that are involved in the process. And if you have the right team together both internally in your design company as well as with your advertising or theatrical partners, you can have some great stuff coming out of it. I think that you basically expand your team to work with the team of the client. And that's when projects really take on a life of their own that no individual is capable of doing.

Do you have any guidelines or preferences in regard to font size and readability, whether for theatrical release, broadcast, or smaller screens?

You know, its kind of funny, but in general we have a really crappy TV here in the office, and after we do some type design we want to make sure it looks good on that crappy TV. I mean, you could do stuff in HD that will look fantastic on an HD monitor, but you also have a lot of people who have different, older, and smaller TVs, and you always want to make sure it works on the lowest common denominator, especially when half the stuff we're doing is still in SD.

So as far as specific specs of how many point sizes, we don't have anything that is that specific because sometimes you have a headline that's a certain size and it's only one word, but if it's three words then it's going to change that rule all together. So, it's a little bit more about what works than our rules.

Figure 3.24a Client: Arts and Entertainment Networks; Project Title: Jacked Auto Theft Task Force; Duration: 00:16.

Figure 3.24b

Figure 3.24c

Figure 3.24d

Figure 3.24e

Figure 3.24f

Figure 3.24g

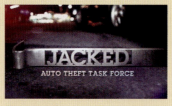
Figure 3.24h

How about screen time?

It kind of follows the same rules as our typographic size rule, which is, you want to make sure it feels right and looks right. Just like with type size, we use a bad monitor, with type timing and also sometimes with scale we'll do a lot of those things in the edit room, which I think is a very important place to say, "Is this on long enough?" So, we may work on the files in 3D or After Effects, but at some point, or often throughout the process, we'll bring it into the edit room and we'll do small adjustments to scale or timing there, because you can get into a level of finesse there that is really where you want to be. You can adjust it so it's just a little bit faster and the other piece is just a little bit slower and it's just a little bit bigger. And you play it down and you make these micro adjustments very quickly, and I think that's where the real magic and poetry really is, when you can make those small finesse changes very quickly. Then we take that information back into 3D or After Effects and implement that information so it's of better quality. It's almost like directing a piece of music. You want to have everything just in the right place, and the only way you can get to that level of finesse is if you have real-time interaction with it.

Do you design while keeping in mind the title safe boundaries?

We still adhere to title safe. I mean, granted, the monitors now don't have such strict or massive amount of title space required, but I think it's much easier to sort of read the typography if it doesn't veer toward the edge of the piece. As long as you didn't put the type up there, you don't want to hide it. So it's helpful to keep it in the general area. So, I think we do follow title safe. Since we do work in a tremendous range of media, we never know where it's going to end up, so if we do a piece that's originally going to be shown on a digital monitor at a conference and is also going to be broadcast in SD later, we want to make sure that we don't create too much work for ourselves by doing something that's specific to one of those mediums. We try to be a little bit more open ended so our client can use it in as many different mediums as possible. When it gets to Web and online in 320 by 240, that becomes very challenging because generally typography, even in SD typography, doesn't work online and generally it has to be redone for small-size Web applications. But more and more clients are going to larger-size Web applications, so it's not so much of an issue.

Can you address any of the motivations behind camera movement or even transition between one shot and another, whether it's hard cuts or dissolves or just general relevance of the use of camera in the work that you do?

When we build tiny worlds for our clients that are very specific, we may have some that are very bare-bones, very clean, very simple, very elegant solutions, and they generally are very hard cuts. And then we have things that are meant to have a feeling of futuristic excitement, and they tend to be much more complicated, so it really depends on what is more appropriate for the project that we're working on.

I think that camera moves in general are pretty distracting unless they're tied into some motivating action. Or your palette is so simplified that there's really not that much else. If you look at some really great title design that's out there, there's just a slight amount of atmosphere and the typography and the camera, and that's all that really exists in the animation of the main title sequences.

Can you elaborate on the relevance of editing in the work that you do? How can you tell a story through editing?

Editing for us has two real major uses. There's one, which is the finessing. It's really hard, even if you have your story and you know that those are the camera angles and those are the shots you want to use. The timing and certain subtle things like scale and color correction that you can address really quickly in Final Cut are essential. I've seen artists work on shots for hours that end up being cut in duration in half because when you get the final piece together it really doesn't need or justify the length of the shot. We create very tight animatics and very specific sort of durations in these things, and we trim it by a frame here or a frame there, but I think you really want to have that ability to go in and interactively work with your piece, which is just not easy to do in After Effects. There are so many layers in there, it makes it so hard to do those finessing adjustments, so people just don't.

So, its almost like you got to get the shot out, you got to get it rendered, you got to get it into Final Cut and you got to finesse it, otherwise it's going to come out clunky.

If you cut a few frames out of someone's reaction, it could go from happy to sad, depending on where you end the cut. In more postproduction-oriented places, it seems like it's more about timing and making the piece feel like a great music composition and flow from scene to scene. I don't think there's that much opportunity to change how the story is told in the edit suite; it's more a matter of finessing it. Because everyone knows that the scene needs to look like this and it's unlikely that you'll discover it in the edit suite, well, you could drop entire shots, but it's unlikely that you'll create an entire shot to fill a gap in the edit suite.

Figure 3.25a Client: Symantec; Project Title: Vision 08; Duration: 00:30.

Figure 3.25b

Figure 3.25c

Figure 3.25d

Figure 3.25e

Figure 3.25f

Figure 3.25g

Figure 3.25h

Figure 3.25i

Do you generally work when you have a score or soundtrack and sound effects already in place? If so, how does it affect your work?

In general, unfortunately, the soundtracks are not done until later on in the project, and we usually work with temp tracks. As soon as we find a piece, we'll start working on the style frames and immediately start working on what we feel is a good piece of music to cut with and to lend personality to the piece. A lot of times the animation will become overly complex just because there's no music associated with it. That's the natural tendency; people think, "Hey, it needs to keep doing stuff," if you don't put a soundtrack next to it. If you put a soundtrack next to it, you realize the design or the style of the frame carries on its own with that music. It's kind of like saying, "Hey, I'm going to paint this painting without red and put the red in later." It's sort of impossible to do because it's such a critical element.

From the beginning we work with those tracks, and it's amazing how often those tracks, once you swap them out with the actual track, the cuts and the beats and the timing still work, because basically a lot of the cuts and motion tend to be more open, more languid, when working with the soundtrack. And as long as it's on 4/4 time, most of the stuff just cuts right to a variety of different tracks if you're close to the same beats.

I highly recommend working with a temp track as soon as possible and then swapping it when you get the final tracks. Voiceovers are a different story. When we get the script and we have a piece that's being written to or being created around a voiceover, we'll generally do a scratch voiceover track here and time it out to that, then get the real voiceover and do some finessing there. I guess it's not that different, you're still working with a scratch track, but you never want to have nothing under there. You certainly never want to present anything to your client with nothing or no soundtrack, because they'll pull it apart.

Can you talk about the use of color and lighting in your work? How is that useful in regard to the emotion you want to convey for a particular client or a particular work?

I think having a controlled color palette is always very helpful, and usually the controlled color palette leads back toward a very specific look of the brand. Let's say you're working with a company whose logo is red or the main title of the movie is red. Chances are you're going to work within a palette of reds and some other colors just so it doesn't get too flat.

I think that controlling the color palette is a challenge for a lot of people. Getting the color palette that is relatively controlled and very brand specific is a great asset toward the piece and making sure that it fits within the larger format of the client's needs. It doesn't speak to movie titles, but it does speak to, "Hey, if I'm going to do this piece for this person and I'm doing it in CG and everything else they did was in Flash or something like that, and I'm doing it in 3D, I can make it match the rest of the body of work and their brand image, just by keeping within the color palette."

Tools like Adobe's Kuler are great for establishing nice harmonies of colors within a narrow palette, but for some odd reason a lot of people don't use it. I think it's a great tool. Another thing that you can do is pull a photograph that may be dominant in reds or something like that, and then pull the colors from the photograph, because one of the things that make a color palette so pleasant is its reflection of nature. I think that if you're on a computer just picking colors randomly you would never find those in a real environment. Whereas if you pull your colors from a photograph, they all seem to work together, because they all came from the same color temperature, lighting, they're all about as saturated, and stuff like that.

Can you talk about the creative process?

Going back to my background in studying design, the first step that I would make in coming up with a new design is sketching—you know, coming up with the basic idea. Sometimes before I'm sketching the composition of a frame, I'm just writing a bunch of words, saying, "Hey, what if we did this, what if we did this, what if we did this?" You can throw out a tremendous number of ideas, you're not on the computer, you just write lines and lines of different ideas, and then you start doodling little compositions and little stories.

A lot of people, when they start just jumping forward and diving into Photoshop or After Effects, basically they'll start down a path and they'll continue down that path. They'll continue to try and make it work even though maybe the idea wasn't so good. Instead, by sketching out all these ideas, you can immediately weed off all these bad ideas and then begin pursuing something that's fairly well defined. You don't want to be defining something in Photoshop; if you have a bad idea there, you can try to make it better, but it's an uphill battle. In coming up with a good idea, coming up with the basic framework of what that idea is going to look like, it's great to work offline and then begin to go into Photoshop.

Even then, once you work in Photoshop and start beginning to add the color and add the nuance and add the detail, I also find it good to go ahead and do a whole bunch of frames and sometimes even start in Illustrator to just figure out the composition with 40 specific frames of how an idea can be arranged, with black and white and really rudimentary shapes representing people or type. Once that's done, move on a little more into Photoshop; once you're in Photoshop it's really about the details. You know exactly what you're going to do and you just need to go in and get the details.

If you start in Photoshop and look for all those different things, you'll never get there, because once you're in Photoshop you expect the frame to have a finish and a polish, and there's no way you're going to come up with 30 ideas or 300 ideas the way you would in a sketch. You're going to come up with two ideas, at most. I'm always encouraging people to spit out as many ideas as quickly as possible and stay out of Photoshop until they really feel strongly about a couple of them, and then work on finessing them there.

What are the most challenging aspects of your work?

The most challenging aspect is integrating client feedback. It's challenging sometimes because you feel it contradicts your idea, and the real challenge is finding ways to incorporate it while improving your idea.

How about your favorite parts?

The favorite part is the unbridled creativity that happens at the very beginning when you're sketching through all these ideas and possibilities, and beginning to shape this world out of nothing. That's just an awesome, great, idealistic part of the creative process.

Figure 3.26a Client: MTV; Project Title: The Word; Duration: 00:15.

Figure 3.26b

Figure 3.26c

Figure 3.26d

Figure 3.26e

Figure 3.26f

Figure 3.26g

Figure 3.26h

Figure 3.26i

How does technology affect your work?

It's funny, as computers get faster, the software seems to get slower at exactly the same rate. Technology allows us to do better and better things, but it's certainly not getting us out of this office any earlier. There are some amazing tools that you can work with right now, but everyone, lots of teams, are working with them at the same time. Motion tracking is now pretty accessible, so getting motion tracking into your project is almost expected if you've got live action. On one hand it's adding possibilities, on the other hand it's adding complexities.

What are your favorite graphic designers, type designers, or motion designers?

I'm a huge fan of someone named Tibor Kalman, who has a great book that I recommend to everybody. It's a little bit about the advertising world and commercial design and keeping your sense of humor.

Who or what inspires you? What is your biggest influence in general?

There are a lot of fantastic Web sites and portals and books and so many great things that influence me in terms of design, but I think that in terms of a specific project it's going to be the client that has a great deal of inspiration in terms of helping us understand their needs. You have lots of stuff out there, but is it relevant to the project you're doing?

What are you working on right now?

Right now we're working on a project for Sprint. And to me it's a really great combination of all the things that are in design. We have live action, there's CG and title design and editing, and all the stuff that makes a project fun.

What we're moving toward is really in the live-action vein and mixing it in with the motion graphics, because I think that creates sort of a bridge. If you look at half the humorous commercials out there, half the products could be swapped. But if you take a story that's humorous or a bunch of live action and create a world that's very, very, very unique, you could tell that same story, or you could tell a better story that's just so specific it's just nontransferrable. For the consumer who's trying to figure out, "Oh, I saw a funny bank commercial, I like the personality of the bank but I can't remember what the product is," if you dial in the design and the look of that world more closely than your average live-action 30-second spot and include something that's very chromatically specific, and very design specific, and very typographically specific, the consumer will tie in that stuff to whatever brand you're working with.

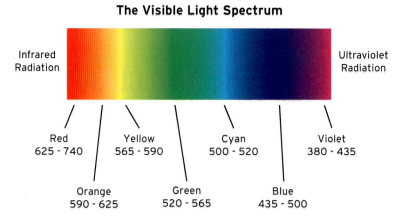

Figure 4.1

It is important to understand which color you should be using in your titles and credits because we experience a psychological and emotional response to colors. When utilized appropriately, colors can evoke moods and emotions that enhance the meaning of the images, whether they are on a movie screen, a TV, or a computer monitor.

For centuries, artists have used the psychology of color to convey an emotional response and mood they wanted to evoke. Think of the use of color in the works of Van Gogh, Chagall, and Degas and the use of color and light in Caravaggio, Rembrandt, and Whistler's works.

Whether you use a color palette because of a personal like or dislike for other colors or with a particular color motivation in mind, you want to make sure that the color choices you make do not conflict with the message you are trying to convey. Or, if the medium and the message conflict, it should be an intentional choice. Understanding a bit of color history, the basics of color theory, and color symbolism will help you find a logical and dependable way to utilize color in your title sequences.

A Bit of History

Aristotle (384 B.C.–322 B.C.)

In **De Coloribus** (translation: **On Color**), possibly attributable to Aristotle's disciples, Aristotle theorizes that colors are derived from following natural phenomena: sunlight, firelight, air, and water. These four elements, mixed with darkness (black) and light (white), create color. Additionally, in the text **On Sense and Sensibilia**, written around 350 B.C., Aristotle identifies a linear sequence of color he deducted from observing the changes in the light during the course of a day, from white to yellow, orange, and red. After sunset, the light becomes purple, sometimes green, then dark blue and black. From his observations, he theorized a linear color system. This color theory was accepted for about 17 centuries.

Leon Battista Alberti (1404–1472)

In **De Pictura** (*On Painting,* 1436), a treatise intended to define the rules of visual arts, Alberti states, "Through the mixing of colors infinite other colors are born, but there are only four true colors—as there are four elements—from which more and more other kinds of colors may be thus created. Red is the color of fire, blue of the air, green of the water, and of the earth gray and ash...Therefore there are four genera of colors, and these make their species according to the addition of dark and light, black or white." Alberti builds on Aristotle's color theory with the exception of white and black, which are demoted to noncolors.

Leonardo da Vinci (1452–1529)

As a true Renaissance man, da Vinci investigated the topic of color. In his **Trattato della Pittura** (*Treatise on Painting*), published posthumously in 1651, he identifies six primary colors: white, yellow, green, blue, red and black. Each color had a direct physical manifestation of the natural world: white for light, yellow for earth, green for water, red for fire, blue for air, and black for night. He also wrote about what would later be referred to as *simultaneous contrast*: "Of different colors equally perfect, that will appear most excellent which is seen near its direct contrary blue near yellow, green near red: because each color is more distinctly seen when opposed to its contrary than to any other similar to it."

Isaac Newton (1642–1726)

Newton was the first person to analyze color and view it as a result of light hitting objects and reflecting colors that are perceived by our eyes. In 1666, he conducted the famous prism experiment in which he demonstrated how light is responsible for color. A prism, when placed next to a window and hit by the sunlight, casts a seven-color spectrum: red, orange, yellow, green, blue, indigo, and violet. In 1704, Newton published **Opticks**, a "treatise of the reflections, refractions, inflexions, and colours of light." Newton rearranged the linear color system into a circular one in which the circular color diagram shows the relationship between primary colors and secondary colors. White is in the center of the diagram, to signify that the sum of all colors results in white light.

Johann Wolfgang von Goethe (1749–1832)

Geothe, in addition to being an outstanding poet and novelist, wrote **Zur Farbenlehre** (*Theory of Colors*) in 1810. He disagrees with

Newton and theorizes that the way we see color is affected not only by the light and the object but also by our perception. Color has "sensual qualities within the content of consciousness," he says. Goethe clearly moved beyond Newton's study of color as physical matter and entered the realm of psychology. He developed a symmetric six-color wheel in which he arranged the colors on a circle to support his color theory. He divided colors into two main categories. The *plus-side colors* (yellow, orange, red) provoke warm, exciting, lively, and comfortable feelings, whereas the *minus-side colors* (green, blue, violet) provoke unsettling, weak, and cold feelings. Goethe also furthered the study of complementary contrasts.

Michel Chevreul (1786–1889)

Chevreul furthered the knowledge of color theory by advancing the concepts of *simultaneous contrast*, the optical illusion that appears to darken or lighten the hues of two bold colors placed in close proximity of each other, and *optical mixing*, the blending of two colors to create a third one.

Symbolism and the Psychology of Color

Color influences our mood and even the way we taste food. Color is deeply rooted in cultural, political, and sociological connotations. These associations are constantly changing throughout cultures, years, and generations.

One common emotional response, originally theorized by Goethe, is provoked by cool or warm colors. Cool colors are the ones close to the green/purple spectrum and evoke distance and coldness. Warm colors, on the other hand, are the ones close to the yellow/red spectrum and evoke urgency, action, and closeness.

Cool colors tend to recede in the background of a screen or Web page, whereas warm colors tend to pop to the front.

Table 4.1 Color's Emotional Response and Screen Depth

	Cool Colors (Purple/Green)	Warm Colors (Yellow/Red)
Emotional response	Coldness, distance	Action, urgency, closeness
Screen depth	Recede	Jump forward

When deciding the color palette for your title sequence, cultural connotations are another factor. Certain colors can acquire a particular significance, depending on the cultural background and codex. Red, for example, is often interpreted as danger, as exemplified by stop signs.

The following are some of the scientific, symbolic, and emotional connotations to keep in mind while you work with color:

- **Color affects our mood.** In a study conducted by Shashi Caan Collective, called *Spatial Color—Live Experiment,* color affected physical activity. The Collective built three identical but differently colored rooms and held a cocktail party in each one. In the red and yellow rooms, people were dynamically interacting, gesturing, and moving around. In the blue room there was little social interaction and the people were more still and calm.
- **Color has cultural and sociological connotations.**
  - **White** is associated with mourning in Japan.
  - **Red** signifies good luck in China but mourning in South Africa.
  - **Black** is associated with mourning in Western countries but signifies honor in Japan.
  - **Purple** is associated with mourning in Thailand but signifies royalty in Europe.
- **Color has political connotations.**
  - *Red:* Labor, left wing, communism, socialism
  - *Green:* Green Party
  - *White:* Pacifism, surrender
  - *Black:* Anarchism
- **Color has a religious connotation.**
  - Blue: Hinduism
  - Green: Islam
- **Color can influence other senses.** A survey conducted by researchers at the Institute of Psychology at Johannes Gutenberg University Mainz in Germany found that colored lighting has an influence on how we taste wine. Wine that was drunk in an ambiance illuminated by red or blue lighting received a higher taste rating than the same wine which was drunk in an ambiance illuminated by green or white lights.
- **Color palettes can evoke places, memories, and personal associations.** Think of colors that evoke a particular childhood memory, season, or place where you spent time. Memory can influence the perception of color; studies indicate that we recall colors as more saturated than they actually were, as though we replaced the original memory of the image with something different. These memory colors do not affect our perception of reality, but they do affect our color preferences. In research published by the *Journal of Experimental Psychology*, Karl Gegenfurtner stated, "It appears as if our memory system is tuned to the color structure found in the world. If stimuli are too strange, the system simply doesn't engage as well, or deems them unimportant." Co-author Felix Wichmann said, "In order to engage or grab one's attention,

bright colors might well be most suitable…If, on the other hand, the aim is more to have an image stick in the viewer's memory, unnatural colors may not be suitable." Based on these studies, while you are working on your title sequence, if you wish to make a particular element endure in the audience's memory, you could try to enhance it with color (for example, the lipstick's vivid red in the **True Blood** title sequence).

- **Color as therapy.** In *chromotherapy*, an alternative medical treatment, color and light exposure is used to heal and restore a physical or emotional imbalance.

- **Color preference is affected by culture and geographical location.** In the book **Eidetic Imagery**, E. R. Jaensch explains that human beings living in hot climates have to adapt to the long waves of light because of the increased amount of sunlight, which could create a different pigmentation in the retina. People affected in this way are referred to as *red-sighted* and their color preference is warm, vivid hues. On the other hand, *green-sighted* people have adapted to a shorter amount of sunlight and have developed a preference for blues and greens. Another study, conducted by Marc H. Bornstein, resulted in evidence that people living closer to the Equator do not distinguish blue from green.

- **Color preference is affected by age.** In the book **Color Psychology and Color Therapy**, color expert and industry consultant Faber Birren states that yellow is the color of preference for children, but their preference for it declines as they grow into adulthood, at which point blue becomes more popular. He says, "With maturity comes a greater liking for hues of shorter wave length (blue, green) than for hues of longer wave length (red, orange, and yellow)."

Take a glance at the following table to see some of the most common emotional, political, and cultural connotations generally associated with colors. Keep in mind that these associations are only a starting point; before you embark on a project you should do research to ensure that you have the most up-to-date information on what colors represent to changing attitudes, generations, and cultures.

For example, even though white has traditionally been associated with mourning in China, brides have started to wear white gowns in addition to traditional red dresses, mimicking Western brides. Or consider the use of violet in Thai Airways' branding. Even though the color violet is culturally associated with mourning in Thailand, the airline's decision to use violet in its branding is most likely dictated by the fact that the target audience for Thai Airways is foreigners who often associate the color purple with luxury.

Table 4.2 Common Emotional and Cultural Color Connotations

	Color	Possible Psychological Responses	Possible Cultural Connotations	Possible Physiological Responses
Warm colors (preferred by younger audiences)	Red	Violence, war, aggression, heat, love, excitement, passion, danger (Western cultures)	Celebration and fortune (China, North Africa), purity (Japan), integrity and purity (India), mourning (South Africa)	Raised heartbeat, increased adrenaline, increased blood pressure, raised temperature; orange and yellow have similar but less intensive effects than red
	Orange	Warmth, light, happiness, nostalgia, energy, enthusiasm	Royalty (Netherlands), Protestantism (Ireland), Hinduism	
	Yellow	Warmth, joy, happiness, excitement, irritation, optimism, wealth	Mourning (Egypt), courage (Japan), royalty (China)	
Cool colors (preferred by older audiences)	Blue	Coldness, coolness, calmness, sadness, somber, clinical, scientific		Slower heartbeat, decreased temperature, relaxed muscles
	Green	Calmness, quietness, coolness, envy, growth	Rebirth and fertility (Celtic myths), sacred (Islam), environmentalism, capitalism	
	Violet	Intrigue, luxury, darkness, power	Royalty (United Kingdom, Medieval Europe), mourning (Thailand), clergy (Western churches)	

Color Systems

Now that you've learned about color's history and cultural and psychological connotations, let's dig into the nuts and bolts of color theory.

A number of color systems are used today; most can be found in common computer applications. The most common color systems are:

- **RGB.** An additive color system that applies to devices using light, such as computer monitors, TV sets, and digital projections. The concept behind RGB is that its primary colors (R = red, G = green, B = blue), when combined, create all other hues. An equal amount of red, green, and blue creates a white light.
- **RYB.** A color subtractive color system most commonly used in visual arts. Its primary colors are red, yellow, and blue, and its secondary colors are VOG—violet, orange and green.

The RGB Color System

Figure 4.2

The Color Wheel

Figure 4.3

The CMYK Color System

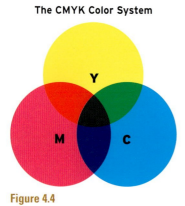

Figure 4.4

HSB Color System

Figure 4.5

- **CMYK.** A subtractive color system used in print design, which can be found when using dyes, inks, and pigments. Its primary colors (C = cyan, M = magenta, Y = yellow, K = black), when combined, create all other hues. An equal amount of cyan, magenta, yellow, and black creates gray.
- **Pantone (PMS).** A color system that utilizes a proprietary system, the Pantone Matching System, or PMS, that allows control over and color matching of its unique color formulas. Historically it has been an industry standard in print design, offering designers tools such as the Formula guides, color chips, and Process guides, but recently, with the introduction of Pantone Goe, designers are able to match solid Pantone colors with their respective RGB values, allowing a precise rendition of Pantone's colors to use in web and broadcast design.
- **HSL (or HSI).** A color system that measures the values of hue (H), saturation (S), and luminosity (L), which is sometimes also called *intensity* (I), of a color. The hue is measured by the position in a circle. The saturation and luminance are measured on a scale of 100 units and are determined by the color's position on the radial line drawn from the center to the perimeter of the color circle.
- **HSV (or HSB).** A color system that measures the values of hue (H), saturation (S), and value (V), which is sometimes also called *brightness* (B), of a color.
- **YUV.** A color system initially developed in the 1950s to allow black-and-white analog televisions to still receive a signal. It is used in NTSC, PAL, and SECAM video standards. It utilizes one luminosity channel (Y) and two chroma channels: blue minus luma (U) and red minus luma (V).

Each color value in a system can generally be translated into another color system, although that might create some differences in the richness of colors. For example, when converting CMYK colors directly to RGB, the colors might look a bit washed out.

When working with computer software, a new document can be created utilizing a specific color mode (e.g., RGB), but you can create design or typographical elements that contain colors picked from a different color system and apply them to the color system in use. This particular case applies when, for example, you are given a style guide, which includes instructions on how to appropriately use the logo, typeface, and color palette of a specific project. If a print designer created the style guide to follow their work done on the logo of a movie or the movie poster, the color palette will most likely display color values in the form of CMYK and/or Pantone colors.

The task of a title designer is to find the corresponding colors in the RGB system. An easy solution is to identify the CMYK or Pantone color in the color picker of your software, using the color system indicated in the style guide provided, and then convert it to RGB. Some color palettes, such as the ones in Adobe Photoshop, simultaneously display the corresponding values in HSB, RGB, LAB, and CMYK, so you could simply enter your value in CMYK and you'll automatically have the corresponding RGB value.

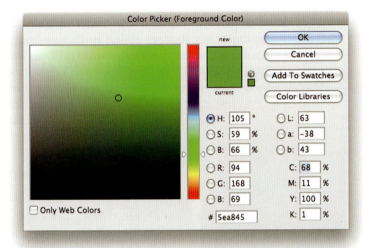

Figure 4.6 Photoshop's Color Picker.

Adobe Illustrator has a similar color picker palette that simultaneously displays the HSB, RGB, and CMYK color values. If you are creating a new swatch color or working in the Edit Color palette, you simply click the pull-down menu to select the CMYK color, enter the known values, and then switch the pull-down back to RGB to know its corresponding values and to use the color in your project.

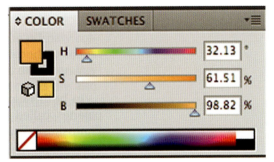

Figure 4.7 Illustrator's Color Palette.

Color has three basic properties:

- **Hue.** The property that distinguishes a color from others in the visible spectrum. The words *hue* and *color* are often used interchangeably.
- **Value/brightness.** A property determined by the amount of black and white added to a color, generally identified as the lightness or darkness of a hue. You create a darker value by adding black, and you create a lighter value by adding white. The following terminology is used when talking about value:
  - **Tints.** Colors mixed with white. These colors, also referred to as *pastel*, tend to produce lighter, softer hues, such as baby blue or peach.
  - **Tones.** Colors mixed with neutral gray.
  - **Shades.** Colors mixed with black. These colors are bolder, richer, and darker, such as navy blue or burgundy.
- **Saturation/intensity.** A property determined by the dominance of its hue. Highly saturated colors are bright and vivid. Less saturated colors are muted. Pure saturated colors are located on the outside perimeter of the color wheel, and less saturated colors are closer to the center of the wheel, where the hue dominates less.

Tints, Tones & Shades

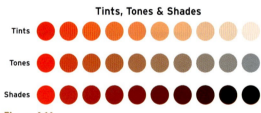

Tints

Tones

Shades

Figure 4.11

Color Harmonies

As in music, where you can experience consonant and dissonant chords, colors can intensify or create tension with each other, depending on the characteristics we've explored so far.

Color harmonies are groups of harmonious colors that you will want to keep consistent when you are designing your title sequences and collateral designs such as posters, postcards, and other materials.

Simple color harmonies might be based on one color, and more complex ones can be based on mathematical rules. The following describe a number of techniques available to create color harmonies, also called *schemes*:

- **Achromatic.** Literally meaning *without color*, these color harmonies present very low values of saturation; therefore they utilize white, gray, and black. Warm and cool achromatic harmonies can be created by adding yellow or blue.
- **Monochromatic.** Literally meaning *one color*, these color harmonies are based only on one hue and its related tints and shades.

- **Analogous.** Literally meaning *similar*, analogous color harmony consists of three colors adjacent to each other in the color wheel. The middle color is generally the dominant color, the second one a supporting color, and the third one is used as an accent.
- **Complementary.** These are colors that are, in the color wheel, directly opposite of one other, such as green and red, purple and yellow, and blue and orange in the RYB color system. Elements designed using pure complementary colors create a visual noise generally called *simultaneous contrast* (see "Color Contrasts: Color and Type Combinations That Work"). Complementary colors are vibrant and they complete each other. In fact, if you mixed two complementary colors, you would create gray. Complementary color schemes can be obtained using pure hues or their corresponding shades or tints.
- **Split complementary.** A variation of the complementary color scheme, split complementary creates a more subtle effect. It uses the main color and, instead of its complement, uses its two adjacent colors. Split complementary color schemes can be obtained using pure hues or their corresponding shades or tints.
- **Triadic.** Composed of three colors located equidistant from each other in the color wheel. Again, they can be obtained using pure hues or shades or tints.
- **Tetradic (rectangle).** Composed of four colors, which are two complementary pairs. If you connected the colors with lines in the color wheel, you'd draw a rectangle.

Analogous Colors

Figure 4.12

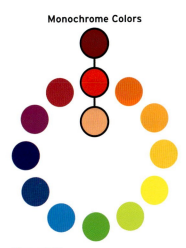

Monochrome Colors

Figure 4.13

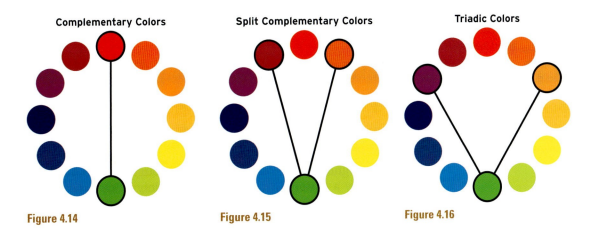

Complementary Colors

Figure 4.14

Split Complementary Colors

Figure 4.15

Triadic Colors

Figure 4.16

The background elements can consist of:
- Solid color
- Patterns, gradients
- Live-action footage
- Animation
- Motion graphics

Think of color combinations that you experience every day: street and highway signs. These signs need to be readable by a variety of people who are moving at different speeds. The most common street or highway sign color combinations are black on white, white on blue, white on green, white on red, and yellow on black.

In the case of title sequences, the reader will most likely be still while the type is animating on-screen. The following are some considerations to keep in mind when you're making your color choices for your foreground and background:

- **Contrast.** When using a color palette that utilizes colors with similar values and saturation, the contrast between foreground type and background color diminishes, causing the type to be less legible.

  When you use two or more colors that have greater contrast, you create some dimensionality. Keep in mind that darker and cooler colors tend to recede into the background, as opposed to brighter and warmer colors, which tend to pop forward.

- **Size.** If you increase the font size of a hard-to-read text/colored background combination, the readability obviously improves.

- **Complementary.**
  Complementary colors as text and background make reading a challenge. On one hand, it intensifies the colors and can definitely get the audience's attention. On the other hand, putting the two colors adjacent to each other creates a vibrating or pulsating effect, making them uncomfortable

Figure 4.20 Lower-contrast colors used as text and background decrease readability.

Figure 4.21 When using lower-contrast color combinations, a larger font size increases readability.

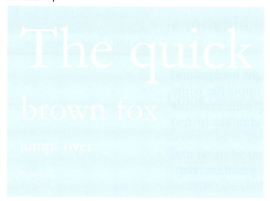

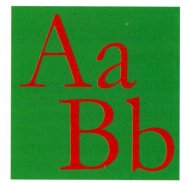

Figure 4.22 Complementary colors used as text and background decrease readability.

to look at and tiring the reader's eyes. They create an effect called *color simultaneous contrast*.

An interesting workaround if you'd like to utilize complementary colors without discomforting viewers is to outline each color with a white, gray, or black line.

- **Black.** If your title sequence will be played primarily in a movie theater, a black background helps blend the dark environment of the theater with your title sequence. The edge of the screen will not be immediately discernable, and you might fully immerse viewers in the movie. This can be particularly effective at the beginning of the movie, when the viewer has not yet fallen into the typical suspension of disbelief on which all movies rely.

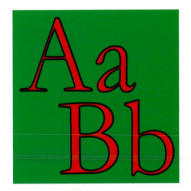

Figure 4.23 When using complementary color as text and background, adding a stroke increases readability.

Afterimage

An *afterimage* is an image created by the brain that persists momentarily in your retina, even after you are no longer looking at the original image. Try this experiment:

Stare at the red square for 20 to 30 seconds from about 10 inches away. Close your eyes and wait 10 to 15 seconds until you see a green square.

Notice that when you focus on a strong stimulus such as the red square, your eyes and brain absorb the color you observed, and the photoreceptors in the eye become overstimulated. The eye contains two types of photoreceptor cells: rods (sensitive to light and dark) and cones (sensitive to red, green, and blue light). These photoreceptors adapt to the image's overstimulation (in regard to both its darkness and its color) and become less responsive to it. If, after staring at the stimulus, you move your eyes to stare at a white surface or even close your eyes, you will experience an afterimage of the inverse or complement of the image. That's because the photoreceptors that are least depleted produce a stronger signal than the overstimulated ones.

Figure 4.24

Why don't we experience this phenomenon every day? Generally the eye moves rapidly when we're observing images. This phenomenon is particularly evident when we stare at a strong stimulus for a number of seconds.

How long does an after image last? Afterimages last for a few seconds to up to a minute. Photoreceptors are relatively quick to adapt to and readjust to the absence of the stimulus.

Does this phenomenon work only with red? This experiment can be done with any colors of the visible spectrum and any shape.

Understanding Light

Through lighting you can manipulate images and typographical elements so that you better produce the desired emotions in the audience.

alternating current arc such as hydrargyum medium arc-length iodide, or HMI. These lights are generally used outdoors because they will match the color temperature of sunlight and moonlight.

The director of photography usually plans which lights to use in different situations, whether the scenes are outdoors or indoors. If a scene is being shot indoors but next to a real or fake window, the director of photography might decide to use all day-light lamps in order to match or recreate the color temperature of the light coming from outdoors. In the opposite situation, if a scene is being shot outdoors but next to a shop, telephone booth, or street lamp, the director of photography might decide to use tungsten lamps to match or recreate the color temperature of indoor lighting.

Sometimes light bulbs can be mixed and matched to create a more subtle variation in the color temperature. For example, the versatile four-banks Kino-Flo lamps (which present four light bulbs) can be swapped to include three daylight bulbs and one tungsten bulb. The result would be still be a dominant blue hue but with a hint of orange to warm it up a bit.

Something else to keep in mind is that when people refer to a light being *cool*, as in its hue, it is not to be confused with blue light being a cool temperature. A light that produces bluish hues is actually a higher temperature, around 5,600K, than a light that produces orange hues, which is around 3,200K.

Color-Balancing Film and Video Cameras

Our visual perception adapts to the different lighting color. We perceive a white T-shirt as white whether we are indoors and using warm artificial lighting or outdoors in sunlight. Our eyes and brain recalibrate what we read as white, based on our own experience and points of reference. On the other hand, film and video cameras need to be guided in recording with the correct color temperature setting. If they are not, they will read that T-shirt as orange under candlelight and blue under sunlight.

- **Film cameras.** Color film stocks have a color temperature rated for tungsten or daylight. With a tungsten-balanced film stock utilizing tungsten lights as illumination, the whites will be reproduced as white. With a tungsten film stock used with daylight lights, the whites will be reproduced with a blue color cast.

  Similarly, with daylight-balanced film stock and daylight lights, the whites will be reproduced as white. With daylight film stock used with tungsten lights, the whites will be reproduced with an orange color cast.

Sometimes the color casts are an aesthetic choice, and sometimes they might be a choice driven by necessity (for example, if the production client has budgeted only for daylight film stock). In either case, with the aid of camera filters or colored gels on lights, you can correct unwanted color casts.

When shooting with daylight film and tungsten lighting, adding an 80A blue filter in front of the film camera lens will correct the unwanted orange color cast. The filter raises the color temperature from 3,200K to approximately 5,600K so that the tungsten-lit scene appears to be now lit for daylight.

Alternatively, when shooting with tungsten film and daylight lighting, adding an 85 orange filter in front of the film camera lens will correct the unwanted blue color cast. The filter drops the color temperature from 5,600K to approximately 3,200K so that the daylight-lit scene appears to be now tungsten-lit.

The same principles can be applied to lighting gels. Clipping a full value of a color temperature Blue (CTB) gel in front of a light fixture will change the color temperature of tungsten lights into daylight. Clipping a full value of a color temperature orange (CTO) gel in front of a light fixture will change the color temperature of daylight into tungsten. This could be a useful tip to apply when color-correcting camera filters might not be available or when you don't have the desired color temperature light fixture at your disposal.

- **Video cameras.** As opposed to recording on film stock, video cameras use tape or digital-based media, which can't be rated for daylight or tungsten. You will need to identify the correct color temperature in the camera settings. Most cameras offer presets that allow the user to select one of two main color temperatures: exterior (6,500K) or interior (3,400K). Sometimes you can even enter the exact number of Kelvin degrees. Depending on the location, set, and lighting, picking the appropriate preset allows the whites to be recorded as white without recording an unwanted color cast.

In addition to the presets, most video cameras allow the user to sample a white element in the frame as a point of reference so that the camera can determine the appropriate color temperature intended for the recorded footage. This feature is called the *white balance*. Refer to your camera manual to accurately perform a white balance.

The ideal place and time to perform a white balance is after the entire set's lighting (including light gels) is in place. Typically a person with a white card will stand at a place in the set where most of the scene's action is performed, so that the person is adequately lit, the camera zooms into the white cards, and the white balance is performed. As long as lighting fixtures are not changed nor gels or filters added between shots, the whites will be read as whites.

Just as with film cameras, camera filters can be added in front of the video camera's lenses to change their color temperature or even modify the set's lighting color temperature.

Something that can be done with a video camera, but not with a film camera, is purposefully faking the white balance to create an intentional color cast, such as the "day-for-night" look, when you are shooting in daylight but you'd like to make your footage look like nighttime.

There are two situations in which you could alter the classic use of white balance with a video camera:

- **Add gels in front of light fixtures after the white balance.** If color temperature gels are added in front of the lights after performing a simple white balance, they will create color casts. If you add colored gels before you white balance, most likely the white balance itself will neutralize the color you intend to keep in the lighting.

- **Add gels or filters in front of the camera lens before the white balance.** If a color temperature gel is added in front of the camera lens before performing a simple white balance, it will create a color cast. For example, if you placed a full CTO gel in front of the lens, the camera will read the orange as the true white and will correct its color temperature. The camera is thinking that it is reading an awful lot of orange in that white and that it needs to correct its color temperature by adding some blue. As soon as you remove the orange gel from the front of the lens, your entire scene will have a blue color cast. This technique is typically useful when you want to create a dramatic effect or even a very subtle effect. You could add a half or quarter CTB gel if you simply need to warm up some people's skin tones or remove a slight unwanted blue color cast.

Qualities of Light: Size, Distance, Angle, and Color

One of the most immediate and dramatic differences in different light sources is the light's hardness or softness. In coming to understand the qualities of a light, a good starting point is to figure out the light's make and model and train your eye to distinguish the quality of the shadow the light fixture produces. Are the shadows dark with sharp edges? Then it's a **hard light**. Are the shadows gray with soft edges? That's a **soft light**.

Typical hard light sources are the sun, a clear glass light bulb, a candle, or light fixtures like spotlights. Hard lights are used in film and video production to create a strong statement. Because a hard light casts such sharp and defined shadows, most three-dimensional details, such as textures or engravings in an object or even skin imperfections, all become much more noticeable. When overused, hard lights could create an extreme, full-contrast look, almost as though the image is a duotone comic book with lots of dimensionality in the frame.

On the other hand, soft light sources include an overcast day, a light that bounces off any reflective or light-colored surfaces, a Chinese lantern, or light fixtures such as zip lights. Soft lights are used in film and video production to light large areas of a set, allowing the actors to move more freely across it. They create a natural look and more subtle statement than hard lights. Because soft lights cast gentle and soft shadows, most three-dimensional details become less noticeable. The light wraps around the three-dimensional object, creating a soft, even, and less dramatic look. The drawback to soft lights is that they are harder to control than hard lights. That's why they are often used in conjunction with flags, which keep light off areas where it's not wanted. When overused, soft lights can create a flat, even look, without much dimensionality in the frame.

On a set, the quality of a light depends on the following:

- **The lamps' size and output.** Light sizes could be as little as 100 watts, all the way up to 5,000 or 10,000 watts (also referred to as 5K or 10K). A small light fixture, such as a 100 watt, will generally create a harder light and sharper shadows than a larger diffused light fixture, such as a 5K.
- **The lamps' model and settings, parameters, or accessories.** There are a number of models within each brand. Some of the most common brands are Arri, Kino-Flo, Mole-Richardson, Dedo, Source 4 Leko, and Light Panels. There are two main distinctions regarding the light's casing: Fresnel and open face.
  - **Fresnel lights** have a built-in lens in front of the light, which helps create a more even light by containing and controlling its beam. They also create sharper shadows and are focusable, meaning you can change the distance between the filament and the lens. Fresnel lights have a knob that can be turned to select two different settings: a *flood mode* (when the filament is closest to the lens and produces a wider spread of light, creating softer shadows) and a *spot mode* (when the filament is farthest from the lens and produces a narrower and focused light beam, creating sharper shadows).
  - **Open face lights** provide a larger light beam, which is useful for creating a soft lighting look. They don't contain a built-in lens, and not all of them are focusable. Some open face lights have lenses that can be placed in front of the light's face, which can further control the quality of light; some lenses are flat or frosted, wide or narrow. The open face lights include the family of soft lights. Some are created by a lighting manufacturer, and some might be created by gaffers.

One kind of soft light that lends itself to be hung over a stage to create an even, soft light across the set is a *space light*. This circular light creates a soft pool light beam and is controlled on its sides by *skirts*, which can be solid (made out of black solid duvatine, keeping the light focused downward) or silk (creating a silky diffused lighting on the edges), and gels can be added to it.

- Larger and increasingly popular lights include *balloon lights*, which are typically used to create a soft, even light on large sets, whether interior or exterior, day or night, and can be easily installed without heavy rigging or cranes because they are incredibly light. Most models are self-supporting, with the space light suspended in the middle of a balloon filled with helium. After the balloon is inflated, it can be elevated as high as the model goes and can be further elevated by a weight-assisted cable.

- **The intensity of light.** The film and video production world uses the word *intensity* instead of brightness. The most common tool used to measure the intensity of light is a *light meter*, which measures incidental light (light that falls on a subject) or reflective values (light that is bounced off the illuminated subject). See Chapter 6 for more on this subject.

  Keep in mind that the intensity of light falling onto an object or subject depends on the angle from which you are looking at it. This is particularly important when you're taking a reading with an incidental light meter.

  The intensity of light is measured in a couple of units:
  - **Lumen.** A light fixture's output is measured in *lumens*, which is the luminous energy created by a source. The light output of other items such as light bulbs and projectors is also measured in lumens.
  - **Footcandle.** When light falls on surfaces, the correct unit of measure is *footcandles* (or *lux*). This international unit of illumination measures the density of light on a given point on a surface. Its measurement is often accomplished with the aid of a light meter positioned on that given point and pointed toward the light source.

  You can manipulate the light's intensity if you modify the following:
  - **Distance.** One instantly gratifying modification you can apply to a light fixture—especially when it's mounted on a light stand—is to change its distance from the subject you are illuminating. The farther you move it, the lower the light's intensity. The closer you move it, the higher its intensity.
  - **Scrims.** When a light fixture cannot be moved, a quick solution is to slide a scrim in front of the light fixture, in the slot

between the front of the light and its barndoors. A *scrim* is a metal wire mesh that, when placed in front of a light fixture, reduces its intensity. A single scrim has a single layer of wire mesh and a green border and reduces the exposure of approximately ½ f-stop. A double scrim has a double layer of metal mesh and a red border and reduces the exposure of approximately 1 f-stop.

- **Gels.** To manipulate the light's intensity, you could use neutral density (ND) gels and diffusion gels. Neutral density gels do not affect the color temperature of the light fixture; they look gray and they decrease the intensity of light, as though you were putting a pair of sunglasses on. They can be found in a variety of weights, from ND2, which reduces the exposure of 1 f-stop, to ND64, which reduces the exposure of 6 f-stops. In addition to ND gels, you have at your disposal a range of diffusion gels. These gels are translucent and they do not affect the color temperature of the light. They can be found in a variety of densities, from light diffusion such as opal gels, which add a slight soft touch to your light without compromising its intensity, to heavier diffusion such as 250. The primary function of these gels is to diffuse lights, but heavier-density gels, which are thicker, reduce the lights' intensity more.

- **Dimmers.** These are external controllers that you can add to lights so that you can control their output. They generally work with the aid of a knob, which you can mark and turn to reduce or increase the light's intensity. Dimmers generally do affect the color temperature by shifting it to warmer hues.

- **The angle of light.** The angle at which you place a light will affect its quality. Imagine a camera and a subject. Place a light right beside the camera and start moving it horizontally around the subject. When your light is in the front, you will benefit from the full intensity of the light. The more you rotate it around the subject, the intensity lowers, but you also create more dimensional light. When you position the light behind the subject, you create a back light; only the rim around the subject is visible. Now go back to the first position of the light next to the camera, facing the subject. Instead of moving it horizontally, raise the light higher or lower and tilt it up or down to keep illuminating the subject. High- and low-angle lighting creates more dramatic effects and deeper shadows than a light that is placed at the subject's eye level or slightly higher.

Functions of Lights

When lighting a set, lights (regardless of their make and model) have a designated name based on their function. One classic lighting scheme is three-point lighting. It consists of a key light, a fill light, and a backlight:

- **Key light.** The main light source of the set or the main source that lights the subject. Its angle and ratio with the fill light determine the mood of the lighting. When placed at an angle from the camera's position, it adds dimensionality to the shot. For a classical three-point lighting setup, the key light is generally positioned at a 45-degree angle from the camera and with roughly a 30–45 degree down-tilt.
- **Fill light.** A soft and lower-intensity light generally used to fill in some of the shadows created by the key light. It is generally positioned at a 90-degree angle, opposite the key light.
- **Kicker.** A backlight, generally a very hard light, that is positioned above and behind the subject, pointing down at them. It creates a hard edge, which helps detach the subject from the background, creating dimensionality. This light is sometimes also called a *backlight* or *hair light* when it is aimed specifically at the subject's hair. A kicker is usually positioned directly opposite the key light, almost as though it were aimed toward the camera but pointed down.
- **Eyelight.** A tiny light that is placed slightly above the camera, generally at a similar angle line to the key light, that helps create dimensionality and create a sparkle in a subject's eyes.
- **Background.** Lights that illuminate the background and further create some distinction and detachment between the subject and background. You will definitely need focus background lights if you are shooting on a green screen, so that the screen will be evenly lit.

Tips for Lighting a Set

When you are lighting a set to shoot footage for your title sequence, whether on a green screen, a stop-motion set, or on location, you should start by doing the following:

1. *Staging/blocking.* Understand the main positions of your characters (whether they are actors, letters, or props) and identify their movements and/or camera movements.
2. *Roughing-in.* Roughly set up position, height, and intensity of the lighting along with the camera(s). Quickly run through the shot with stand-ins and verify that the lights are in their correct positions and that the right lights are being used.
3. *One at a time.* Turn off all the lights and turn on each light, one at a time, to verify their effectiveness. Start from the key, then go to the fill, kicker, and any other additional lighting you have. Make changes if necessary, then slowly turn on the lights again, and again make any necessary changes.
4. *Fine-tuning.* Add colored or diffusion gels, move the light stands' positions if they are in the middle of a shot, and refine the angles of the lights.
5. *Rehearsal.* Perform a full rehearsal with the talent and any necessary camera movements.
6. Shoot!

Emotive Lighting

By orchestrating a set of light fixtures, which fill particular functions and possess specific qualities, we obtain a lighting *style*. Lighting styles are inevitably responsible for suggesting moods and evoking emotions and psychological states dictated by the content of a scene. Two common lighting styles are *high key* and *low key*. These styles are not to be confused with hard and soft lights, although they play fundamental roles.

A low-key lighting scheme is dominated by deep shadows, and the few illuminated areas are well exposed or sometimes overexposed. To achieve this lighting scheme, hard light sources are often used in conjunction with minimal or no soft lights. The contrast ratio between bright and dark areas of the scene is high; sometimes parts of the talent's faces or parts of the set are obscured and dark. Visually, high contrast ratios add depth and dimensionality to the frame. Emotionally, they evoke urgency and high stakes. It's no surprise that low-key lighting was used at the beginning of the century in German Expressionist films, then later adopted and heavily utilized for the film noir of the 1940s and 1950s. Today, low-key lighting is usually associated with crime, horror, mystery, and psychological films.

A high-key lighting scheme is characterized by an overall brightness. The majority of the frame is well (sometimes overly) lit, with very few shadows. This lighting scheme presents a low contrast ratio between the key and fill lights. The fill light's intensity, in fact, is raised to one similar to the key light so that it creates an overall bright, flat, and even look, without casting any major shadows on the characters or on the set. This low-contrast look evokes upbeat moods and focuses on nuances rather than making a hard statement. High-key lighting is usually associated with the look and feel of musicals and comedies.

Similarly to the *mise-en-scene* decisions of what you'd like to compose in the frame or not, deciding what to light and what not to light can have a profound effect on and evoke different emotions in the audience.

A good exercise that will quickly train your eye to lighting is to observe and analyze paintings and even photographs. Try to pay attention to the light source(s), the effect of light on skin tones and objects, and the kind of shadows they cast. Can you identify the position and angle of the key light and even the fill, kicker, or background light? Are they a soft or a hard source? Does the composition present low-key or high-key lighting? Being able to recognize at a glance the effects produced by different lighting setups will inform and educate the way you approach lighting in your own title sequence.

Computer-Generated Lighting

Now that you know about film lighting in the real world, understanding how most of the industry-standard software programs deal with lighting will be easy. Similar to real-world lights, CG lights need a bit of artistry in their arrangements. In a way, you have fewer limitations and less setup time. You don't have to put lights on stands or rig them to an overhead grid. You can simply place any light wherever you'd like in your composition, using 3D coordinates and manipulating a few parameters.

On the other hand, adding lights to your project might increase your render time and sometimes even your screen preview. As with real-world lighting, a good way to start is to add one light at a time, find its desired type of light, position, and point of interest (where the light is aimed), and then add all the additional lights. If you think you have overdone it, turn all the lights off, then turn them on one at a time. Verify that each one is effective, see how they work together, and modify them if necessary.

One major difference to keep in mind when working with CG lights is that their position in the 3D environment does not affect the lights' intensity as it does in the real world. In CG, you can move a light closer or farther away from the subject, but the intensity will remain the same. If you want to affect the intensity of CG lights, you need to change their intensity value (as we discuss shortly).

Just as with lighting in the real world, start by roughing in a key light, then a fill light, and then you can further articulate the set by adding a backlight. Depending on the software you are using, you might need to explore and modify the light's properties to obtain the lighting style you want.

In Adobe After Effects you can add a light to your composition by selecting **Layer | New | Light**. A pop-up window displays the light's options. To begin with, you can pick one of four types of lights:

- **Spot.** Your typical spotlight resembles the real-world spotlights used in theatrical lighting. In your composition, the wireframe outline of a cone visually represents the spotlight's position—the point being the apex of the light, which can be modified through its own properties. The base of the cone represents the direction and wideness of the light beam.

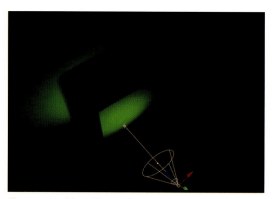

Figure 4.26 After Effect's Spot Light.

- **Parallel.** A directional light that emits a parallel light beam that mimics the effect of the sun's light. Its distance from the subject it is illuminating doesn't actually affect the range of influence of the light (as happens with the spotlight; when you move a spotlight closer to the subject, the cone of light shrinks, and when you move it away from the subject, the cone of light widens). To manipulate the parallel light effectively, you can change its point of interest and its intensity.

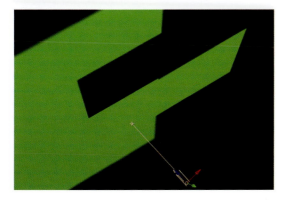

Figure 4.27 After Effect's Parallel Light.

- **Point.** This lights creates an omnidirectional illumination in the 3D space, like a bare light bulb.
- **Ambient.** This light creates a flat, overall illumination in all directions and doesn't have an actual source point in the composition. In fact, this light doesn't even have transform properties, so you cannot even move it. When you want to create an even lighting across your composition, maybe in addition to your key, fill, or a color cast, this is the light of choice.

Figure 4.28 After Effect's Point Light.

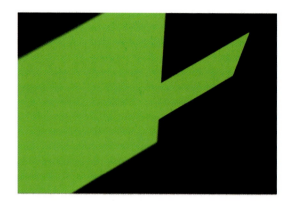

Figure 4.29 After Effect's Ambient Light.

Figure 4.30 After Effect's 3D Layer Icon.

To see your lighting setup in action, you might want to import or create other elements in your composition. You might start with a simple solid. Make sure that you turn any elements that you want to illuminate with a light into a 3D layer by clicking its 3D layer icon (the one that looks like a cube).

Each light has a variety of options to modify according to your own taste or project necessity:

- **Intensity.** Similar to a light fixture's wattage, this option regulates the intensity of light. There is no direct measurement of the light's intensity other than your own judgment. Move your mouse pointer over the canvas to read the RGB value of your light through the Info palette, and avoid reaching an overexposed true white light (R = 255, G = 255, B = 255) to keep within the ranges of broadcast-safe color.

- **Color.** This is like adding a colored gel in front of the light fixture. You can click on the color well to dynamically select your color, or click on the color picker and select a color from another element of your composition.

Figure 4.31 After Effect's Light Options.

- **Cone angle.** A wide cone produces a wide spotlight, and a narrow cone produces a narrow spotlight. The light's cone angle can range between 0 degrees (invisible) and 180 degrees (very wide cone angle). This feature is similar to, but with wider ranges than, the flood/spot setting of a real-world light.
- **Cone feather.** If you'd like to add a soft edge to your spotlight, this is the place to do it. A cone feather of 0% creates a very sharp edge, as opposed to a 100% one, which creates very soft and blurry edges. Keep in mind that when you increase the cone's feather value, you will visually decrease the cone angle at the same time, to make up for the pixels it needs to blur the edges. To compensate for it, you might want to consider readjusting the cone angle after you have reached your desired cone feather setting. Do not confuse this feature with soft lights in the real world. A cone feather will soften only the edges of the light beam, not the light itself.
- **Cast shadows.** This option can be on or off, and it cannot be keyframed. If you want the light to cast shadows on layers stacked below (in z-space), the ones you are illuminating, keep it on. If you don't want this light to cast any shadows, keep it off. Remember that if you're not getting the result you're looking for, you might need to do some troubleshooting. In After Effects, if you are trying to recreate a spotlight illuminating an object, which casts a shadow onto another object, but you are having trouble achieving that effect, check the following parameters:
  1. First, check to see whether the material options of the layer you are lighting has the **Cast Shadows** property on.
  2. Reduce its light transmission to **0%**.
  3. Check to see whether the material option of the layer you are trying to cast a shadow onto has the **Accept shadows** property on.
     That should do the trick. Now you should have a proper working light and shadow.
- **Shadow darkness.** This regulates how dark you'd like the light's shadow to be. Make sure that this property is set to at least 50% so that you can visualize the shadow on your composition. This property could be somewhat compared to the properties of hard and softlights in the real world. If you'd like your CG light to have a softer shadow, then set its **Shadow darkness** to a lower percentage. If you'd like to recreate the impression of a hard light, then increase the percentage.
- **Shadow diffusion.** This regulates how you'd like the shadow to be diffused. It is particularly noticeable around the edges of the cast shadow. It is advisable to start with a lower setting (even at 0 pixels) and then fine-tune it as necessary.

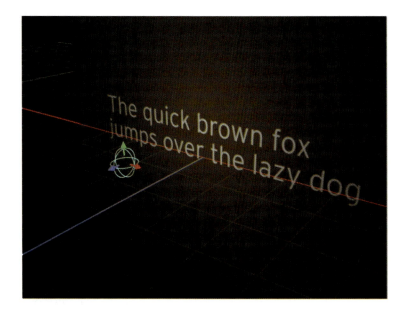

Figure 4.35 Motion's Point Light.

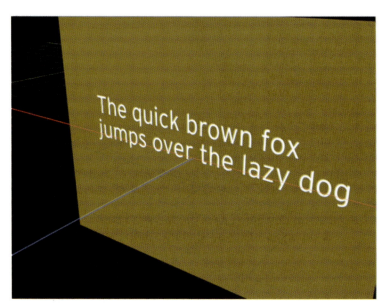

Figure 4.36 Motion's Ambient Light.

Each light has different properties than the ones in After Effects. In Motion, all lights can be modified by changing their color and intensity. Point lights and spotlights can be changed by modifying their:

- **Falloff start** (point and spot)
- **Falloff** (point and spot)
- **Cone angle** (spot only)
- **Soft edge** (spot only)

Figure 4.37 Motion's Spot Light's HUD (Heads-Up Display).

Using Photoshop Layer Styles with Type

With the variety of potential colors and shapes in a background, whether animated, footage, or even a solid color, you will need to employ a number of additional effects on type to keep it readable. Additionally, type effects will help add that level of professional slickness necessary to help your titles stand out and be memorable.

Photoshop's live-editable layer styles are useful on a number of levels. First, as a design effect, they are quite useful in easily recreating a wide variety of light, shadow, glow, texture, and depth effects that come from the real world. Second, layer styles now comfortably integrate with Adobe After Effects to make integrating them in animation much easier than before.

Adding and Adjusting Layer Styles

To add a layer style, highlight the layer you want to apply it to and click the 𝑓𝑥. icon. You'll choose an effect, and now below your layer you'll see a heading for **Effects**, and then below that you can find the name of the effect applied. If you want to delete it, you can drag it to the Trash like a layer. To duplicate the effect with the same setting on another later, **Option-click** and drag it to the layer that you'd like to apply it to.

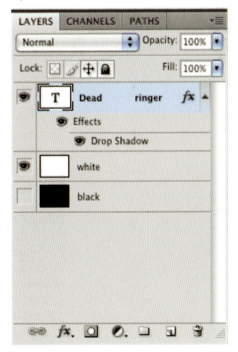

Figure 4.38

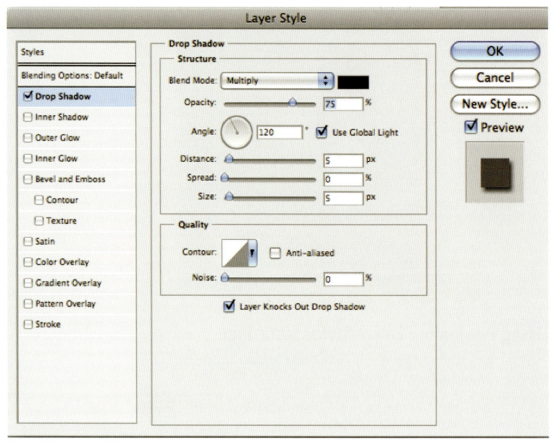

Figure 4.39

Whenever you apply a layer style, the dialog box specific to that layer style will open.

The Layer Styles

Now let's go through what each layer style does and the options for each.

- **Drop Shadow.** Creates a shadow behind the layer based on the shape of the layer.
- **Inner Shadow.** Creates a shadow that falls inside the contents of the layer.
- **Outer Glow.** Creates a glow that extends out from the contents of the layer.
- **Inner Glow.** Adds a glow from the edge of the layer inward.
- **Bevel and Emboss.** Creates a false depth based on highlights and shadows.
- **Satin.** Adds interior shading to create a glossy surface on the layer.
- **Color Overlay.** Lays a color over the layer contents.
- **Gradient Overlay.** Places a gradient over the layer contents.
- **Stroke.** Creates an outline along the edge of the layer.

Using Global Light

Figure 4.40

Drop Shadow, Inner Shadow, and Bevel and Emboss use an artificial light source that can be synced across all the layer styles that use a light source. It's called **Use Global Light**, and you'll see a checkbox to the left of it to turn it on. Below you'll see the three effects we've mentioned, with a synced Global Light and the same effect.

In this example the layer styles' light sources are synced with **Use Global Light**.

Figure 4.41

In this example the layer styles' light sources are switched off and at varying angles.

Figure 4.42

Contour

Drop Shadow, Inner Shadow, Outer and Inner Glow, Bevel and Emboss, and Satin all have **Contour** settings controlling the shape of the shading. Each of these is controlled with a Bezier curve. You have 12 contour presets, as

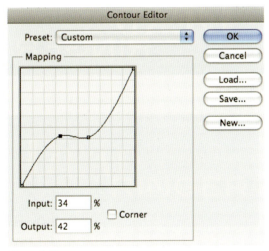

Figure 4.43

Figure 4.44

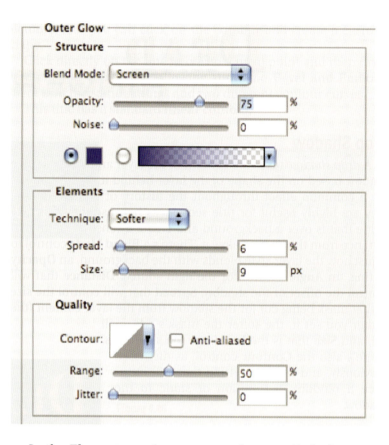

Figure 4.52

In the **Elements** section, you can choose a **Technique** (your choices are between a sharper **Precise** mask or a feathered edge **Softer** technique) and slider settings for **Spread** and **Size**. **Spread** and **Size** have the same functionality as they did for **Drop Shadow**.

Finally, under **Quality**, you have **Contour** controls, with an additional **Range** control that will adjust the amount of effect that the **Contour** will have on the glow, and a **Jitter** control for adding a natural randomness to the gradient in a glow.

Inner Glow

At first, it might be unclear what the difference is between **Inner Glow** and **Inner Shadow**, but as you go through the controls, you'll see that this effect has a more additive lighting effect, which is easier to use with subtlety than an **Inner Shadow**.

Figure 4.53

The controls will almost exactly resemble **Outer Glow**, with the exception of the **Spread** being replaced by a **Choke** control, for the same reasons as mentioned earlier, when we were comparing the controls of **Drop** and **Inner Shadow**.

Bevel and Emboss

Although many of the layer styles are used to add a bit of depth to layers, **Bevel and Emboss** does an excellent job recreating many effects of sculptural type you have seen in countless places. A **bevel** adds shading to the edges of the layer to either push it forward or back; an **emboss** will do the same thing by adding shading from the outside of the layer to push it forward or back.

Figure 4.54

The first setting you choose is the **Style**; the bevels will work along the edge of the layer, and the embosses will work from the area immediately around the letters.

Figure 4.55

Outer Bevel   Inner Bevel   Emboss   Pillow Emboss

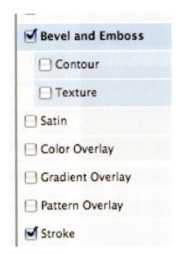

Figure 4.56

Figure 4.57

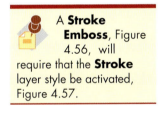

A **Stroke Emboss**, Figure 4.56, will require that the **Stroke** layer style be activated, Figure 4.57.

After you have chosen a **style**, the next setting is for **Technique**, which gives you choices (**Chisel Hard**, **Chisel Soft**, or **Smooth**) of varying strength for how the chosen **style** will be achieved. You have a slider for the amount of **depth,** which will control the strength of the shading; a choice of **direction** (**up** or **down**); a slider for size, which controls the strength of the bevel; and a slider for **softness,** to add fine control of the **Technique** choice.

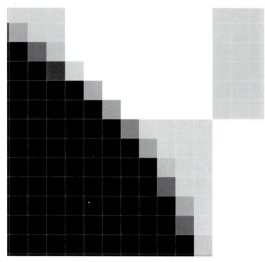

Figure 4.65

Figure 4.66

The reason we can avoid permanent rasterization of our type in After Effects is that After Effects' effects are nondestructive, meaning that they can be applied and removed without permanently being applied to the graphics. Photoshop's Smart Filters and Layer Styles are the only "live" effects.

What Is a Raster Image?

A *raster image* is a digital image in which the pixels are specifically assigned to exact locations in a grid. Since each pixel can be any of millions of colors, having the pixels specifically assigned to exact locations in a grid means that they are capable of a photographic image quality. However, it has a major limitation in that it will become distorted with enlargement, so when you use raster images, knowing the sizing is crucial.

Film and video are media that rely on photographic images; therefore, in most cases we should be working with raster engines and raster files. The same is true for type. Since type in most cases only needs to be graphic and not photographic, it is optimal for us to have type in a vector format, where size changes will not reduce quality. Photoshop and After Effects use *continuous rasterization* for type, so the type is sourced to the software as vector imagery and continuously rasterized to maintain maximum quality.

Photoshop is the world's most popular raster image editor. However, the type engine is vector information that is continuously updated and referenced by the software, so there is no quality loss from resizing. Unfortunately, if you want to use many of Photoshop's effects, you will have to go ahead and perform a full rasterizing of type layers, thus converting them to standard graphics layers and limiting your text's size. Throughout this book I'll demonstrate ways you can take advantage of After Effects to avoid ever having to rasterize the type in Photoshop. When using raster effects with type, you can get photographic textures and effects to work with your type. But nearly every raster effect can be achieved without having to rasterize the type graphics permanently.

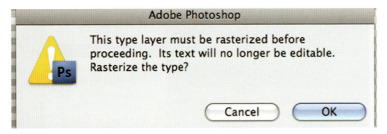

Figure 4.67

What Is a Vector Image?

A *vector image* avoids the entire issue of quality loss by not specifically assigning pixels to their locations; rather, vector images use **Bezier paths** to map out the shape of the image and reassign pixels as the path size changes. This leads to cleaner edges, and though they will never look like photographs, in most cases for type we either won't need photographic-styled imagery or we can find a workaround using masks, or some other combination of effects.

In short, it's totally acceptable to perform the typesetting part of your title work in animation software such as After Effects or Motion. If you need to typeset using Photoshop, you can, but avoid using Photoshop's effects, since there's likely an equivalent in After Effects that will not detract from the quality of your image.

Figure 4.68

Tutorial: Using Stencil Alpha to Cut Out a Texture

1 One issue that often comes up is wanting to do a photographic texture for type. The problem is, of course, our recurring issue of needing to avoid rasterizing, and the way we can do that here is to use a **blend mode** called **Stencil Alpha**. In After Effects, create a new **composition**, import the texture you'd like to use, and place a type layer above it.

1 Open the document **deadringer.psd** in Photoshop. You will see that the type layer has the **Inner Shadow** and **Gradient Overlay** styles applied.

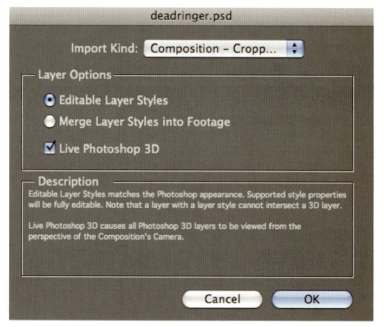

2 Import the document into After Effects as a **Composition Cropped Layers**. When you come to the **Photoshop Import** window, select **Editable Layer Styles** and click **OK**.

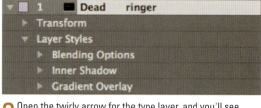

3 Open the twirly arrow for the type layer, and you'll see **Transform** and **Layer Styles**. Open **Layer Styles** and you'll see the same layer styles we set up in Photoshop. Let's open **Gradient Overlay**.

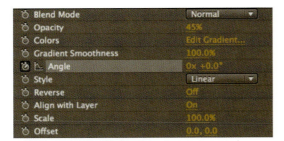

4 You will find keyframe tools for animating the same parameters that we initially set up in Photoshop. For a quick example, let's set a stopwatch for **Angle**. Go to the **2** second mark and give the **Angle** three revolutions.

5 **Done**-You'll get this ceiling fan-styled shadow movement throughout the type. Take a few minutes and try animating several different layer style parameters with After Effects.

Tutorial: Adding Animated Illustrative Elements to a Main Title Card

Using a simple, animated illustrative element can make the difference between the movie logos that people remember and ones they will forget. In the following tutorial, we'll animate an organic plant element as part of a movie logo.

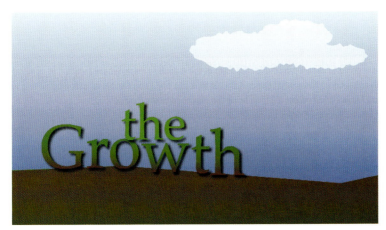

1 This scene was designed with Illustrator. Let's begin by locking the background layer. Let's add a new **Shape** layer to extend the *e* into a growing and ominous plant leaf.

2 We'll use the **Pen tool** to create the leaf. Press **G** on the keyboard and then look at the new buttons that arrive on the screen. You'll see a star icon next to a half-circle icon; choose the star, which tells After Effects that we are creating a **shape** and not a **mask**. Set the **Fill** to match the green of the *e*, which you can do by clicking on **Fill** and using the **eyedropper** from the color picker. Set the stroke to **No Stroke** by clicking **Stroke** and choosing the square with the red slash.

After Effects' new **Shape** layer function allows users to create Bezier shapes that can be animated over time. However, it sounds very similar to **Masks**, which are also Bezier shapes that can be animated. So what's the difference? Think of **Shape** layers as being like a **Mask** over a *Solid* layer, with the addition of **Animators** dedicated to them. **Masks** are designed to cut out layer content; Shapes are designed to create content.

If you would like to use the same project management system for a project where you will use Motion instead of After Effects, you can still apply it in the same way, though you might want to name the folders **Motion Project** and **Motion Renders**.

- **Original Art.** In this folder we will keep any elements that are provided from the client side or any research elements such as images you found on the Web. We will **not** import any of these files into our actual project; we keep only provided or reference material here. For example, in a moment I'll demonstrate how to convert a movie poster file into a graphic for our title sequence, so I'd keep the original file in this folder and the converted file in the Photoshop folder.
- **Photoshop.** In this folder we will keep all of the .psd documents we plan to import into After Effects. If you plan to work with Illustrator, you should name this folder Illustrator instead or, if you are going to use both, make a Photoshop folder and an Illustrator folder.
- **AE Project.** When you save an After Effects project, it will create an .aep file. Keep all your .aep files for this project in here. You should use the **Increment and Save** function in AE periodically so that you have an archive of files to look back through. **Increment and Save** does a **Save As** function except that it skips the part where it asks you to name the file and simply adds a number at the end of the file name. You might want to label your files so that you know which one is current.
- **AE Renders.** When you render a file in After Effects, send it to this folder. You can purge the content of this folder when you are ready to archive your project.

In OSX, to give a file a color-coded label highlight the filename, go to the **File** menu from the Finder, scroll to the bottom, and choose the color you want, Figure 4.70.

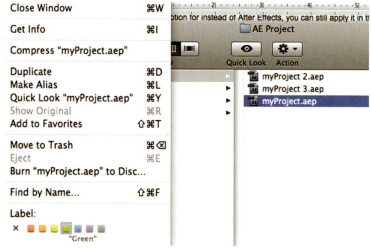

Figure 4.70

Working with the Graphic Design Department

The titles in your movie will often reflect the same look as the posters, invitational cards, and other print material that will be used to promote the film. In the old days, when titles were not as valued a marketing commodity as they are today, the print materials would sometimes follow the titles by some period of time, to the point where they wouldn't match at all. Now, since these two elements can happen simultaneously, it makes it much easier to keep them in sync.

300 dpi Becomes 72 ppi

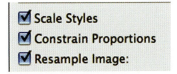

Figure 4.71

When a motion graphics artist receives material from the print department, several things will need to be changed. If the print material comes first, it must have its resolution reduced. Print usually uses 300 dots per inch (dpi) or higher. However, screens have the advantage of needing much lower resolution, 72 pixels per inch (ppi). When lowering resolution in software such as Photoshop, we must be very careful to avoid destructive processes.

When you are adjusting the scale of image in Photoshop you should be quite careful about the three check boxes above. Let's say that we are going to shrink down a movie title logo from a poster.

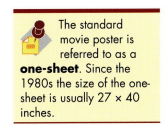

Figure 4.72

The standard movie poster is referred to as a **one-sheet**. Since the 1980s the size of the one-sheet is usually 27 × 40 inches.

Resizing a Movie Poster Logo

1 To downsize our poster logo, first go to **Image | Image Size** and turn off **Resample Image**. Resample Image allows the software to warp the image into whatever dimensions we give it (which is something we will rarely want at this point). Leave **Scale Styles** and **Constrain Proportions** on. In most cases we will want **Constrain Proportions** on because that will preserve our dimensions.

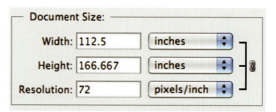

2 Now, under **Resolution**, change it to **72**. Notice that the width and height of the document have become huge. That's because we have **Constrain Proportions** on but Resample Image off. Leave **Constrain Proportions** on, and turn on **Resample Image**.

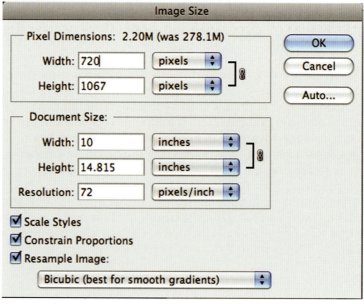

The difference between **Image Size** and **Canvas Size** is that Canvas Size only addresses the size of the workspace (or canvas), not the contents. **Image Size** affects both.

3 Now you have unlocked the ability to enter in **Pixel Dimensions**. Under **Width**, enter **720**. Hit **OK**.

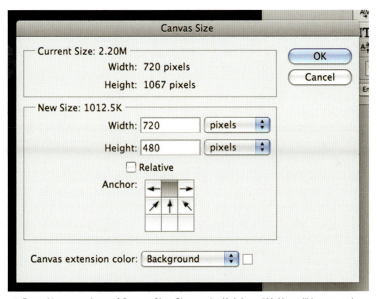

4 **Done**-Now go to **Image | Canvas Size**. Change the **Height** to **480**. You will be warned that this will crop the image, but in this case there's nothing I want below the 480 mark so it is okay (if there was something below I would have to do some resizing). Since the logo in my example comes from the top of our document, I moved the **Anchor** to top center.

Setting Up in After Effects
Composition Settings

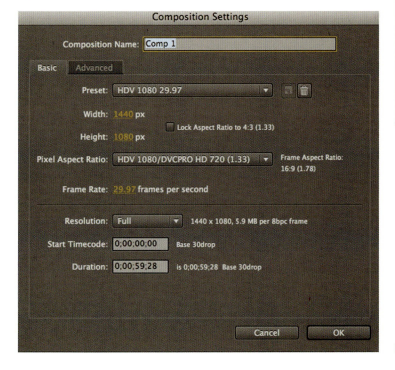

The world of film has become so much more diverse in the past decade and movies can be projected in so many different formats now that your setting could range from standard small DV to 4K and higher sizes.

Figure 4.73

At the beginning of any motion graphics project, particularly a title sequence, it is very important for the designer to have a meeting with the producer, director, and editor to discuss what the final output will be.

Ideally, you will be able to work in the format that matches the final output, but that might not always be possible. Working with 4K footage and animated type will cripple even some fairly high-end systems, and on the ones it won't cripple, it could make After Effects or Motion run so slowly that the movie's production could grind to a halt. So, you can work with lower resolutions until the clients approve the piece and then output the high-resolution footage. How?

First, remember that if your type is vector, you can resize it at any point nondestructively. If you are animating elements as part of your title sequence, if they are vector, again, resizing is not a issue. With raster elements there's room for more concern.

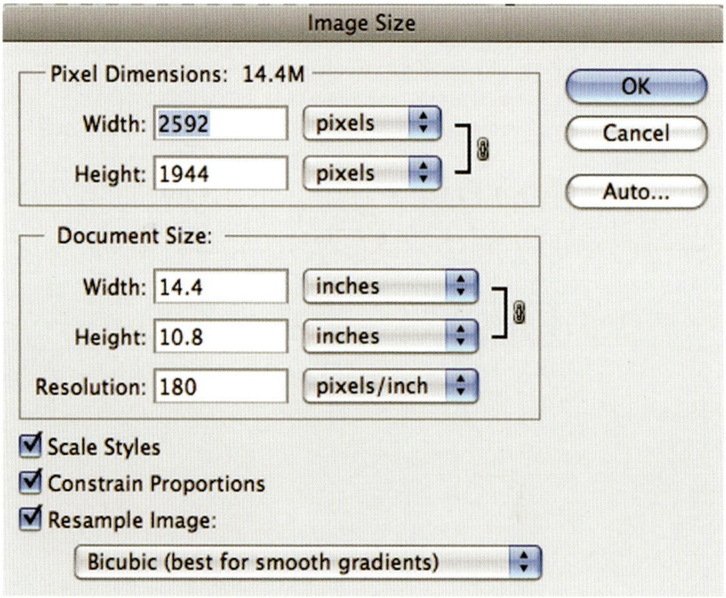

Figure 4.74

With the image being prepped, you will notice that the resolution is set to 180, which is more than double 72 ppi. Since video will be 72 ppi, After Effects will read the document purely from the number of pixel dimensions, and this image is 2592 × 1944, making it large enough to be part of a 2K film document later. But if we put it into a 720 × 480 document, we have to bring the Scale way down to make it work well in our lower-resolution document, but by doing this we have freed ourselves to make it larger later.

Tutorial: Making a Preset

In creating a title sequence with After Effects, there are a number of ways to do the same things, and we can take advantage of some workflow accelerators to save serious time. One of these is to make a **preset** for your animation so that we don't get stuck in repetitive tasks.

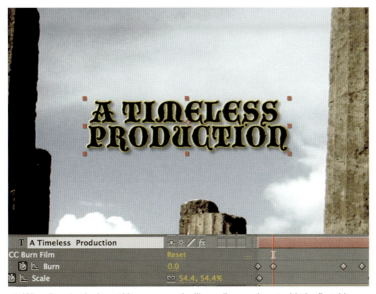

1 When I am beginning a title sequence, I will usually experiment with the first title until I find something I like. In this case, I've settled on using **CC Burn** to make the text appear and a **Scale** that begins at **50** percent and ends at **70** percent.

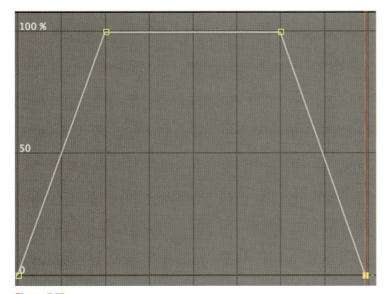

Figure 7.75

A standard fade up and fade down are used often on titles. There are numerous **Transition** effects in After Effects, but the **Opacity** tool also does the trick. When doing a fade up/ fade down, you need four keyframes. The first one set to 0, the second set to the max opacity. The third should repeat the maximum opacity, which will pause the opacity effect for the length of time between the two keyframes, and the fourth should return it to 0, Figure 4.75.

Figure 4.76

Figure 4.77

2 Press the **U** key on the keyboard, which will bring up your animation parameters. Highlight the **CC Burn** and **Scale** tools. Drag and drop them into the **Effects and Presets** menu. You will be prompted to enter a name. I called it **Augustus_TS**.

The **Add/ Remove Keyframe** button will add a keyframe that repeats the last value entered, if there are no other later keyframes for that parameter. So this is a quick way to add a keyframe that will pause an animation, Figure 4.76.

3 **Done**-Now we can apply the settings throughout. So, put in your next title and drag and drop our **Augustus_TS** preset on it and it'll match the previous title. What's also pretty great about this is that if the title needs tweaking, you can change the keyframe values after they are applied. In the case of the next title in this sequence, I had to lower the **Scale** to between **30** and **50** percent to keep the larger title between the two columns.

Open in Editor

One of the most useful commands for working with Photoshop and Illustrator sourced documents in After Effects is **Ctrl-E** (or **Command-E**). This will open the layer in its editor, which is the program that was used to create it. So, your computer will then launch Photoshop or Illustrator, you can make your changes, and save. Jump back to After Effects, and voilà! It's updated to accept your change.

If it hasn't updated—and sometimes it won't because After Effects stores a lot in your RAM and will only return to the source files if it needs to—highlight the update information in the **Project** window and go to **File | Reload Footage**.

Figure 4.78

TED 2009: A Case Study

Motion Graphics Studio: Trollbäck + Company
Creative Director: Jacob Trollbäck
www.trollback.com

Figure 4.79 Jacob Trollback.

The content, sound effects and motion graphics in this piece achieve a sense of unison I've rarely seen. Can you elaborate on the creative process while you were working on this opening?

Many years ago I did a three-dimensional type animation for TED8. Many people have told me that it is their favorite of my TED openings. Since the 2009 conference was a jubilee of sorts—the 25th year since the first conference—I thought it would be fun to go back to the roots, as all the early conferences were explorations in moving type, and also give the type geeks something to enjoy.

The conference had 12 themes that we wanted to feature. The goal in all our work is to find clever ways to make an emotional connection, so here we wanted to load the type with meaning according to the themes. For example, *Discover* is a DNA spiral swooping upward, and *Engage* interacts with it in a choreographed dance. *Invent* forms a curious shape—later to be found to be a *T*—and *See*, *Predict* and *Dare* merge into the word *Reconnect*. After that, *Reconnect* splits into several strands of *Grow* that form an organically spreading shape, only to be intercepted by the word *Dream* that brings us into a **2001**-inspired white space. More themes enter and line up in a kind of large meta-type that spell out *The Great*. But these letters turn out to have yet another dimension. As they rotate around their own axis, we see that they are three-dimensional objects that read differently from another angle.

I have worked with Michael Montes for 15 years, and we have an innate understanding of how music and motion can and should support each other. We create the pieces with a strong idea of what the thrust should be, and Michael finds a way to put this into sound.

Everything in this piece works elegantly, efficiently, and poignantly, from the Mac booting-up sound effects, the Discover DNA, the white flash frame after the dream sequence, until the reveal of the conference's title. How much preparation and testing went into this project? What was the decision factor that led to the type treatment in 3D?

I came up with the rotating three-dimensional type for a title sequence for the movie **True Lies** many years ago. Ironically, Peter, one of our 3D designers, had made a similar discovery by himself and actually advanced the idea with type that you can read from three directions. The playful surprise seemed perfect to reveal the word *Unveiling*.

Figure 4.80a Still frames from TED 2009, created by Trollbäck + Company.

Figure 4.80b

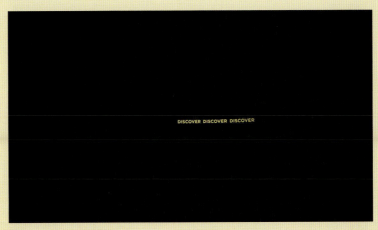

Figure 4.80c

Figure 4.80d

Figure 4.80e

Figure 4.80f

Figure 4.80g

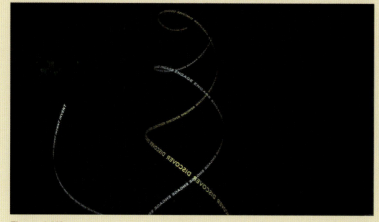

Figure 4.80h

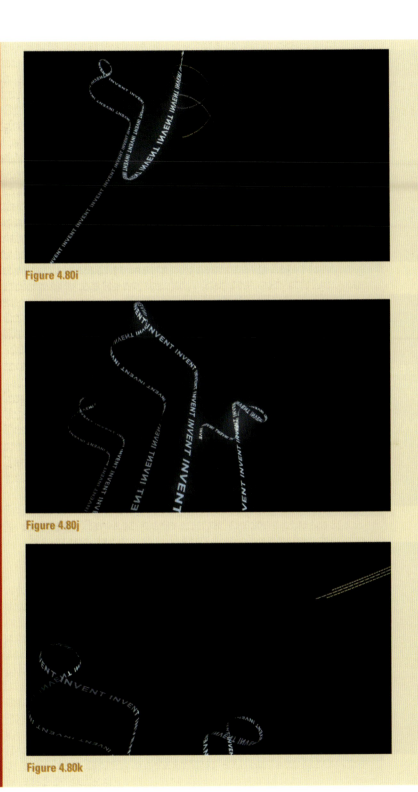

Figure 4.80i

Figure 4.80j

Figure 4.80k

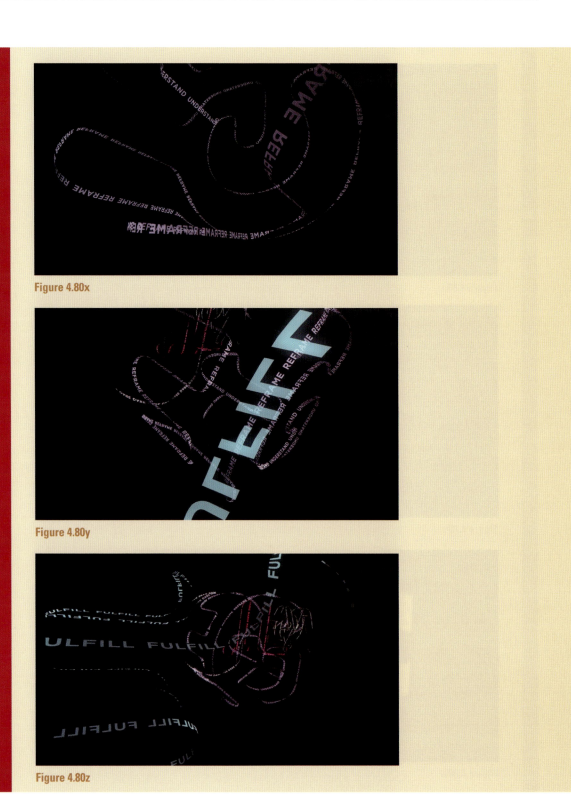

Figure 4.80x

Figure 4.80y

Figure 4.80z

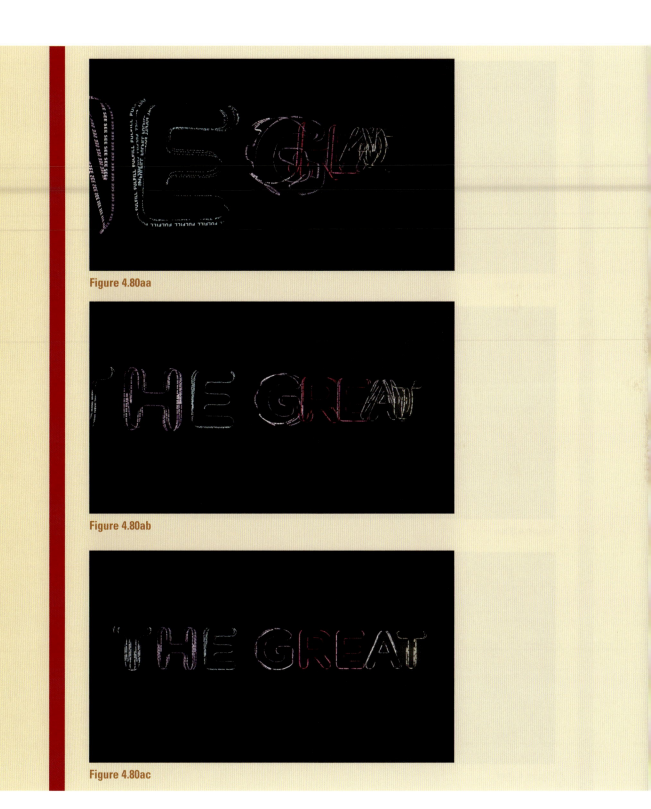

Figure 4.80aa

Figure 4.80ab

Figure 4.80ac

What did the project timeline look like, from beginning of the project to the deliverable?

I think we spent about two weeks on concept, and then about another week refining the final concept when it was chosen, and production was about two weeks. It was fast turnaround. And that probably affected the lack of changes and the direction the client was going in.

Since the spot was going to be used at the Sundance Festival between each of the film sections—as they were promoting the drink there—and was also going to be played in flight in Virgin America—as they became the first airline to take this drink on board—they had to have the commercial in a very short time. That's why the timeline was kind of fast and furious. It gave it a kind of definite "We have to have it done by this time to have it by this time."

How does the use of camera move the story forward?

The camera movement on this commercial was defined by the concept: a drink or a bottle spilled over onto a napkin or a piece of paper. So you are following all of these trails no matter how far they go across this infinite-sized piece of paper.

We wanted the camera moves to be flexible enough to rotate: not just follow a line but actually spin around 180 degrees, over the z-axis and the y-axis, but also to have a little bit of movement, a slightly handheld effect, but not too much.

The distance of the 3D camera from the paper stays essentially the same. The individual objects have a different z-space value which gives them a slight offset when things move, like having textures moving separate from the background.

By pulling those elements off separately by 100, 200 pixels each, we had the capability to use a little bit more flow with the camera. That then revealed more of the differences between those 3D layers. If we kept all the elements flat, then the camera moves would have pretty much just made it all, and I think that would have been boring.

I think we took a good decision because to randomly move the camera would have been the easy choice. We would have ended up with a more lazy, storytelling kind of view, instead of a distinctive drunken feel to it.

The only forced camera move that had to be done was right at the very end when we come in on the logo. The design element of the devil's face here in the background bleeds in. But it is barely there, and as it gets darker toward the end of the commercial, you can see it actually becoming quite heavy, which is nice I think, it has got a nice imposing feel to it. The end frame is actually my favorite of the piece because of its dark texture and because it gets a little more foreboding. I now have this image in my head that I can't get rid of.

The camera move on this last shot was actually a trick: It resulted from a two-dimensional rotoscope. This was because coming from 3D and revealing the two-dimensional bottle got a little too complicated. So inside essentially there's another composition, and I just rotoscoped five or six frames to reveal it. And in the new composition there's just another 3D camera that's just slightly moving in. So that was really the only twist.

The French background of Paris, that was really quite nice. Was it done by a designer of yours?

No, actually a designer called iStockphoto! We found some fantastic high-res illustrations of Paris landmarks and we just acquired them, layered them, and repositioned them so they would fit the HD and the SD versions. We then filled them with texture, which I originally intended to do in paper form with the text on it, kind of like the dark design.

But in the end it was a little too dark overall, and you couldn't see much of the detail because the texture was taking over. But they worked really well and they took a little while to render, especially the Eiffel Tower, there's so much detail in that. Everything else was provided.

Figure 4.83a Still frames from Le Tourment Vert, designed by Energi Design.

Figure 4.83b

Figure 4.83c

Figure 4.83d

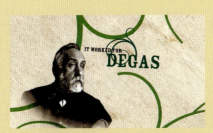

Figure 4.83e

Figure 4.83f

Figure 4.83g

Figure 4.83h

Figure 4.83i

Figure 4.83j

Figure 4.83k

5

IMPORTING TEXT AND OTHER FILES INTO AFTER EFFECTS

Adobe After Effects was designed for working with information that was created in other software packages, even though over the years Adobe has added more generative capabilities within After Effects. Creating type in After Effects is a completely acceptable way of working, but many designers choose to bring the type in from other software such as its sister programs, Photoshop and Illustrator. There are a few workflow considerations to take into account when you're importing layers into After Effects.

Workflow Considerations

Importing Files into After Effects

After Effects has four different import types. They are listed here, with explanations of what each one is meant for.

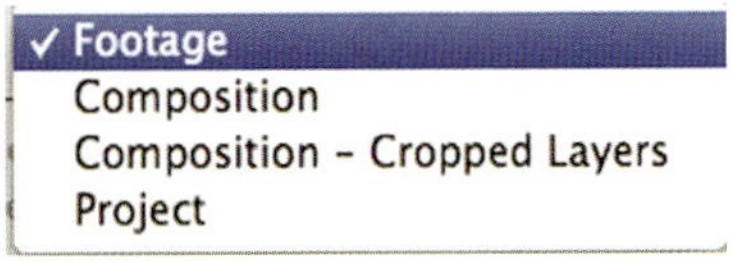

Figure 5.1

Footage

Importing layers as **footage** is used for bringing in items one at a time. Basically, you use **footage** when you either don't want multilayer information or you want a single layer of a multilayer document. The following list gives you an idea of what I mean:

- Video files, since video files are not in a multilayered format
- Audio files
- Photoshop or Illustrator files when you want to flatten them as you bring them into After Effects
- Photoshop or Illustrator files when you only want one layer of a multilayer document
- Image files that don't have separate layers
- Motion Timelines (.motn files)

Composition

There are two import types for **Composition**: the standard Composition and Composition **Cropped Layers**. When you want

doi: 10.1016/B978-0-240-81419-3.00005-2

to bring a Photoshop or Illustrator file into After Effects and have the separate layers treated as separate clips in After Effects, the Composition setting is the correct way to go. When you use Composition, the **Anchor Points** are set in the center of the document.

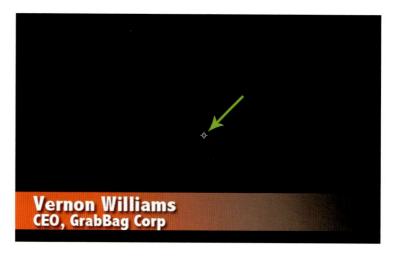

Figure 5.2 Notice that the Anchor Point for every layer is set to the center of the document when you import with Composition.

This is useful for documents where you have rotation animations that will rotate around the same orbit. Also, **Composition** is a good choice for when you want to use an effect such as **Shatter**, where the effect will take elements of the layer beyond its immediate area.

Composition Cropped Layers

In most cases, for title sequences you will want to choose this setting for multilayer Photoshop and Illustrator files. It will set the anchor points to the center of each layer.

Figure 5.3 Notice how when you use Composition Cropped Layers, it places the anchor points where the center of each layer lies.

Project

After Effects can import projects, which is used for the purpose of bringing elements from one After Effects document into another. It will place the files inside a folder, and those elements can be accessed in the current project.

Special Considerations for Text Layers

If you are importing a Photoshop document, and you'd like to make changes to the type, you can use the **Convert to Editable Text** option from the **Layer** menu. This takes a Photoshop type layer and makes it type that you can edit in After Effects. This option is not available to you if you make your type layer with Illustrator. But of course there is a way around that.

Convert to Live Photoshop 3D
Convert to Editable Text
Create Shapes from Text
Create Masks from Text
Auto-trace...
Pre-compose...   ⇧⌘C

Figure 5.4

Tutorial: Editing Type from an Illustrator Document

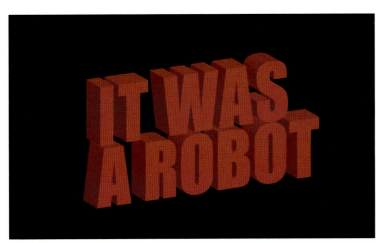

1 Let's say that I want to change this title so that the *S* lines up with the *T*. Here's how we can fix that. From After Effects, press **Ctrl-E** (or **Command-E**), and your OS will open Illustrator.

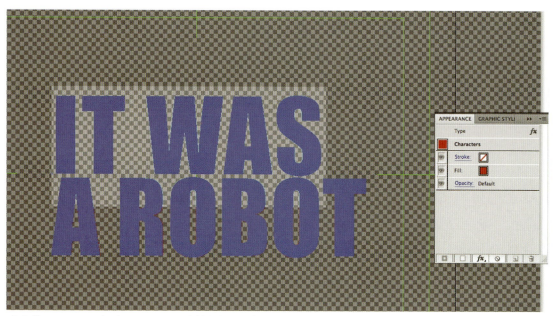

2 In Illustrator, open the **Appearance** panel. Click the eye icon for the **3D Extrude and Bevel** effect to temporarily turn it off. Open the **Character panel**.

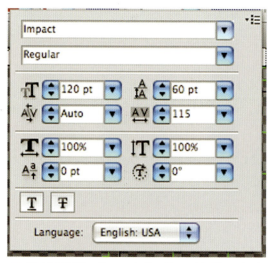

3 Highlight **It Was**. Change the **Tracking** to 115. Now check to make sure that we have lined up our *T* and *S*. Make the **3D Extrude and Bevel** visible again and save.

4 **Done**-Return to AE and you might see your type updated, but you might not. If not, select the type in the **Project** window and either right-click or Control-click on the layer and choose **Reload Footage**. This forces AE to refresh the connection to the layer and update.

Creating Title Cards

The term **title card** (or **intertitle**) comes from the old days when a literal card would be stationed in front of a camera and photographed. These were the dominant devices used to convey dialogue between characters during the silent era. How far we have come! This practice is no longer the method used, but **intertitles** themselves are still very much in use for artistic effect.

Title cards typically are not placed over footage that is part of the main narrative. Titles that are placed over the footage that are part of the actual film are usually referred to as **supers** or **supertitles,** referring to the title being superimposed over the image.

Creating a non-moving title card is fairly easy, a simple matter of using the text tool of your chosen software to place type on the screen. However, using After Effects opens up a world of opportunities for adding animation to a title card.

Tutorial: Animated Title Cards

In this example, we'll make an animated title to tell the audience the location of our story.

1 If you are making the title as a card and not a super, you can set the timeline to the exact length needed for the film. Depending on the length of the title, you need to be sure that the composition will be long enough for the audience to read. So, for our title, which will say *Glasgow, Scotland,* let's make it 6 seconds long.

After Effects has tons of menus; rather than sift through them every time you need to bring up a new one, use the Workspace for Text. Look at the upper-right corner of the screen, open the drop-down menu for **Workspace**, and select **Text** (see Figure 5.5).

Figure 5.5

1. Font Family
2. Font Style
3. Eyedropper
4. Reset Colors
5. No Fill/Stroke
6. Fill
7. Stroke
8. Switch Stroke and Fill Colors
9. Point Size
10. Leading
11. Kerning
12. Tracking
13. Stroke Width
14. Stroke Position
15. Vertically Scale
16. Horizaontally Scale
17. Baseline Shift
18. Tsume
19. Faux Bold
20. Faux Italics
21. All Capitals
22. Upper/Lower Caps
23. Superscript
24. Subscript

2 Type your title. Set the appearance you want using the **Character panel**. Set the chart above for how to adjust your type in After Effects. What we decide to use here is the foundation that will be animated when we animate this title later.

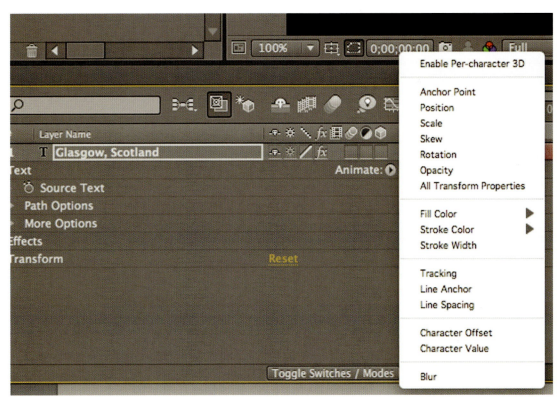

3 When you are happy with the appearance of the title, open the text layer. You will see a button for **Animate**, which adds type-specific animation tools to your word. Choose **Tracking**.

You will notice that **Position, Scale, Anchor Point, Rotation**, and **Opacity** are repeated in the Animate menu. In the Animate menu, these tools affect the **individual letters** (Figure 5.6). The tools of the same names in the **Transform** menu will move the entire body of type (Figure 5.7).

Figure 5.6 Type animated with **Transform | Rotation**.

Figure 5.7 Type animated with **Text | Animate | Rotation**.

4 When you add an **animator** to your type layer, it will add **Animator 1** and **Range Selector 1** to your layer. Below **Range Selector 1** are the keyframe tools for the **Tracking** animator we've just added. Set a keyframe at the 0 mark with the **Tracking Amount** set to **0**, and then at the **6** second mark, set the **Tracking Amount** to **6**.

Enable Per-character 3D	
Anchor Point	
Position	
Scale	
Skew	
Rotation	
Opacity	
All Transform Properties	
Fill Color	▶
Stroke Color	▶
Stroke Width	
Tracking	
Line Anchor	
Line Spacing	
Character Offset	
Character Value	
Blur	

5 To the right of **Animator** 1 you will have a button called **Add**. Click there and choose **Property**. The **Property** list will open. Choose **Scale**.

6 **Done**-From 0–1:00, animate the **Scale** from **0** to **100** percent. At the **5** second mark, create a new keyframe, set it to **100** percent; at the **6** second mark, make it **0**. Now you've got a pretty slick title card.

Tutorial: Title Card-Based Title Sequence

Title sequences based on cards can be made quickly with After Effects.

1 Set up the composition to match the length you need for your title sequence. In this case let's set it to **60** seconds. Import the background footage and place it at the bottom of the layer order in our timeline.

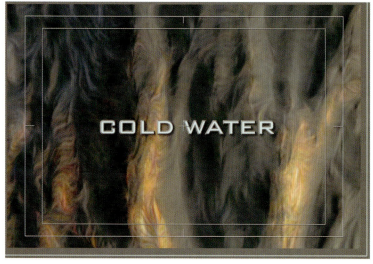

2 Use the **Type tool** to create your title. Modify your text with the tools in the **Character panel**.

3 Trim the title down to the length we need it to be; in this case, trim it to **5** seconds.

4 Go to **Animate** and choose **Blur**. Set keyframes to go from a blur set to **26** at 0, and at the **1** second mark, bring the blur down to **0**. At the **4** second mark, insert a blank keyframe, and at the **5** second mark, increase the blur back to **26**.

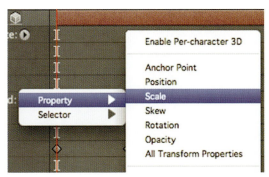

5 Go to **Add** and choose **Property | Scale**.

6 Click the chain-link icon to unlock the **Scale**. Highlight the first **100** value and make it **–100**. The type should now be facing the opposite direction. Don't start the stopwatch for **Scale**.

Use the **Range Selectors** to make an effect appear on letters one at a time.

7 Open **Range Selector 1**. Start the stopwatch for **End**, and set it to **0** percent. At the **1** second mark increase it to **100** percent. At the **4** second mark set a new keyframe, and reduce **End** to **0** at the **5** second mark. We will now use this animation template for the rest of the title sequence.

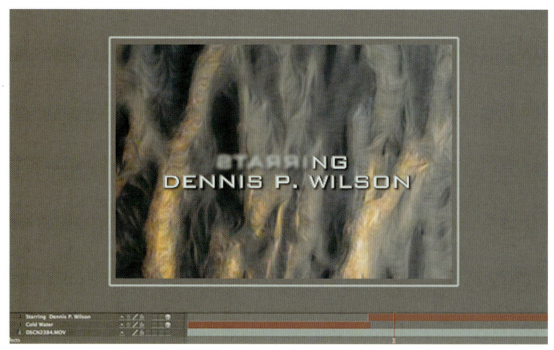

8 **Done**-Now we can duplicate our first title for the remaining titles. Press **Ctrl-D** (or **Command-D**) and it will duplicate your layer. Move it down so that it begins after the first title ends. Double-click the text, and type the next title. Repeat this process for the rest of your title sequence.

Tutorial: Creating a Lower Third Title

Lower third titles are very commonplace and are reasonably quick to create with After Effects or Motion. The term **lower third** comes from the location where the title is positioned on the screen: the bottom third. The reason for this is that the lower third is designed not to interfere with what is being shown onscreen but to supplement it. Originally, on TV and in film lower thirds were only used as a way to supply absolutely necessary information; now they have become a way of implementing some creative design as well as branding.

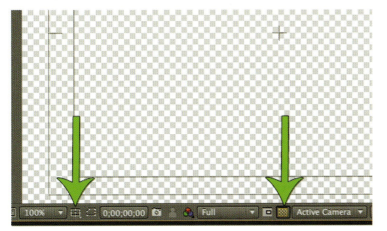

If you are relatively new to After Effects, you might not be familiar with *alpha channels*. Alpha channels are extra channels added to the RGB channels that will keep track of blank or semitransparent pixels. Even if you are importing a multilayer document from Photoshop into AE, you are using alpha channels; any blank space needs an alpha channel. In the case of importing a Photoshop document, the software uses the alpha channel without necessarily making you aware of it.

1 Begin by making a new composition that matches the size of the footage over which it will be placed. Often the designer is not the same person who edits the project, so the designer will have to set it up to be easily integrated into an editing project. Turn on your **Title/Action Safes** and the **Transparency Grid**. Since in this lesson we will go over how to prepare this title for use in a project being edited on Final Cut Pro or Avid Media Composer, it is important to keep our eyes on what our **alpha channel** will be doing.

2 Next, let's create a background. Create a new **Shape layer** by selecting the **Rectangle tool**, and place your background in the bottom third along the **Title Safe** line. I used a **gradient** for the **fill**, and a **stroke** set to black.

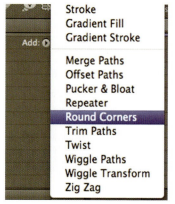

3 This is an optional step, but often lower-third titles can feel like they cover too much area, and one way around that is use a lower opacity as part of the gradient. Open the **Gradient editor** and choose one of the top markers. You'll see a percentage for **Opacity**, so you can go ahead and lower it.

4 **Shape layers** have the ability to add parameters similarly to the way you can do so with text layers. Open the **Shape layer**, and click **Add**. Use **Round Corners**.

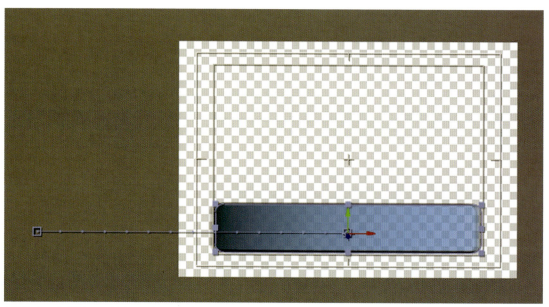

5 My favorite TV lower thirds are the ones that build rather than do something like a **Fade Up/Fade Down**. Now, keep in mind that you don't want this to be cheesy or to feel overly animated. Avoid the **Effects | Transitions** in most cases. In this case, I put the rectangle in **3D Mode** by activating the 3D switch (it looks like a cube) and for the first 15 frames I use **Position** keyframes to animate it from being completely off-screen to its center frame spot.

6 Now add in a keyframe animation of the **X Rotation**. At the 15-frame mark I placed my first keyframe with **X Rotation** set to **90** degrees. At the **1** second mark, I changed the **X Rotation** to **0** degrees.

7 Turn on **Motion Blur** (via the Motion Blur switch, which is the series of overlaid circles). You have to turn on the large switch to enable it in the entire composition, and the smaller one to activate it for specific layers.

8 Now add the text layer for the title. I have the name of the person speaking in a larger point size than his description. Now turn on the **3D switch** and the **Motion Blur** switch.

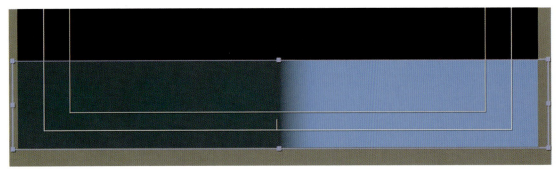

4 Click and drag out your rectangle, making sure you cover up a comfortable distance above the **Title Safe** mark. Now we have to fix that gradient.

5 Adjust the number values for **Start Point** and **End Point** until you like the way the colors transition. Also, you can click **Edit Gradient** to bring up the sliders for your gradient. The following is what I have settled on.

6 Now we will carefully set our type. You'll want to choose something bold and large enough to read on your screen size. For optimal clarity, use a sans serif typeface with a bold style. Remember, people must be able to read this or else you will just annoy them. Unlike our previous example, you might even be giving them very important information.

7 This is optional: I added **Effect | Perspective | Bevel Alpha**, with a very slight setting to help the type read better. It's very subtle, but we want our type to be as legible as possible.

8 Set keyframes for **Position** to have the type scroll from right to left. Make sure the sentence goes from being completely off the screen on the right side to being completely off the screen on the left side. Now, it is important that it move incredibly slowly to be easily read. My sentence had 13 words with 55 characters, so my keyframes were set at the **0** second mark and **30** seconds.

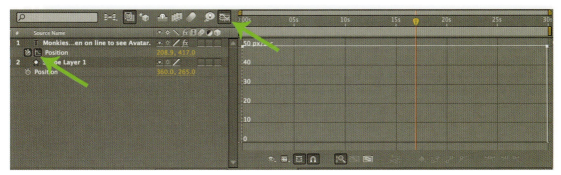

9 Check the **graph editor** to see the speed, which you can find by enabling the **graph editor** switch at the top, and then activate the **graph editor** switch next to the **Position tool**. My title is traveling at approximately 50 pixels per second.

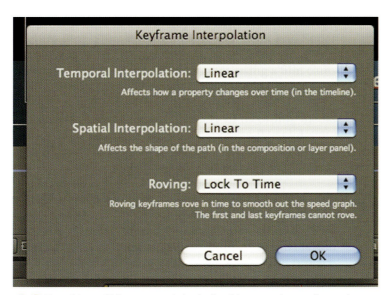

10 To avoid your title's movement behaving in odd ways, make sure that you have the correct **keyframe interpolation**. Highlight your **Position** keyframes and go to **Animation | Keyframe Interpolation**. Make sure that both **Temporal Interpolation** and **Spatial Interpolation** are set to **Linear**.

☐ 4:3 or 1.33:1
☐ 1.66:1 (scaled down to match the SD height)
☐ 16:9 (scaled down to match the SD height)
☐ 1.85:1 (scaled down to match the SD height)
☐ 2.35:1 (scaled down to match the SD height)

Figure 6.6

Formats and Aspect Ratios

Before you start working on your project, you need to determine which format you are going to deliver your final video render in. If you are creating a title sequence for a client, the client will make the decision. But if you are creating a title sequence for a friend or for your own demo reel, you'll need to choose the best format to suit your needs. This decision will not only affect the graphic elements you create, it will also affect the format you shoot in, your camera decisions, and the aspect ratio for your frame.

The **aspect ratio** is the relationship between the height and the width of your frame and is important to know before shooting footage or creating graphics for your title sequence.

In film cameras, each film format utilizes a different aspect ratio. The aspect ratios for 8mm, Super 8mm, and 16mm film are 1.33:1 (or 4:3). Super 16mm aspect ratio is 1.66:1, and 35mm aspect ratios are 1.33:1, 1.85:1, or 2.35:1, depending on the lenses, camera mattes, and cinema projectors.

When you are working with video cameras or in digital postproduction, the horizontal and vertical pixel dimensions of your project and frame format determine your frame size and aspect ratio. For example, SD NTSC video is 720 pixels wide and 480 pixels tall and its aspect ratio is 4:3. HD video dimensions are either 1280 × 720 or 1920 × 1080 pixels, and the aspect ratio is 16:9. Common video frame sizes are shown in Table 6.1.

Table 6.1 Common Video Frame Sizes

Width	Height	Screen Aspect Ratio	Description
640	480	4:3	An early standard for analog-to-digital video editing
720	480	4:3	NTSC DV and DVD image dimensions
720	486	4:3	NTSC SD video dimensions used for professional digital formats such as Digital Betacam, D-1, and D-5
720	576	4:3	PAL SD video dimensions used for digital formats such as Digital Betacam, D-1, and D-5 as well as DVD and DV
1280	720	16:9	HD video format
1920	1080	16:9	Higher resolution HD video format

In After Effects you can create a new composition by choosing **Composition | New Composition**. Pick your composition settings from the **Presets** pull-down menu, and pick your custom frame size.

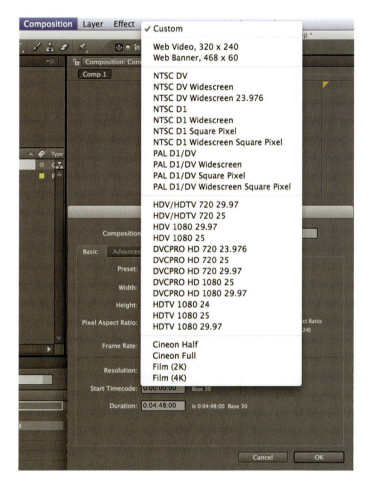

Figure 6.7 In After Effects you can pick your custom frame size from the presets pull-down menu in your New Composition window.

In Motion you can create a new project by choosing **File | New** and either picking one of the project **Presets** from the pull-down menu or setting your own custom frame size.

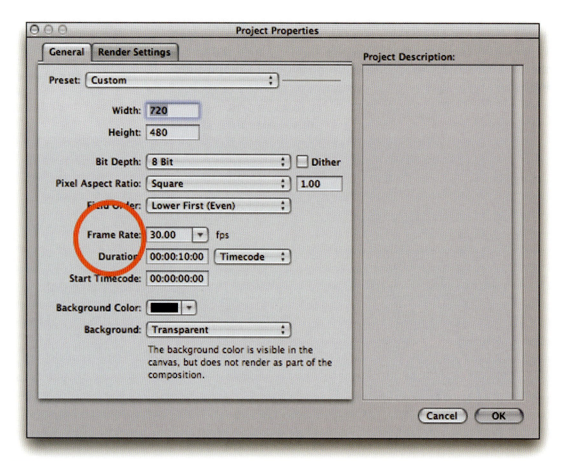

Figure 6.10 In Motion you can set your project's frame rate by choosing **File | New** and selecting **Custom** from the project preset pull-down.

Table 6.2 Common Frame Rates

24 fps	Film, certain HD formats, and certain SD formats use this frame rate; this can also be 23.98 fps for compatibility with NTSC video
25 fps	SD PAL
29.97 fps	SD NTSC
59.94 fps	720p HD video frame rate; this can also be 60 fps

Compressing and Expanding Time

Recording at speeds other than the default speed creates a temporal effect that changes how the moving image is perceived. The following are two common situations in which you will perceive a time compression or expansion:

- **Slower frame rates (e.g., 9, 12, 16 fps) produce fast-motion shots.** In fact, if the playback frame rate is higher than the recording frame rate, the action will appear to move faster. For example, images recorded at 12 fps (low frame rate) and played back at 24 fps will create a fast-motion effect. In this case it will take 1 second to play back 2 seconds of recorded material. Think of the early silent films, which were shot at 18 fps and played back at 24 fps, creating that typical fast-walking movement á la Charlie Chaplin.

- **Faster frame rates (e.g., 36, 48, 60 fps) produce slow-motion shots.** If the playback frame rate is lower than the recording frame rate, the action will appear to move slower. For example, images recorded at 48 fps (high frame rate) and played back at 24 fps will create a slow-motion effect. In this case it will take 2 seconds to play back 1 second of recorded material.

Figure 6.11 Slow-motion and fast-motion shots.

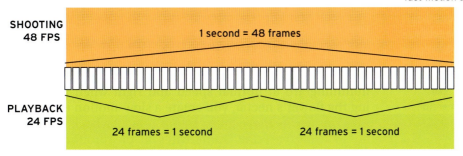

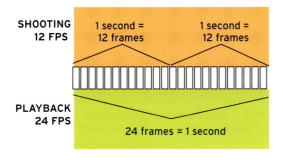

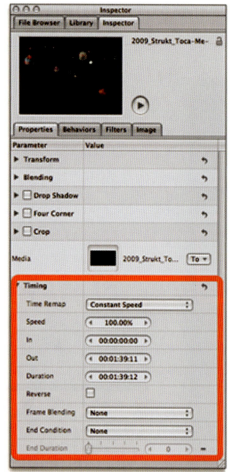

Figure 6.14 In Motion you can access the Time Remap feature through **Inspector | Properties tab | Timing**, where you can select **Constant speed** from the **Time Remap** pull-down.

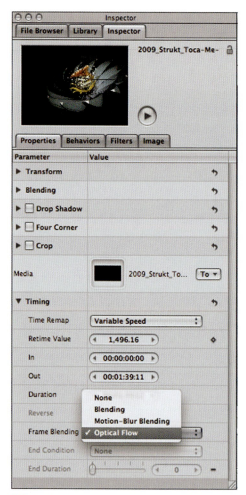

Figure 6.15 In Motion you can access the Variable Speed Time Remap feature from the **Inspector | Properties** tab, were you can also pick the powerful Frame Blending option called **Optical Flow**. Different from a motion-blur frame-blending algorithm, Motion's optical flow algorithm determines the application of the blur on the extra frames created by the slow-motion effect by analyzing the clip's directional movement of the pixels. The result is a significant increase in the image quality of the slow motion.

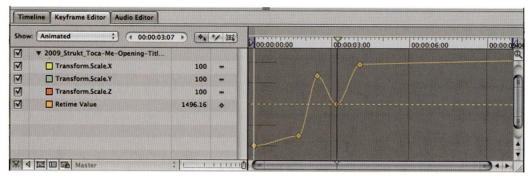

Figure 6.16 In Motion the velocity curves and keyframes can be modified in the **Keyframe Editor** tab in the timing pane.

Lenses

Whether you use a real or a computer-generated camera, one of the first decisions to make is what lens to use. By deeply understanding how to use and modify your lenses' parameters, you'll be able to master the look and feel of your final title sequence.

Camera lenses have three main features that you'll want to take close note of: **focus**, **f-stop**, and **focal length**. These three features respectively allow you to modify your image sharpness, exposure (whether it appears darker or lighter, underexposed or overexposed), and framing.

Focus

Adjusting the focus of your camera lens allows you to control whether your frame is sharp (in focus) or soft (out of focus). Both film and video camera lenses have focus rings, which allow you to focus on objects at different distances from the camera. Keep in mind that you can focus only on one distance at a time (exceptions are wide-angle lenses, where most of the frame appears in focus; see the subsection called "Focal Length" later in the "Lenses" section).

In film cameras, lenses' focus rings are often labeled in meters and/or feet. They display intervals from the closest point where the lens is able to focus to the farthest. If, for instance, the focus ring is set to 8 feet, the plane of **critical focus** will be 8 feet away; all objects 8 feet away from the camera will be in focus, and objects in front of or behind the plane of critical focus will appear out of focus. The farther something is from the plane of critical focus, the more it will be out of focus. This is referred to as *depth of field* (see the section, "Depth of Field").

Video camera lenses often have an unmarked focus ring. Focus measurements generally appear on the camera's viewfinder or LCD screen and are measured by arbitrary values (e.g., 0–99), which do not correspond to feet or meters but can be used as a point of reference to record the focus at a given time during the shot or to perform a **focus pull** during a particular shot (see the section, "Camera Movement").

After Effects and Motion cameras do not have focus rings. Instead they have a focus parameter, which you can adjust manually to achieve the look you are seeking.

In After Effects you can change the **Focus Distance** parameter, located under the camera options in your timeline; it is also accessible from the main camera settings window, which can be opened by double-clicking the camera layer in the **Timeline** panel or selecting the layer and then choosing **Layer | Camera Settings**. Similar to most of the parameters in After Effects, you can keyframe the focus distance so that within a given shot you can manipulate when and how quickly your image shifts from soft to sharp focus, or vice versa.

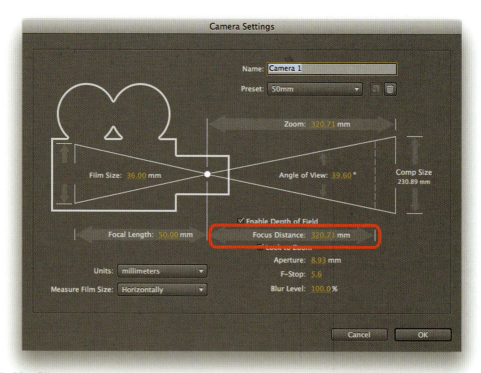

Figure 6.17 In After Effects you can change the Focus Distance parameter from the main camera settings window.

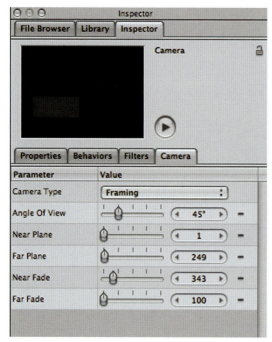

Figure 6.18 In Motion you can change your **Near Plane** and **Far Plane** parameters in the camera's Inspector tab.

Motion doesn't have a focus parameter per se. If you select your camera (either in the layers tab or in your timeline tab) and then take a look at the **Inspector | Camera** tab, the **Near Plane** and **Far Plane** parameters allow you to set the pixel limit of the layers you want to display in front of the camera (**Near Plane**) or far away from the camera (**Far Plane**). For example, increasing the Near Plane parameter to 100 pixels will avoid layers positioned 100 pixels in front of the camera to be visible. The **Near Fade** and **Far Fade** parameters will allow you to fade the object's visibility based on the **Near Plane** and **Far Plane** pixel values, resulting in a smoother transition.

Aperture and F-Stops

F-stops are numerical values used to control the amount of light that each lens allows into the camera, therefore affecting the exposure of your shot. Think of your eyes when they react to a bright environment; the pupil reduces its diameter to allow less light to reach the retina so that you are able to see a correctly exposed image. The opposite happens when you enter a darker environment; your pupil expands in diameter to allow as much light in as is necessary or possible. A camera lens is constructed in similar fashion. Located in the back of film lenses you can find the iris, a metal diaphragm that closes and opens depending on the f-stop values that you select on the f-stop ring. This aperture regulates the amount of light reaching the film plane. If the f-stop is not set properly, it will cause your shot to be overexposed (the image will be overly bright) or underexposed (the image will be overly dark).

You can find an f-stop ring on film cameras, but video cameras don't have one. Depending on the model of your video camera, you might find a wheel, commonly identified as the *iris*, which allows you to change the f-stop value of your exposure. Generally the f-stop value is indicated in the viewfinder or LCD screen of your video camera.

Depending on the film lenses and video cameras, f-stop numerical values can range from 1 (or "open" in video cameras) to 22 (or "close" in video cameras), 1 corresponding to a larger diaphragm opening (allowing more light in, as for filming in darker areas), and 22 corresponding to a smaller opening (allowing less light in, as for filming in bright sunlight). Lower f-stops allow more light in; higher f-stops allow less light in.

*f*1   *f*1.4   *f*2   *f*2.8   *f*4   *f*5.6   *f*8   *f*11   *f*16   *f*22   **Figure 6.19**

To determine the correct exposure, and therefore the f-stop, a cinematographer uses a *light meter*, an instrument that measures *incident light* (light that falls on a subject) or *reflective light* (light that is bounced off the illuminated subject). Most light meters have a parameter to set before taking a light reading: the Exposure Index (EI), also called ASA (American Standards Association) or film speed, which rates how sensitive a film stock is to light.

For video cameras you need to check the manual or online resources to find out at the ASA at which your camera has been rated and the equivalent EI if your camera uses film stock.

In After Effects you can set or change your exposure by changing the f-stop parameter in the **Camera Settings** window. Make sure that you check the **Enable Depth of Field** box so that you can access and modify the f-stop. When you modify the f-stop, the **Aperture** parameter changes to match it. As opposed to real-world cameras, After Effects' f-stop values range from 0 (changing the Aperture to 504400, creating a darker exposure of your composition) to 1,429,795 (changing the Aperture to 0, creating a brighter exposure of your composition).

Figure 6.20 In After Effects, in the **Camera Setting** window, make sure that you check the **Enable Depth of Field** box so that you can access and modify the F-Stop, Aperture, and Blur Level parameters.

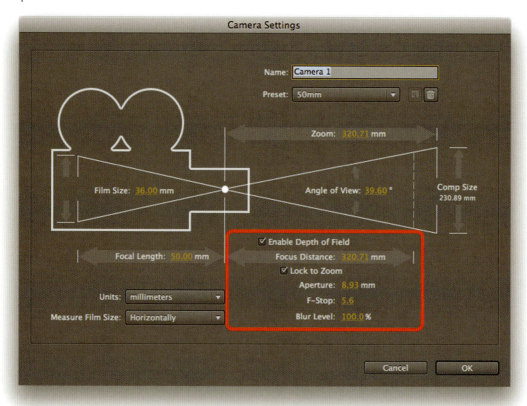

Focal Length

The *focal length* is the measurement from the center of the lens to the film plane. (In film cameras it corresponds to the point where the light entering the lens reaches and exposes the emulsion of the film.) It is usually expressed in millimeters (mm). For example, if a lens is a 25mm lens, it will be physically shorter than a 50mm lens. Visually, it translates into how wide or narrow a view the lens provides; a lower value such as 10mm provides a wider angle of view, and a higher value such as 70mm gives a narrower angle of view.

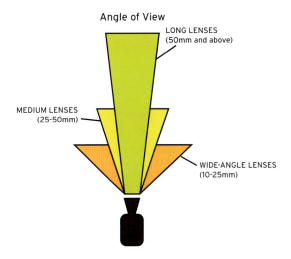

Figure 6.21

Lenses fall into two main categories: zoom and prime. *Zoom lenses*, most commonly found in video cameras, have a variable focal length and they are identified in terms of their range (for example, a zoom lens ranging from 70–300mm is referred to as a *70–300 lens*). *Prime lenses*, most commonly found in film cameras, have a fixed focal length and can be grouped into three main categories:

- **Short lenses** (or wide-angle), ranging between 10mm and 25mm
- **Normal lenses** (or medium), ranging between 25mm and 50mm
- **Long lenses** (or telephoto), ranging from 50mm and up

In After Effects you can decide which lens you want to use by selecting one of the presets from the preset pull-down in the **Camera Settings** window, or you can select your own by changing the **Focal Length** parameter on the lower left part of the window.

Figure 6.25 In After Effects click on the **Enable Motion Blur** composition switch at the top of the **Timeline** panel to enable or disable motion-blur rendering for previews. Then you can enable motion blur for each layer individually by clicking the **Motion Blur** icon on the corresponding layer.

Remember that you can modify the render settings in the **Render Queue** panel to enable or disable motion-blur rendering for your final output.

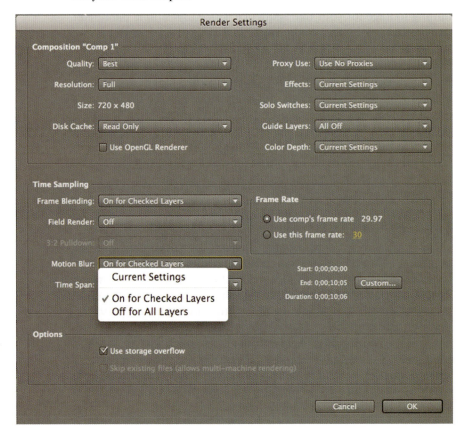

Figure 6.26 In After Effects you can enable or disable the Motion Blur from your **Render Settings** window.

In addition to the Enable Motion Blur switch, After Effects offers you the option to change the composition's shutter angle. You can affect the shutter angle by choosing **Composition | Composition Settings** (or typing the shortcut **Command+K**) and selecting the **Advanced** tab. As with film cameras, the **Shutter Angle** setting in After Effects is measured in degrees, but its values range from 0 to 720° (rather than 360°). A value of 1° creates almost no motion blur and results in a sharp image, as opposed to a value of 720°, which creates a large amount of motion blur. Explore the different settings to see how they change the look and feel of your title sequence.

Figure 6.27 In After Effects you can change the composition's shutter angle by choosing **Composition | Composition Settings** and selecting the **Advanced** tab.

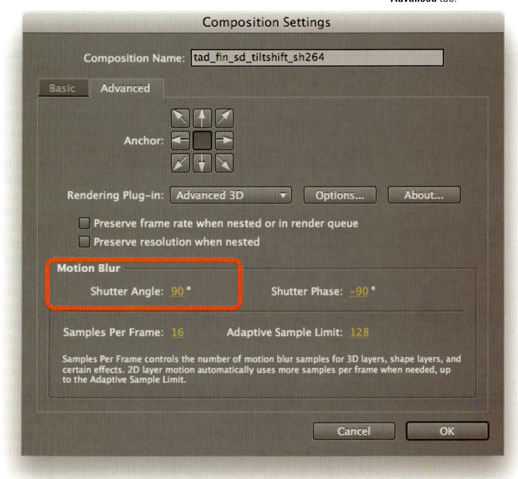

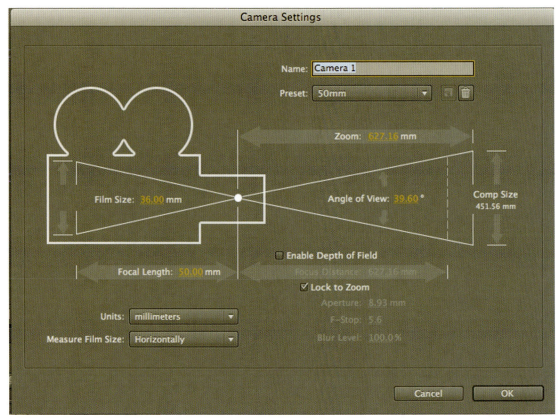

4 Next we will create our virtual camera. Create a new **camera** layer by going to **Layer | New | Camera**. Use the preset for 20mm. This will give us more options for taking advantage of the virtual camera's **Depth of Field** effects.

5 Now that we have our **camera** layer, add your first text layer. Flip on its **3D Switch**. Place it behind the first cloud in **Z** space.

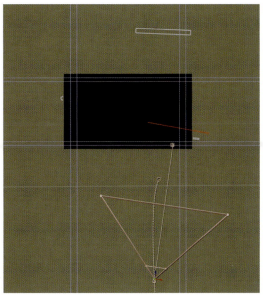

7 Animate the camera traveling through the scene, using both the **Point of Interest** and **Position** to move the camera to each cloud. Have the camera pause for **3** seconds at each cloud to allow for the animation of each title.

6 With your clouds and text layers highlighted, go to **Layer | Transform | Auto-Orient** and **Orient Towards Point of Interest**. This basically means that the clouds and text layers will turn to face the camera wherever you place or turn the camera.

8 **Done** - In that 3-second window, during the first second animate the cloud's **Opacity** from **100–0** while you animate the text's **Opacity** from **0–100**. This will give the impression that the cloud goes away to reveal the title. Hold the animation for 1 second, then have the cloud reappear by animating the **Opacity** from **0–100** (also fade out the title at this point by setting the **Opacity** to **0%**).

Pop!Tech 2008: A Case Study

Motion Graphics Studio: Trollbäck + Company
Creative Director: Jacob Trollbäck
www.trollback.com

What was the main concept and inspiration for this conference's opening titles?

We were discussing scarcity and abundance and they felt like very organic concepts to us, so we spent a lot of time looking at nature references, and that led to thoughts on different organic ways to construct the type.

Were there any challenges that came up when you were combining live action and motion graphics?

We shot all ink, powder pigment, and ferrofluid, which is a really cool oily, magnetic liquid, with the RED camera. We also created and shot some plastic letters that we poured ink into. There actually weren't any huge issues with combining the live action with the type in After Effects. We do it all the time. Don't get me wrong, it took time and was a pain. Christina Ruegg and Stina Smith, two extremely talented designers and animators, did all that hard work.

The choice of imagery that creates (Abundance) and destroys (Scarcity) the type is very effective. How were you able to balance and integrate visual imagery and typography in such a manner?

Well, the idea that the word **Scarcity** would dry out and disappear was central to the idea, and that is setting the stage for **Abundance** to come in with a bang. We discussed color a lot, and while we ended up with a mostly monochromatic piece, we really liked how the red exploded onto the scene, like a flower bursting into life.

The seamless integration of type and imagery, storytelling, and editing in this piece definitely provokes an emotional reaction in the audience. Can you elaborate on that?

In all our work, we are trying to make people feel something. All our inspiration comes from insightful moments and experiences. We try to distill all that emotional power into small injections of pure emotion. The [sound]track, once again by Michael Montes, definitely helps.

Anything else you would like to add?

Like all good communication, the piece is strictly curated and choreographed, but the goal must always be to make it look effortless.

Figure 6.43a Still frames from "Pop!Tech 2008", created by Trollbäck + Company.

Figure 6.43b

Figure 6.43c

Figure 6.43d

Figure 6.43e

Figure 6.43f

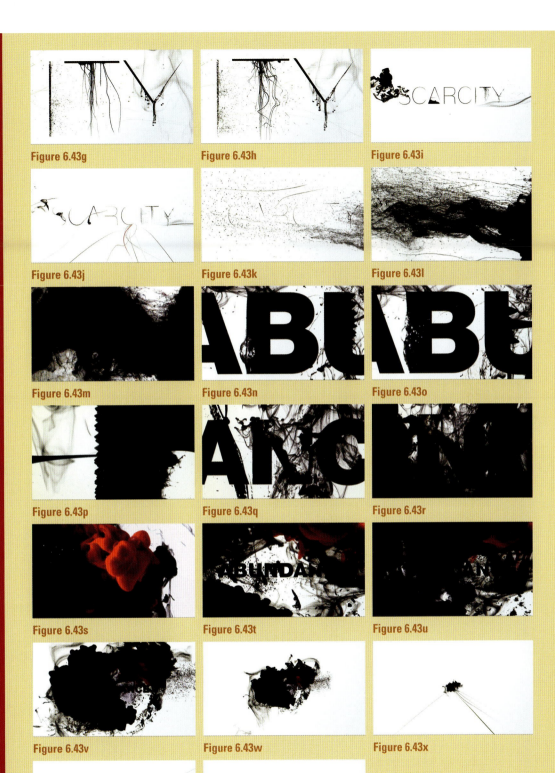

Figure 6.43g

Figure 6.43h

Figure 6.43i

Figure 6.43j

Figure 6.43k

Figure 6.43l

Figure 6.43m

Figure 6.43n

Figure 6.43o

Figure 6.43p

Figure 6.43q

Figure 6.43r

Figure 6.43s

Figure 6.43t

Figure 6.43u

Figure 6.43v

Figure 6.43w

Figure 6.43x

Figure 6.43y

Figure 6.43z

Interview: Ben Radatz on Title Design

Motion Graphics Studio: MK12
Creative Director: Ben Radatz
www.mk12.com

Figure 6.44 Ben Radatz.

Can you talk a bit about yourself and your background?

I'm a pretty easy read; work is also my hobby, so I spend an unhealthy amount of time behind my desk. I have a great wife, a couple of dogs. Solid roof. No complaints.

I moved to Kansas City in '94 to attend KCAI in the hopes of becoming a Disney animator, but it wasn't long before I'd forgotten about that and was off tinkering with early versions of Premiere and After Effects, making experimental type and collage animations. I was usually more interested in seeing how far I could push the software than I was the actual content of the work itself, but that gave me a good library of techniques and ideas that I was then able to apply to more substantial work.

As a senior I was awarded the Princess Grace Foundation's **Young Filmmaker** Award, which afforded me a full year to work on my senior thesis project—this pretentious, confusing, 20-minute-long abstract live-action/animation hybrid thing. But it went over well on the festival circuit, and that gave me the post-grad encouragement I needed to continue making my own work.

How did MK12 start out?

MK12 started out as something entirely different than what it is now. While I working part-time at my first animation job, I got a call from an investor who had been referred to me by a professor at KCAI. He'd been following the success of Napster and other media portals and wanted to build something similar, and he hired me to design it. Not knowing anything about Web design, I recruited several of my KCAI friends/fellow filmmakers-turned-Web-designers. We'd work on the site by day, and at night we'd come back in and work on short film projects, a few of which became the work we're still best known for.

A year later, the investor wasn't seeing a profit and bailed out, leaving us jobless. He was kind enough to let us keep our machines, though, and we took our small reputation, set up shop in my old apartment, and gave it a go. Our exposure in film festivals eventually lead to calls from networks and agents, and we gained momentum from there.

Commercial work has always been a means to an ends for us; we're all filmmakers and artists at heart, and the work we're paid to do affords us the ability to continue on with our own projects. Not that we're any less proud of our commercial work, though; we're fortunate to have worked on some great jobs with some very talented people. But it's usually only because of our in-house work that we're able to work on jobs we like.

How did you get to specialize in motion graphics, and in particular, film titles?

As with most things we do here, by accident. When we got started, the term *motion graphics* wasn't all that prevalent, and it hadn't occurred to us that we'd be able to make a living at it. We figured that we'd be doing the same as before, more or less, only now with clients instead of a boss. But festivals like ResFest and Conduit—along with cheap workstations and an abundance of bored ex-rave-flyer designers—gave motion graphics some momentum. Add to that an army of jobless animators and title designers displaced by the closing of the bigger title companies, and overnight, boutiques with ironic names became the new agency go-to.

Much of the early work we did got swept up in all of that, and though we'll argue when called motionographers, it's where we found our core audience.

A lot of our in-house work is type-driven and experimental in nature, and that's gotten us some attention from feature directors wanting title sequences or animated vignettes in their films, and we're often afforded a lot of trust in our interpretation and execution of the job, which usually leads to a better piece overall, leading to more calls, etc. We love creative collaborations with like-minded people, and we really feel at home working on films.

And if you look back at our work, it's not hard to spot our love for title sequences. It's an art form for which we have a tremendous amount of respect and admiration, the pioneers of which aren't credited nearly enough in the pages of pop-art history.

How do your life experience, interests, and passions influence your work?

We don't like to think that we have a "house style"; almost every piece that we make is the result of some new tangent or meme bouncing around the studio at the time. And we acknowledge that the best work often comes from personal experience and interpretation, so we try to create an environment in which everyone is welcome to pursue their own tangents and influence the creative direction of the studio.

And many of our influences are defined by our geography: The Midwest is a treasure trove of flea markets and obscure mythology. Summer months spawn road trips down unmapped service roads, uncovering lost ephemera and absorbing the nuances between county lines. And being in Kansas City itself is a source of inspiration. It's a cornerstone of American folklore, but for more obtuse reasons: cabaret, jazz, the Mob, Jesse James, Disney, Pollack, Benton, Burroughs. The list goes on. It's good energy to plug into.

What are your guidelines/preferences in regard to font size and readability for theatrical releases, broadcast, and/or smaller screens?

There really aren't set guidelines for designing on-screen type anymore; any game you play these days, for example, uses type that challenges legibility, even on the biggest HDTVs. We usually just use common sense: design it as we wish, throw it on a couple of TVs or a screen, and adjust as needed.

In film, font size is almost always dictated by lawyers and agents; every name is assigned a percentage of the main title based on his or her role in the film. So it is a bit more restrictive than television in that regard, but we just work around it.

What kind of guidelines (if any) do you receive from the studios in regard to title card order, font size, or size distinction between executives, main title, and primary and secondary talent?

The title card order is always dictated by the studio, and there's definitely a science to it that we'll probably never understand. And that's fine with us; our concerns are compositional and narrative; names are just text at that point.

What are your general guidelines to determine the duration of each title card?

Again, that's usually dictated by the studio. Most single cards run for 3–5 seconds, with gang cards up for 7 or 8 seconds.

Do you have any preferences and/or motivations in regard to transitions (dissolves, camera movements, hard cuts, etc.) from the titles to the film (or vice versa) and from one title card to another?

It all depends on the type of film we're working on. Some call for choppier, more staccato pacing, others for graceful camera moves and a softer tone. We usually go out of our way to avoid cuts, though; we just feel that there are far more interesting ways to get from A to B. But we're certainly no strangers to hard cuts—they have their purpose also.

It's usually up to us to propose a transition from the titles into the film, and we'll work back and forth with the editor until we have something that everyone's happy with.

Can you talk about the use of color and lighting in the work you do?

Most of the work that we do inhabits a hybrid live-action/graphic/2½D world, and we're always testing new recipes for getting those elements to work together. When we shoot we have a pretty good idea of how we'll be working the footage into the overall mix, and we'll usually light accordingly. But we don't have a set technique that we take from one project to another; unless we've hit oil, we'll usually shelf a technique after having done it once. It just helps keep the work fresh and us entertained.

Can you talk about the relevance of editing in the work you do?

We usually replace the word *editing* with *pacing* when we work on a project; as I mentioned, we generally prefer continuous camera moves and graphic transitions over hard cuts. I suppose the only reason behind that is to do something different and unpredictable. But as a viewer, it's also nice to feel as though you're immersed in a larger world, of which you're only seeing a fraction. More so than with edits, continuous action implies this well.

Do you generally work on your titles with the score already in place? If so, how does that affect your work?

There's no real standard here, and our jobs are pretty evenly split between having music up front and adding it on at the end. If we don't have music to work with, we'll speak with the composer (or to whomever will be licensing the music, if that's the route) to get a feel for what the mood and tempo of the score will be. We don't work with a temp track, because that has a tendency to influence the work, even when you're mindful of it. So instead we'll work on good-sized chunks and then tie them together once we're able to.

If we had it our way, we'd have the track from the start. Music (and audio in general) is such a big character in any animated piece, and it gives us an opportunity to really play up the relationship between the visuals and the track. But it seems to work equally well the other way; since we're not able to exploit the nuances of the track, we'll put our efforts elsewhere. It just comes out differently—not bad, just different.

At what point in the production/postproduction process of a film do you generally get involved?

Most of the title work we've done has been with Marc Forster (*The Kite Runner, Stranger than Fiction, Quantum of Solace*), and he likes to lock in his team as early as possible, so we usually have plenty of time to knock around ideas. In terms of actual work, though, that comes at the end of the production, not only because we often need yet-unshot footage to work with but also because it is important to us that the director feels involved in the process and pleased with our direction, which is usually impossible during production. We're the least of his/her concerns when shooting.

As a creative director, can you elaborate on the dynamics with your team of designers, 3D artists, and illustrators?

We're a fairly democratic studio in that anyone here with a good idea has the opportunity to influence the course of a project, and we've mastered the art of passing projects around the studio so that everyone can add to them. Most of us are generalists and are able to develop full shots (or in some cases full projects) on our own, so our pipeline can stay fluid, and we don't keep a set blueprint for working through a job. That spontaneity helps us approach each project from a different perspective, which almost always translates well in the final work. Narrative pieces are the exception, though, as it's important to establish a solid pipeline to ensure narrative and visual continuity.

In either case, we'll either make sure that everyone is privy to the same thoughts and information, or we'll appoint a creative lead, the responsibilities of which are to filter and interpret the collective thoughts of the studio, not necessarily dictate the aesthetics of a project singlehandedly.

Is there a typical length of time you are given (or a minimum amount of time you request) when you work on a title sequence project?

We'll usually know about a title sequence project long before we start working on it, so at least we can get some ideas going, but in terms of actual production, it's usually a two- to three-month affair.

Can you elaborate on the research you do in your projects, and how it affects your work?

Our ideal working scenario is to develop projects from the ground up, which gives us an opportunity to inject our own interests and influences without competing with an existing idea or style. In cases like these, our research is probably already done, or at least well under way. We have a cache of ideas and techniques on the back burner, waiting for the right project. And more often than not those are informed by our own personal interests and experiments.

If research is required, we do try to limit ourselves to nonvisual (or at least nondesigned) material so as not to influence our general direction. On *Stranger Than Fiction*, for example—in which Will Ferrell plays an auditor with OCD—we did a lot of research into what actually constitutes compulsive behavior and used that to inform our designs. And because he does work for the IRS, we dug up our old tax returns for further inspiration.

What are your main goals/objectives when you are working on a title sequence?

Most important is that the director is happy with our work, because at the end of the day, it's their film, and while we do make films of our own, a title sequence is not the right venue for our personal tangents, unless called for. And it matters that the sequence is an accurate reflection of the film itself; perhaps not so much in content or texture, but more in spirit. A title sequence usually sets the tone of the film, so it's important that we communicate that clearly.

We'd hope that the sequence is progressive, novel, and poignant. And then, of course, we'd hope that it's our best work to date.

What are the most challenging aspects of your work?

We try to avoid doing the same thing twice, so the biggest challenge is probably developing new techniques, especially given the turnaround of most commercial work.

What are your favorite parts or aspects of the work you do?

Meeting and working with like-minded people and learning from them. Finding the right aesthetic or technique for a project. Brainstorming good ideas.

How does technology affect your work?

We're a small studio in a midsize town; we wouldn't be here if not for affordable technology and the means to work with people on the coasts or overseas. We try not to let technology describe our work, but it certainly enables it.

Throughout your career, approximately how many titles (or type-oriented motion graphics) have you worked on?

Not counting our own films, we've produced three title sequences and contributed graphic animation to four features.

What are your favorite titles you've worked on?

Not to speak for everyone here, but I'm sure we'd agree that *Quantum of Solace* was at least the most memorable, in that it was more of an experience than a job. We shut down the studio for months, learned new software, produced some fantastic early designs, stayed out in London, talked gun safety with Daniel Craig, ran a three-day shoot on one of the most famous stages in the world, and met the Princes at the premiere. And Marc Forster is about as genuine and inspired as they come, so it's always great to work with him. We shot the sequence with Simon Chaudoir, whose work we'd been drooling over years before. In all, a very deep and immersive project, all of which really informed the outcome of the piece.

What are your favorite titles (if different from the ones you worked on)? Favorite graphic designers, type designers, or motion designers? Favorite font (either from a font foundry or custom-made)?

Not surprisingly, the Bond titles will always be favorites around here, as with all the work of Binder, Ferro, Bass. A fairly predictable list, truth be told, but is so for good reason.

David Carson designed a font called Thaitrade, which was our house font for almost seven years. It has a great presence and honesty … a very stable font. But we've now side-graded to Univers, just to switch things up.

Do you have any advice that you'd like to give to novice title designers?

Don't think of yourself as a title designer. Good title sequences really are works of art, and that should be your focus. The screen should only be the outlet, not the medium.

What are you working on now?

We're currently working on a new short film to be released sometime in the spring of 2010, and we just wrapped up a cinematic for Harmonix's next iteration of Rock Band. And we'll be doing some in-film animation on a currently top-secret feature, which will probably be in theaters early next year.

7

SOUND IN MOVIE TITLES

Characteristics of Sound

Before we get into using sound as part of title sequences, there's something to be gained from getting a little background on sound itself. Every sound possesses three main characteristics: **pitch**, **tone**, and **amplitude**. We can distinguish one sound from another based on these three characteristics.

Pitch

Pitch is dependent on **frequency**. Frequencies are basically a number of cycles and repetitions over the course of a period of time. A high frequency will have a wave that represents more repetitions in the same period of time than a lower frequency.

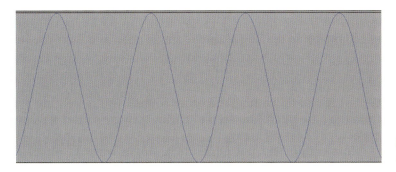

Figure 7.1 This frequency was set to 440 Hz.

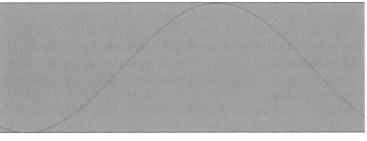

Figure 7.2 This frequency was set to 1 Hz.

doi: 10.1016/B978-0-240-81419-3.00007-6

feel some unease, as though something in the scene is not right, meaning that the suspension of disbelief may become fractured.

Famous film editor Walter Murch, author of one of the great books on filmmaking, **In the Blink of an Eye**, is also known for developing classic sound design and audio production techniques. One of his famous techniques involved creating the correct audio environment for a scene. In the 1970s Murch developed a technique whereby he would take a sound recording device and a playback device and bring them both, with the sound from a film, to a location that matched the one that the film was trying to recreate. He'd play the original sound back, allowing the space to have the effect it would have on the sound if it had been recorded originally in that environment. He'd take the two recordings and decide between how much of the effected sound should be heard in the scene and how much of the original sound should remain.

Today we have all kinds of audio plug-ins to develop the exact kind of sound we want. However, the audience must believe the sound when they hear it.

When you work on a title sequence, you are creating a reality. What does the moving type **sound** like? Are the words heavy? Do they clink or bang when they land on-screen? Because we are dealing in a very abstract realm, where large letters appear, that doesn't mean that we can ignore synesthesia. The environment we build must engage the audience and make them feel as though there is some level of reality present. If a title zips by the front of the camera, it should **whoosh**, right?

Sound in Postproduction

Postproduction is the final stage of the filmmaking process before the film is released. In this phase, the film is edited, the visual effects are generated, and the sound is finalized. There are numerous stages to finalizing the sound as part of the postproduction process.

The Sound Edit

While an editor is editing a film, he or she is also cutting, arranging, and adding various sound elements. For example, if a character's face is not actually facing the camera when she is speaking, the editor can go to a different take of the actor saying the same line or something different. Sometimes the original recordings will be flawed, and it might be necessary to perform additional dialogue recording (**ADR**). If needed, ADR is used to replaced flawed recording or performance from an actor. Also during the edit phase, sound effects are recorded. Sometimes a process known as **foley** is used, whereby an engineer will record sound effects while watching a movie, to sync the sound effects to what he sees on-screen. So, for footsteps, the engineer will wear shoes that are similar to the actors' shoes and walk across a surface that is similar to the surface that was in the shot.

The editor might also have a sound editor or sound effects editor who will supervise this part of the process so the editor can remain focused on the more major issue of editing the film.

The Score

A *score* is an original piece of music composed to work directly with what happens on-screen. A score is quite different from a *soundtrack*, which is where popular music is played during parts of the movie. The score is meant to highlight narrative moments; it is sometimes meant to sit behind what is happening and at other points drive the narrative forward.

The Mix

Film editors are usually capable mixers, but they will take the audio mix to a mix professional to finalize it. All the sounds have to be mixed together to create a completely believable audio environment. Also, the mixer is responsible for processing every element so that narration, music, dialogue, and sound effects all sit correctly together.

Audio Integration with After Effects

Though After Effects was not exactly designed as a software package for purposes of mixing and editing audio, it's still quite friendly toward a variety of audio formats. Music or sound effects can be easily imported and integrated into your timeline. After Effects supports the audio file formats listed here:

- **ASND** – Adobe Sound Document.
- **AAC/M4A** – Advanced Audio Coding.
- **AIF** – Audio Interchange File Format.
- **MP3, MPEG, MPG, MPA, MPE** – Moving Picture Experts Group formats.
- **AVI, WMA** – Windows formats.
- **WAV** – Waveform.

When you are working with an audio file, it can only be imported as **footage**. Files will keep their native duration. There are a number of places where you can activate and deactivate the audio. You will only hear the audio through your speakers during a **RAM Preview**.

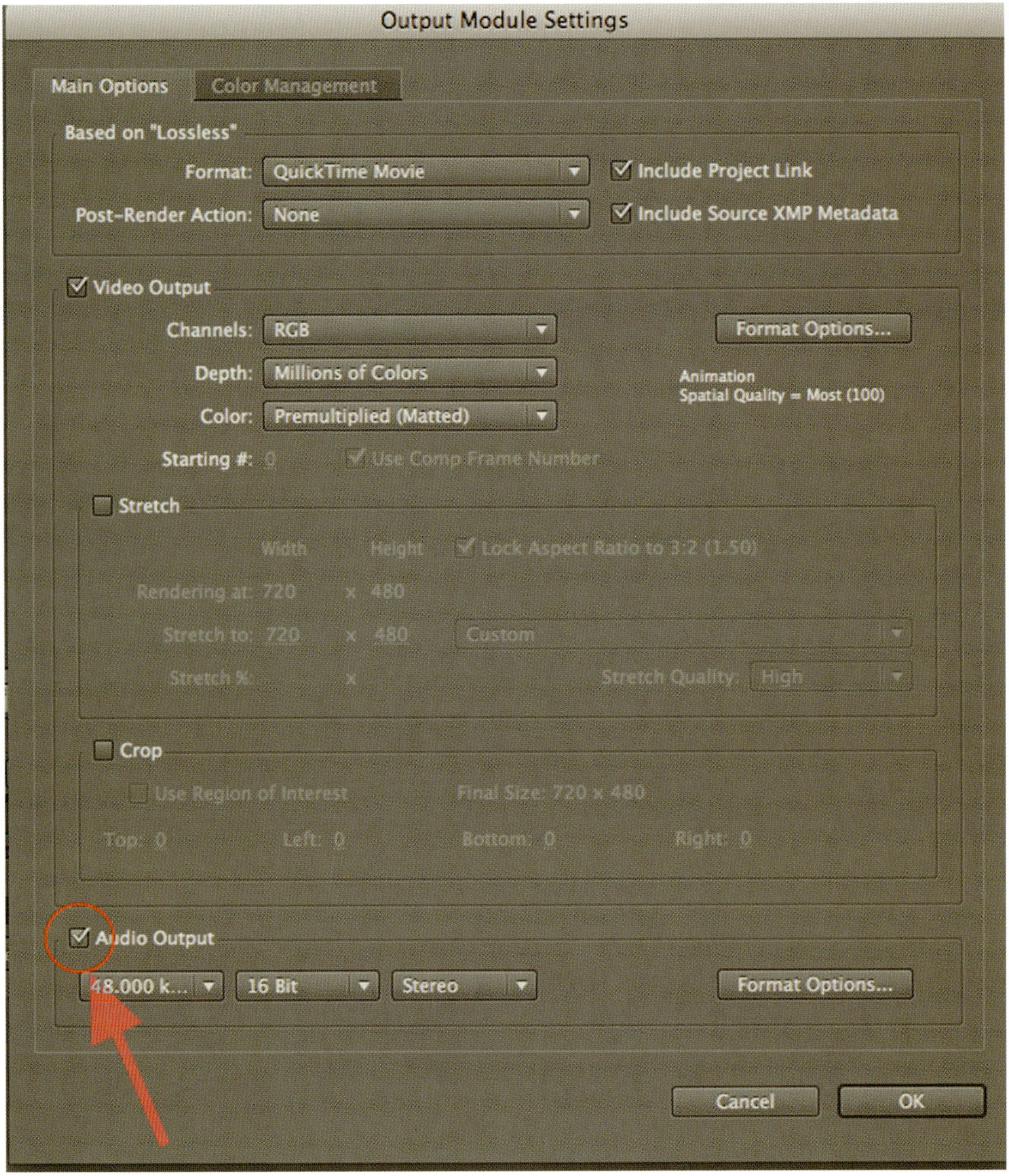

Figure 7.9

Finally, Adobe realizes that After Effects is not often used with final audio. So, by default when you render, your audio is switched **off**. If you want the audio embedded in the video file, you would have to open the **Output Module Settings** dialog and, at the bottom of the list, make sure that there's a check on **Audio Output**.

Adding Sound Effects and Music to Your Title Sequence

I'm not trying to plug my previous textbook here or anything, but it does present an opportunity to demonstrate adding music and sound effects to a title animation. For the supplemental videos for that book, I created an opener with type animation and sound design. In the following tutorial I'll take you through the full process of adding music and sound design to a type animation.

For a quick sound design lesson, let's start by downloading the free audio editing application Audacity from sourceforge .audacity.net.

Tutorial: Introduction to Sound Design: Making a "Whoosh"

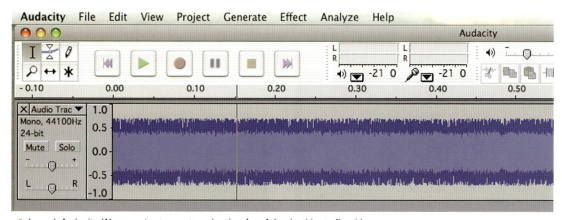

1 Launch Audacity. We are going to create a classic **whoosh** for the titles to fly with.

2 Go to **Generate | White Noise**. White Noise is basically static, a random signal. Think of it as a block of marble from which we can sculpt our sound. A window will pop up asking you to specify the length. Set it to **0.5** seconds.

5 **Done**-Lower the level of our "woosh" sound effect until it sits nicely with the music. Try adding it to the other words as they fly on screen. Adjust the **Stereo Mixer** effect accordingly, based on the direction in which the words come on screen.

Synching Sound with Type Using After Effects Expressions

Typically with After Effects, when you want to make one parameter dependent on another, you'll use *layer parenting*, but parenting has its limitations. For example, if you want to use an effect instead of Position, Scale, or Rotation, you'd have to use an *expression*.

Expressions use a code language to give you a whole lot of versatility where you give your layers special instructions or hook just about any parameter to any other parameters. Many professional After Effects designers don't take enough advantage of what an expression can do for them.

Now, to sync our audio to animation, we will first convert our waveform into keyframes and then employ an expression to get better control of them.

Tutorial: Synching Sound with Type

1 Set up your After Effects composition and set your type layer. I'm going for a 1980s style here, so I wanted a big-sounding action
movie.

2 Import your audio and place it in your timeline. Open its twirly arrow to see the **Waveform** parameter. You'll have to click the
waveform's twirly arrow to make it appear on screen.

Urbanicity: A Case Study

Motion Graphics Studio: Energi Design
Creative Director: Steve Holmes
www.clickenergi.com
© Energi Design

What was the main concept and inspiration for Urbanicity–Air?

Urbanicity is still a work in progress. It regards the pitch for a documentary on urban issues. There were a series of titles that we were going to come up with for the different stages of the show. One was on energy resources and damage to the planet, others about urban destruction, graffiti, or damage to property. Lots of different ideas. I wanted to create them with the utmost flexibility and later on add a lot more depth to them. That's really where these two titles came out because they both stand alone very, very well and display very unique techniques, especially the 3D one.

The first one is more on the nature side of things, a story telling about clean air, essentially, going from bad to good, pointing out how we can change the world as it is at the moment.

It is a transition done with interesting time remapping. It relied a lot on stock footage suitable for time remapping, which was great. The clouds moving in the background, the grass growing in the foreground, the wind turbines were all stock footage elements. In fact that dust is as well, but I didn't time-remap that.

I just wanted to build this sort of journey, from bad to good essentially, and make the color reflect that. You have this very dark and angry, almost fire-looking start to it, where the clouds are obviously just filthy. There's no good there; when you look at that and think about breathing, you want to cough.

A lot of the line art imagery actually came from a book called Neubau Welt, which is an entire library of phenomenal vector art all on one CD. It's an incredible library; I love it. This was a good starting point because it really gave us a good artwork to play with, and that's where the crane idea came from, by the way.

I thought: "What's going to stand against the background of that much dirt?" and I figured that something digging or pulling or mining would have been really cool. It got the job done quickly because the stock art was adding a certain amount of detail to it, which I think worked really well. The dust was added over the top, just to give that choking feeling to things.

And then the scene goes from mining and fossil fuels to electricity, which is a healthier form of power but has a visual impact on the countryside, with these massive towers and wires.

We wanted to take it on from there so you get to the wind-powered section, where you have turbines that pull the power in. They look a little more like trees and can be a little bit more hidden in some respects, and blend a little bit more into the environment. They stand alone without being connected to other items.

As we move from there to now, the grass is starting to grow again, the colors change, we've got water that's falling, and a general clean feeling to it. We've animated the swirls on the logo to reflect the growing of the grass. We've also duplicated the grass clip four or five times, just to add a little depth to it. There were some really nice elements that ended up working. For instance, the water that goes behind the grass in the foreground; I think it's kind of cool. I think the end result in this journey from dark to light just worked. The concept and the timing of it all didn't take too much as it was a very linear process.

Each episode is going to have its own title based on the theme of the content. So if this takes off, we would have to figure out different ways to approach those. To maintain a similar feel of vector and vectorized footage and the same thematic approach, we have to think how that might work.

Figure 7.10a Still frames from Urbanicity–Air, created by Energi Design.

Figure 7.10b

Figure 7.10c

Figure 7.10d

Figure 7.10e

Figure 7.10f

Can you talk a little bit about the use of colors?

There was a lot of color to start with, and when you got to the end point, because of these textures, you couldn't see that much difference between start and finish. So, I took a step back. I was trying to get as simple as possible and make the end look very, very clean and make the beginning look the complete opposite.

The posterization of the clouds in the background, for example, had many levels, and I added more colors in each of those, so it became harder to differentiate between the changes in the air as there were too many colors. It was a very detailed, very gradual shift. So, I took everything back a few steps and went right back to two colors, then I went up to four and I think we ended up with six, to give it a bit more impact.

There's a lot of black on the foreground, while all the graphics in the back are essentially white or very light. These are the main colors, and everything else in between had to sit quite happily in the middle, either in front of it or behind it, in terms of good versus bad.

The fact that the hillside covers the fire effect, which almost had a forest fire feel to it, as if there's burning going on there—I wanted to cover that up as we move forward in time. That's now hidden, so we get more to the blue, which is good.

Having drastically changed the now hidden color, the fire, we slightly introduced that fire color here in the turbines. But then as the 3D angle changes they slightly change as well—there's actually one gradient over the top of the whole piece here—and because of the way the camera moves, certain elements appear in one color and as they move they become the other color. I think that was the kind of feeling we wanted to achieve here. We thought much on how to give a different impression from when you first see the object to when you last see it. That is a lot healthier, if you like, because it has changed its own color space.

In the end it's all very simple, really: It is mostly blue and there's just a little bit of detail in the grass; everything else is very clean. It was quite a simple process, all about marking the difference between start and finish, when you can really see clean versus not, and everything is in the same color space.

Would you agree with the statement that basically you're a storyteller?

I think this word defines a lot of our work. I don't know if that's something we tend to do a lot or we get a lot, but it's mostly a process of beginning, middle, and end, and what's the story in between. I guess most commercial pieces are like that. I enjoy taking my art for that journey, if you like, and figuring out the best way to approach a story. I think sometimes it is best to present something with a story.

This piece is only 15 seconds long, but you get that sense of history and evolution, people caring about the environment, and visually, at the end you might want to say: "I want to live there." It's all very beautiful there, it's green and lush, while in the beginning you realize how the different things work.

Even in such a short space of time, if you could tell a good story or figure out the best way to represent that change, it massively helps the piece to get done. You end up with a good resolve rather than focusing on one element and saying: "Here's the title, here's a few turbines, here's some clouds, how do we make that last 15 seconds?" which is what we see a lot of people do. Too many artists try to take a series of elements and make them last as long as possible.

If you try to go a little bit deeper and add some narratives, I believe it helps hugely, and I would say a lot of our projects are based around that idea. I think it's good to start and finish with a transition.

Can you talk about the other Urbanicity titles—Derelict?

This one's a little bit more surreal. It was as much a technical challenge as anything. I was trying a technique that finally worked very well, and while this is great, I spent much time seeing how far things could be pushed and tested. I think with part of this project the technology was driving the concept. I knew what I wanted to see and I wondered if I could get there.

Figure 7.11a Still frames from Urbanicity–Derelict, created by Energi Design. **Figure 7.11b** **Figure 7.11c**

Figure 7.11d **Figure 7.11e** **Figure 7.11f**

Figure 7.11g **Figure 7.11h** **Figure 7.11i**

Figure 7.11j **Figure 7.11k** **Figure 7.11l**

I started by adding the glowing swirls onto the floor and they blended in so nicely. The end was more about freedom and imprisonment and the feeling of it. Hence, the dove and the shadows.

The thing I really liked about this is the original shot that just had a small beam of light in the corner. When I added the glow effect to it, the look was then very golden. I wanted to take the whole room and move it into the same color space but also take all the elements and just blend them completely in, so that they would look like they're shiny and they're gold, as if there is some value in them. Not material value, but more the feeling of success, like there's light at the end of the tunnel. There's a golden highlight to this dark feeling, there [are] things [that are] bright and shiny.

There's a positive feeling to the elements that are being animated here. The swirls could have been black and grungy, and so everything else. Just by introducing this light, which almost illuminates the room, I think we just really added a very nice element to it; it made it stand out.

The fireflies at the end of the room are actually just periods: that's animated type. They're not particles or anything else, they're just text. And that was again a technical challenge. Looking in hindsight now I could have used a particle emitter to add more of them and give them some blur, but initially it was just: "Let's figure out an easy way to do this." By having them glow, and given the text animation properties of After Effects, the blurs could be keyframed very quickly and apply random opacity levels, so they do tend to flicker. You can catch them occasionally; they fade in and out just as real fireflies would. This was a nice effect, it's almost like they're adding the color to the end of the room. It's not just them trying to blend in, it's almost like they are actually lighting the space. Without those the project needed something, it needed something like dust, so they might be fireflies, they might be just dust particles if we'd have added more. Things that slowly move in the 3D space, just to add some depth to it. It was more of a technical concept challenge as well as a graphical playground, if you like.

If I'd have gone back and revisited this piece, I probably would have made it a bit darker on the start, leading into the light as it progressed, like the end of the tunnel, where the light is. The shadows from the window at the end of the room would also be darker, and the logo would stand out a little bit more.

In this piece the camera movement is simulating a person exploring the space, with sort of handheld moves. How does that fit in your piece? And about the use of depth of field, as it is a little more evident in this piece, why have you decided to maximize its use here?

On the previous piece the depth of field was consistent and mathematically coherent. That piece was created so that the camera moves and its focal point were exactly positioned. The camera moves were sort of fast, and then they would slow down, and then fast and then slow; during those slow periods of about 200 pixels the point of focus was pretty much dead in the middle, so that the item that was coming into focus was always in focus during the slow move, and then the zoom would go to the next object, which would come into focus just at the right time. Everything was laid out to the pixel. The camera just moved backward and everything worked.

This project, like you say, was very human, and that was what I wanted. It was almost like someone was picking himself up off the floor. It's the first time they stood up for a while, and they lean to one side, and then they come across it to the other side, then turn and realize there's hope here. Something is growing and it's bright, there's life and it's almost like walking out the door, knowing that around the corner things are going to be better.

This is always something I like doing—not just thinking in terms of slow movements, or handheld feel to it - this was even actually adding a person into the mix, which I thought was kind of cool, and having him start low down.

All this was just done with a series of keyframes for both the position and the focal point of the camera, which do shift independently of each other. I might have used the [After Effects] null. I'm not sure, but I believe they were just keyframed independently. I then applied random values to both of those parameters in order to get this sort of swaying effect, where they appear to be independent from each other.

The result is that the front might be doing the same movement, but the position would change accordingly, so there's a wonderful realization that a camera is always mostly fixed pointing in a certain place, whereas with the human head, you always have so many angles of choice; plus you've got the eyes, added to that which is another 180 degrees in each direction.

There's so many points of rotation there that sometimes handheld camera moves in the computer can't really achieve that feeling. It's harder to make that work and be believable than maybe moving it as you're seeing through someone's eyes, as in this case. And that's why here and there there's an occasional shift, because it's not just the head moving but maybe a flick of the eye. This was cool, actually—a very good challenge.

I like the moves at the end, but again, just going back to it, once the positions were done, I would measure the distance from the camera to the logo and then adjust the depth of field when it comes into it, and make sure that everything else moved accordingly.

I did want that feeling of realization that someone's holding onto this door and reads the sign; it worked nicely.

I'd love to develop this one a little longer and try to have the person move in and go through that door. And as they do, the brightness would have marked the transition to the intro of the documentary.

When you are working on a variety of projects like these, how do you keep your creative juices flowing?

Well, obviously going out on the bike and clearing my head up in the mountains is great. It helps. Sometimes it feels like your creative pipeline has a block, and it is building up. You know it's there, so sometimes you just need to blow that pipeline out, and I think a good bike ride and some sunshine is always a big help for me.

I like to go and see a film; I'll just take an afternoon off, drive into the city, which in itself is kind of different, because you are taken from the environment of a studio, with a small number of people, and a small town feel kind of thing, and then you get into the city. All of a sudden you are surrounded by a lot more visual information, and that in itself gives me a lot of ideas. I see the way colors are in storefronts, or what people are wearing, or what kind of bag someone bought from a store and how that is colored, or something like that.

I sometimes get the most inspiration from bizarre things, so I'll go and sit somewhere and have coffee and watch people as they walk by, and see color or shape or something that catches my eye. I would then sketch that or take a note. It's quite bizarre sometimes, people and their color: their clothing color, their fashion choices, what they're holding, what they're riding or walking, or what shoes they're wearing, stuff like that can sometimes just tweak the senses enough for you to say, "Oh, that's interesting."

On the other side of things, going to movies and watching titles. The color and framing, the camera and the angles that they used. Occasionally I'll see a single shot and say, "That's just the angle I was thinking of, or the way that that color shows up at that angle," or something like that. And then you have the titles and they always give you some sort of inspiration. It's not that I go to the movies to get that inspiration, but it's more that I find some inspiration in most movies.

When I'm abroad, I will bring back from every trip probably four or five design books, every single time I go away. And sometimes the books are so big and heavy I have them shipped over, because they're too expensive to put in the suitcase. There are a few stores off the back of Covent Garden in London where I could spend all day. They tweak the senses very, very well. The color of them, the book covers themselves, the subject matter; I get a lot of joy from that. I like those stores because books are all around you and there's books seven or eight shelves up that you have no hope of even getting to, and you look at them and go, "I want that one!" It's beautiful; I love it. Some of my favorite books I got them from there.

How does the inspiration that you get from outside influence your work?

I think it gives me the ability to look at the project from a different angle. I sometimes find myself as if I'm in a one-way street and the project is blocking the way. I then realize I'm only going at it from one side.

Sometimes if you step away from it and come back later with some sort of inspiration, which changes your thinking or your approach, you find yourself in the same place, but it's like with floating. You are able to move around and look at the same thing from a slightly different angle: from the other side, or climb up a ladder and look at it from here. And that's how it actually feels when I come back to a project; I've got that new sense of how to look at it. And that is really cool. It doesn't happen a lot, but sometimes you reach the same block so many times that you need that.

I really enjoy projects when you end up taking a different step, and thinking, "I never thought of that before." All of a sudden it clicks, and that's how a lot of projects have done well, by the way.

Like with the absinthe one; I was in France and got a chance to see some of the history of this particular product, and some of the artists associated with it, and to go into the area where it was consumed back in that time. To get a geographical feel for it helped much as well. To just come back and say, "Okay, we have a texture, we have a logo, we have a bottle" —that is so easy to do.

How does research affect your work?

I think a lot of problem solving goes through agencies these days. A lot of the work that we get is quite specific in terms of the project and has a more direct vision. The product is already established or there's a general feeling for what it is going to look like.

It's very rare that I have to do massive amounts of research, and absinthe again is a classic one. The research was enjoyable mainly because it was a subject matter in which I was interested and was geographically somewhere I was interested in. It drew me into a desire to actually research it myself and to look at what I could add to the project in doing so.

But a lot of projects that we get are more straightforward in that respect. I don't want to disrespect anybody in any way by saying that, but a lot of them are predefined. I would like to have projects that do require more research so I could learn more about them and offer more to the project. But the budgets are never there for that kind of work. And that's why that sort of stuff tends to go through an agency, because they will set aside $10,000 or $15,000 just for research and then do the work. And only after that they will come to someone like me and say, "Hey, can you do the work? We've done the research."

Occasionally, research-wise, I will look into how things had been done previously. I maybe ask myself how a design was done—in case I'm doing a redesign, for example—or how it looked in the past, why it looked that way in the past, if it feels dated, what do I need to change, what is the sort of feel of typography that would go with that particular design, is that an historical choice as opposed to a personal choice. These are all possible questions I might ask.

8

ESSENTIAL TECHNIQUES

Timing

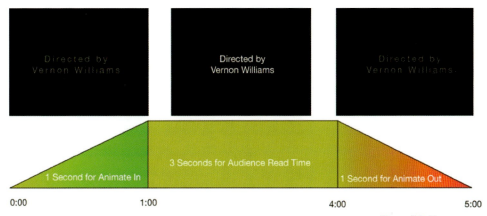

Figure 8.1 How can we set up an average speed title with enough time for animating in and out and audience read time?

It's crucial that we allow for the right amount of time for each title. I have a formula that I apply to every title sequence I do. First, for an audience member to have enough time read one title (that's average in length), they will need roughly 3 seconds. However, that's only the time it requires to be legible to the audience. Looking at Figure 8.1, in order to time it so that we have enough time to do an animated arrival and departure from the screen, we need to add 1 second at the beginning and at the end to allow for this, which puts us at 5 seconds.

Now, this is true only, of course, if the title is not legible during the animate in and out. If it is, then as long as the audience has 3 seconds or close to 3 seconds to read the title, you are safe.

Now, with these considerations in mind, we can begin.

doi: 10.1016/B978-0-240-81419-3.00008-8

Fade Up and Fade Down

The single most common title sequence animation is the classic **fade up and fade down**. After Effects (in addition to most editing packages) gives you several ways to do this simple move. We'll go through a couple variations.

Tutorial: The Basic Move

1 Even your most complex type animations will usually integrate this move as part of their effect, so this is more of a building block technique. With text layers in After Effects we can achieve our effect with either the standard **Transform | Opacity** or **Text | Animate | Opacity**. Remember that the **Text | Animate** versions of the **Transform** effects go by character, not the entire word. But with **Opacity** it will look the same.

2 Place the playhead at the point where you'd like your type to fade up. Start the stopwatch for **Opacity** and set it to **0%**.

3 Go to the **1** second mark. Set the **Opacity** to **100%**.

4 With keyframe animation software, the computer is calculating all the frames between keyframes for you, but when you want the value of something to remain the same, you need a keyframe that repeats the previous value so that the software knows how long to keep the value the same. So, for our **Opacity**, from 1 second to 4 seconds we need to keep it at **100%**. So, at the 4 second mark, click the **Add or Remove Keyframe** button in the far left column.

5 **Done**-To complete our animation of **Opacity**, at the **5** second mark, return the percentage to **0**.

Fade Up and Down by Character

Whenever you use a text animation effect that needs to address a single character at a time, the most efficient way to approach that is via the **Text | Animate** menu. Every one of these effects creates an **animator.** The animator will contain the added effect as well as **range selectors**. Range selectors are brackets that allow you to animate which letter or letters has an effect applied to it at one time.

Figure 8.2 In this example, you can see that the *O* has a lower opacity effect. It is surrounded by the two range selector brackets to isolate the effect to the single letter.

Figure 8.3

If you open **Range Selector 1** for the **Opacity** animator, you will see you can keyframe the percentage for **Start** and **End**. In addition, you can use **Offset**, which will take the difference between **Start** and **End** and move it through the word. If you want to have it reveal one letter at a time, you will have to use the **Text | Animate** effect. Here's how you can do that.

Tutorial: Fading Up and Down by Character

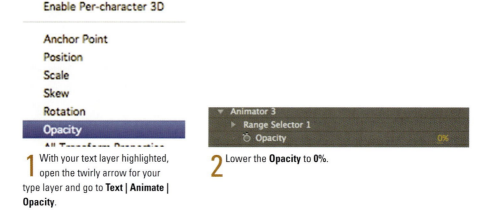

1 With your text layer highlighted, open the twirly arrow for your type layer and go to **Text | Animate | Opacity**.

2 Lower the **Opacity** to **0%**.

3 **Opacity** can be a little confusing here. Start the stopwatch for **Start**. Set it to **0%**. Why are we doing it this way? Well, to reveal the letters one at a time from left to right, we must gradually hide the effect of the 0% **Opacity**. So, as the **Start** bracket passes a letter, it reveals it.

4 At the **1** second mark set **Start** to **100%**. The word will be completely revealed. Notice that the two brackets are both at the end of the word, basically making the **Opacity** effect completely hidden.

5 At the **4** second mark, click the **Add or Remove Keyframe** button for **Start**. This will keep the **Start** range selector at 100% for that time period.

6 **Done**-Return the percent for **Start** to **0%** at the **5** second mark. It will now go back through the word and remove it from the screen.

Tutorial: Shaped Fade Up and Fade Down

In this next tutorial we'll approach this task again, this time doing a reveal that shows how the fade up and fade down move from the middle of the word in and out, in a radial shape.

1 From the **Mask Shape** tool, choose **Ellipse Tool**.

2 Make a tiny elliptical mask between the two words. On other titles, choose the space that is closest to the center without being over a letter.

3 Press **MM** on your keyboard. At the **0** mark, start the stopwatch for **Mask Expansion**.

4 As we did in the previous two tutorials on this topic, we'll keyframe to reveal the title from 0–1 seconds, hold from 1–4, and fade out from 4–5 seconds. At the **1** second mark, increase the value of **Mask Expansion** to reveal the whole title. Click **Add or Remove Keyframe 4** seconds to hold the value, and at **5** drop it to **0**.

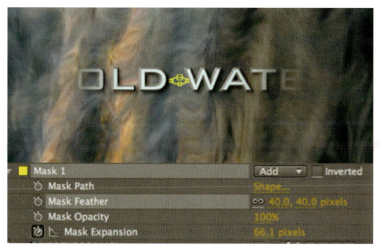

Note: When we added the **Mask Feather** value, we did not start stopwatches. In After Effects only start a stopwatch if you plan to **animate** the value. If you don't just apply the effect and give it a number, you will see it, but it won't move on you.

5 **Done**-To really finish off this effect in a handsome way, we should soften the edge of our revealing shape. On **Mask Feather,** increase the value to **40** pixels. That will nicely soften the edge.

Tracking

Perhaps second in popularity to a **fade up and fade down**, animation of **tracking** is very common. A **tracking** animation involves adjusting the spaces between letters. Here's how to do it.

Tutorial: Tracks

1 Alright, I know this example is a pun, but aren't textbooks supposed to have lame puns? Anyway, highlight the type layer and open its twirly arrow.

2 Put both layers into **3D Mode**.

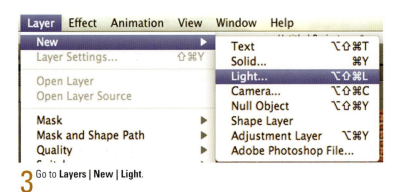

3 Go to **Layers | New | Light**.

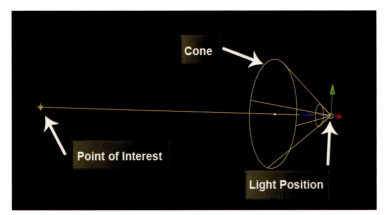

4 The light's interface is similar to that of a camera layer. It is controlled by the devices above. The **Point of Interest** controls the direction the light faces. The **Cone** controls how far out the light will spread. The anchor point controls the position of the actual light. For right now adjust the **Point of Interest** setting to turn the light away from the title.

5 Open the twirly arrow for the **Light** layer. Under **Transform**, start the **stopwatch** for **Point of Interest**. Also, under **Light Options** start the stopwatch for **Intensity**. Lower the **Intensity** to **0%**.

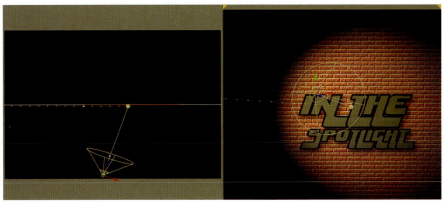

6 **Done**-Go to the **1** second mark. Move the **Point of Interest** to face the title. Also increase the **Intensity** to **100%**. Now you'll see the title revealed.

Text Bounce

This next tutorial is based on one of the very first techniques I learned for text animation. Although it is nothing mind-blowing anymore, I think that it helps new users think "outside the box" when it comes to what you can do with type. No fancy text menu stuff here; rather, just scale and opacity.

Tutorial: Make Your Text Bounce

1 Highlight the **type** layer and make sure that the center of the layer is the center of the word; the quickest way to do that on a type layer is to **center-justify** it with the **Paragraph** panel.

Tutorial: Wiping Your Title

1 First a basic mask wipe. Highlight the **Rectangle tool** and put a mask over the text layer.

2 Adjust the mask so that the right side has an angle. You can use the **Selection tool** to move points. At the **1** second mark, start a **stopwatch** for **Mask Shape**. Set **Mask Feather** to **20** pixels, and start the **stopwatch** for this parameter as well.

3 Using the **Selection tool**, highlight the two points on the right side. Go to the **0** mark in the timeline.

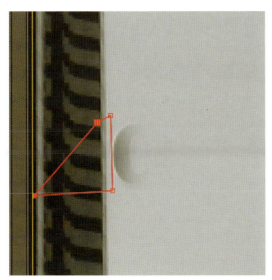

4 Drag the two points to the left, and pass the points that are already there. Also, you'll see that there's some of the *C* left over. To remove it, drop **Mask Feather** to **0**.

5 **Done**-There you have it, a simple wiping effect. Adjust the size of your mask if you need to.

In-Scene Wipes

I've seen this effect quite often lately, where objects within the scene are used as part of a wipe, so here's a basic version of that effect.

Tutorial: Creating In-Scene Wipes

1 Let's begin by pressing **Ctrl-D** (or **Command-D**) to duplicate the footage layer.

2 Create a **mask** over the building on the top footage layer. It can be a **garbage matte**; the only thing we need to be careful of is the right side of the building.

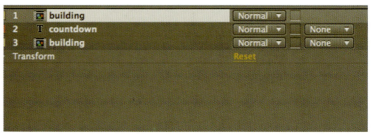

3 Move the **building** layer with the cutout above the title.

4 Move the **title** over to the left side. It will end up behind the building.

5 Now set keyframes for **Position** on our two building footage layers at the **1** second mark.

6 **Done**-Now, at the **1:10** mark, move both layers to the left and it will reveal the title. We'll discuss a number of techniques in this book in regard to integrating type into scene elements.

Extreme Zoom-In Effect

Type layers being vector can be a real advantage. In this tutorial we'll do a huge zoom-in effect.

Tutorial: Creating a Zoom-In Effect

1 Start a stopwatch for **Scale** at **100%** at the **0** mark. Set another to keep it at **100%** until the **2** second mark. Also at the **2** second mark, start a **stopwatch** for **Position**.

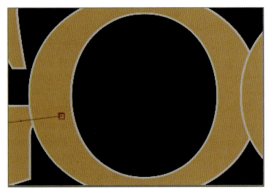

2 At the **4** second mark, increase the **Scale** to **3000%**. Adjust **Position** so it appears that the *O* is coming toward the camera.

3 We can use this as a transition to a scene. Create an elliptical **mask** over the footage layer inside the *O*.

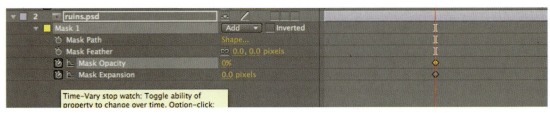

4 Start the **stopwatch** in the **Mask** tools for **Mask Expansion** at the **2** second mark. Start the **stopwatch** for **Mask Opacity** and set it to **0%**.

5 Go to the **3** second mark, make **Mask Opacity 100%**, and make **Mask Expansion 500** pixels.

6 **Done**-You might want to add a **Mask Feather** to soften the edge of the mask. This versatile effect is very useful for thrillers and adventure-themed movies.

Falling into Place

Effects where type falls into place are fairly easy to achieve. We begin with our fade-up and fade-down technique.

Tutorial: Falling into Place

1 For this effect I am starting from an existing animation that we did for the tutorial previously in this chapter, "**Fade Up and Fade Down by Character**." That lesson focused on using a **range selector** with **Opacity**. We animated the **Start** bracket to reveal our letters.

2 Whenever you have already animated one parameter with a range selector, we can easily add in another parameter using the same range selectors. Start by going to **Add | Property** and choose **Position**.

3 Now with **Position** still highlighted, drag upward any letter that is within the brackets. Here I decided on the *A*, but it doesn't matter which letter you choose as long as you do it to a letter that is on the inside of the **range selector** brackets.

4 **Done**-Add on **Motion Blur** to give the effect some high-end veneer.

Exploding Type

Sooner or later everyone will need to blow up some type. Here's one method for approaching this task.

Tutorial: Exploding Type

1 One secret to animating anything that explodes is to start from the ending. In a moment you will see why. In this timeline the video in the background has an explosion that we are synching to, so we will need to keep that in mind.

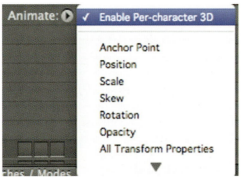

2 On your timeline, leave the playhead at the mark where the explosion in the background has finished (about the **5** second mark). Open the **type** layer, and click the option for **Enable Per-character 3D**. This gives us the 2.5D options for the characters in our type layers.

3 From the **Animate** menu, choose **Position**.

◷ Position	38.0, 0.0, −668.0

4 When you are using the **Per-character 3D**, you have three number values for **Position** instead of two. The third number value here is **Z Position**. Adjust this number until it is so high that the type comes toward the camera and then passes it.

5 Start the **stopwatch** for **End** in the **range selector** for **Position**. Make it **100%** at the **6** second mark, and at the **4** second mark reduce it to **0%**.

6 Go to **Add | Property | Rotation.** Give it three revolutions on each axis. Now this will work from our existing keyframes for **End** in the **range selector** for **Position**.

7 **Done**-Now, for one last touch, go to **Add | Property | Blur** and set it to about **3**, and it'll add a nice blurring effect as the letters come toward the camera. Feel free to experiment with adding other effects to augment this exploding type effect. As you might have predicted, give it a shot with **Motion Blur.** All you have to lose is more time spent rendering.

Stop-Motion Titles

With the success and recognition of **The Fantastic Mr. Fox**, there's been more interest than ever in stop-motion animation. *Stop motion* is the effect of taking still images of the same subject, shot one frame at a time, with subtle movements of the object occurring between shots. When these shots are played back as video, the object appears to move on its own. In this tutorial I'll go through a couple of techniques that use stop motion and stop-motion-related techniques.

Tutorial: Classic Stop Motion with Modern Equipment

1 You'll need a digital camera and a tripod or table pod to do a stop-motion technique like this. For this title, I wanted to create the effect that the letters were dispersed and then come together. For that technique, I arranged the letters for the last frame of the title assembled first and then worked backward.

2 So, using a standard digital still camera, I shot frames at three per setup at first, to create slower movement, and then toward the end I switched to one per setup, to speed it up.

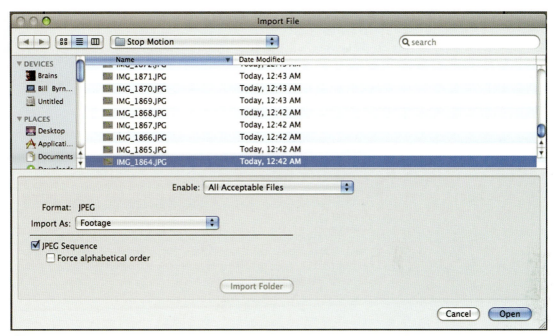

3 Use your favorite means of importing photos into your computer, and put them in an accessible folder. Import the first image of the sequence into After Effects (as **Footage**) and check **JPEG Sequence**. This is the beauty of this effect: digital cameras number the images, and AE can read a sequence of numbered images as footage.

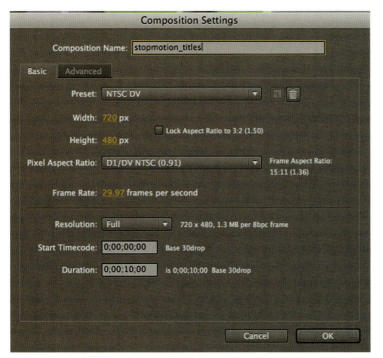

4 Create a new composition using the **NTSC DV** preset. Put the image sequence in this new timeline. You'll have to **Scale** it down to about **22%**.

5 Now, we have to reverse our footage so that it moves in the intended direction. **right-click** or **Ctrl-click** the layer and choose **Time | Time Reverse Layer**.

6 Our image sequence is about 1 second and 22 frames long, so we'll have to manipulate its time setting by enabling **Time Remap**. **right-click** or **Ctrl-click** the layer, and go to **Time | Enable Time Remapping**.

7 The **Time Remap** effect allows you to set keyframes for the frame that is showing at a specific point in the timeline, and between keyframes it will adjust the speed accordingly—faster or slower to match the instruction of your keyframe. Have a keyframe set to **1:21** at the beginning of the timeline. Set a second keyframe to **0:00** at the **3** second mark.

8 **Done**-To finish the effect, I've set another keyframe at **4** to keep the title up for a second, and then a final keyframe set at **1:22** at the **5** second mark.

Fine-Art Techniques

Rather than stick to the most obvious techniques, a little inventiveness goes a long way. In this section I'll demonstrate a few ways in which fine-arts techniques such as sketching and painting can be used in a title sequence.

Tutorial: Painting or Writing Text on Screen

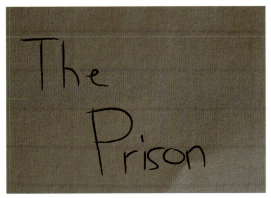

1 To create this horror-film-style handwritten or scrawled effect, I started with a pencil texture brush in Illustrator, and I put every brush stroke on its own layer. Note that this is one of **many** ways to get a write-on effect; we will address several in this book.

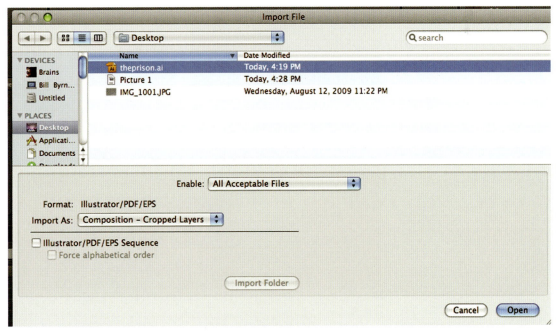

2 Import the file into After Effects as a **Composition Cropped Layers**.

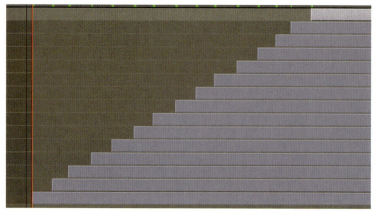

3 Arrange the document so that every 10 frames another brush stroke comes up.

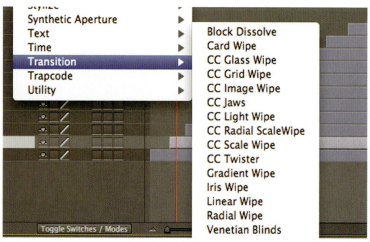

4 Though few, there are some gems in the **Effects | Transition** menu. Apply **CC Radial Scale Wipe** to your strokes.

5 This next step will be somewhat time consuming but worthwhile in the end. Turn on **Reverse Transition**. Place the **Center** point where you'd like the stroke to begin. Set the **Completion** percentage to **100%**. Go to where the next brush stroke begins and decrease to **0%**. Now it'll look like your letter's stroke is being drawn on.

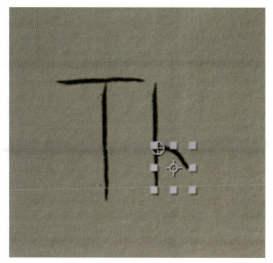

6 **Done**-Though the last few steps were tedious, it's looking great. In the end it will have a totally authentic feel. Skip the *O* and the bulb part of the *P*, which won't look great with the **CC Radial Scale Wipe** transition effect on it, so it'll work just fine popping on.

Tutorial: Write-On Effect with a Font

If you prefer not to draw your letters but still want a handwritten effect, you can still use After Effect's **Eraser** to do the job.

1 Start by using a font that looks somewhat handwritten, to keep the effect believable.

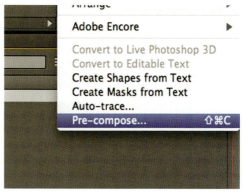

2 You can't apply the **Eraser** to the text layer right away, so we'll need to **pre-compose** the layer. Go to **Layer | Pre-compose**, with the text layer highlighted.

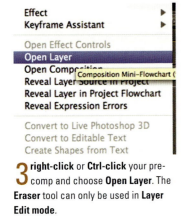

4 Now you can apply the **Eraser** tool.

3 right-click or **Ctrl-click** your pre-comp and choose **Open Layer**. The **Eraser** tool can only be used in **Layer Edit mode**.

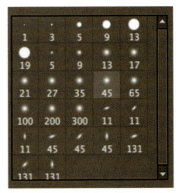

5 Choose a brush that will be thick enough to erase the entire stroke of the letter in simple motion. Every case will be different, but for this one I am using a 45 pixel soft-edged brush. Switch over to the **Paint** panel, and choose **Write on** under **Duration**.

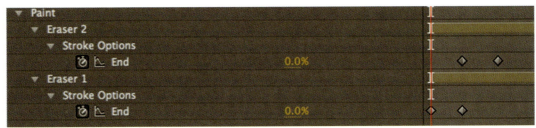

6 Use two **Eraser** strokes to erase the *T*.

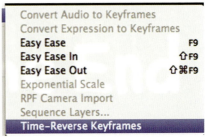

7 The **Eraser** tool defaults to making your strokes simultaneous, but you can press the **U** key to reveal the keyframes. Next, arrange the keyframes so that they come in the order you want.

8 Highlight keyframes for the **Eraser Stroke Options** and go to **Animation | Keyframe Assistant | Time-Reverse Keyframes**. Repeat this process throughout the whole title.

9 **Done**-So, though complicated, there are numerous approaches for a write-on effect.

Tutorial: Painterly Effects

Similar to the rather lovely titles that visual artist Jeremy Blake created for the film **Punch Drunk Love**, I wanted to demonstrate how effective simple color use can be. This lesson shows how we can use paint splatters to reveal something that is hidden by negative space.

1 In Illustrator I have created a document in which large watercolor brush strokes are separated onto different layers.

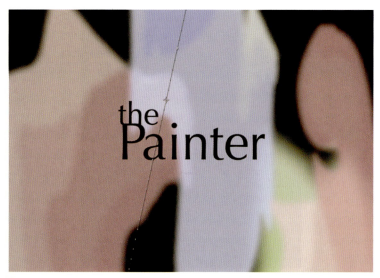

6 **Done**-The truly exciting part of this effect is how revealing the negative space creates the letter forms. Experiment with different amounts of blurs and glow effects to get the most out of this effect.

End Scroll

End scrolls with huge lists of names slowly scrolling might seem like an easy proposition in After Effects, but it can be surprisingly difficult, especially when you're dealing with video. Here's a tutorial with some basic tips up front.

Why Are End Scrolls Harder with Video?

The main reason end scrolls are more difficult with video has to do with separate field rendering. Every still image on video shows a half image, which is designed to smooth out the motion. However, with text scrolls this can lead to an incredibly ugly and somewhat disagreeable strobing effect. Editing software such as Final Cut Pro and Adobe Premiere have text tools in place to compensate for this issue.

Typefaces

Thin-stroked, serif typefaces will not work well for end scrolls. Keep it simple with a bold, sans serif typeface to get a nice clean result.

Effects

Motion Blur and **Continuous Rasterize** can either help or hinder. Experiment with these and see what has the best effect.

Processing and Setting

Title designers who end up typing the credits should charge more per hour. Most situations should have the producer or assistant producer sending you a Word file with the titles in it. Normally I don't recommend that title designers be pushy, but in this case, insist that the end credits get sent to you after they have been checked and double-checked for spelling and to make sure every name is included. It is much easier to fix mistakes before you start than after.

Then I recommend moving the titles over to Illustrator. When you're done, import that document into After Effects.

Tutorial: Animating an End Scroll

CAST

Kevin   Vernon C. Williams
James   Stephen Cooper
John   Michael East Brandis
Thomas   Ken Caldwell
Francis   Jack S. Chango
Arthur   Dennis Paul Van Der Wilson
Michael   Nathan Wind

CREW

PRODUCER   J.P. Mint
DIRECTOR   Bob Aloo
WRITER   Mare Joman
COSTUME DESIGNER   Rebecca Florida
CINEMATOGRAPHER   Elinor Marie Byrne
COMPOSER   Dave Kwon
PRODUCTION DESIGNER/
ART DIRECTOR   Christian Samplon
1ST ASSISTANT CAMERAPERSON   Wip Kinger
2ND ASSISTANT CAMERAPERSON   Suzanne Byrne
2ND ASSISTANT CAMERAPERSON   Fritz Hausmangler
STILL PHOTOGRAPHERS   Antone Roblemo
PRODUCTION COORDINATOR   King Lazer Hands
AST. PROD. COORDINATORS   Melu Kist

1 Do your typesetting in Adobe Illustrator; it's much easier to manage than trying to do it in After Effects. Open the sample document **endscroll.ai** to check it out.

2 Import our sample document as a **Composition Cropped Layers**. Change the **Composition Settings** so that it's a **20** second timeline.

3 Animate the **Y Position** to scroll the type. I've set my keyframes at **0** and **19:22**. Tweak the keyframes back and forth a little; this will have an impact on how much flicker is visible.

4 Only use this step when you are dealing with video. It's unnecessary otherwise. Option-click the **Position** stopwatch and enter this expression: **[Math. round(position[0]),Math.round(position[1])]**. This expression tells the **Position** tool to only move the title in full pixel increments.

▶	Bilateral Blur
▶	Box Blur
▶	CC Radial Blur
▶	CC Radial Fast Blur
▶	CC Vector Blur
▶	Channel Blur
▶	Compound Blur
▶	Directional Blur
▶	Fast Blur
▶	Gaussian Blur
▶	Lens Blur
▶	Radial Blur
▶	**Reduce Interlace Flicker**
▶	Sharpen
▶	Smart Blur
▶	Unsharp Mask

5 This one is another step that is only for video. Add **Effects | Blur and Sharpen | Reduce Interlace Flicker**. I set the softness on mine to **0.6**. Keep it very low.

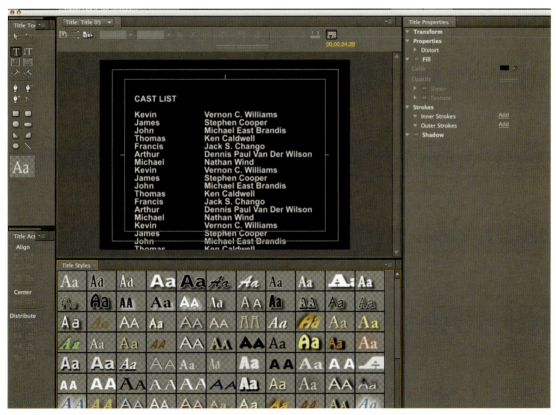

6 **Done**-If tweaking these keyframes leads to you pulling out your hair (you wouldn't be the first), there's a great Title Designer tool in Premiere Pro that blends MS Word-style word processing with automated tools to make this process much easier.

FAMOUS MOVIE TITLE TECHNIQUES

The *Sopranos*-Style Wipe

The memorable title sequence for **The Sopranos** features a very subtle but effective type animation. In this tutorial we will recreate that motion.

Tutorial: Creating the *Sopranos*-Style Wipe

1 To match the look and feel of the *Sopranos* intro, I am using treated footage from the New York/New Jersey area, and the title of this project is displayed in Franklin Gothic Bold. Move *The Narrows* off-screen to the left side.

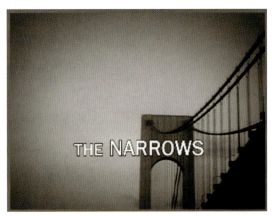

3 **Fifteen** frames later, move it to the center of the screen. Preview it. It doesn't look like much yet. At **4:15**, add another **Position** keyframe to hold it in its place, and then at **5:15** move it off-screen to the right.

2 With the type layer still highlighted, go to **Text | Animate | Property | Position**. Start a **stopwatch** for **Position** where you'd like it to begin. I started mine at **3:00**.

4 Enable **Motion Blur** in the timeline and on our type layer.

5 Now you will start seeing this effect look closer to the *Sopranos* titles. Now, the *Sopranos* title sequence also has a little skewing to it, so go to **Animate | Add | Property | Skew**. Start the **stopwatch** for **Skew** at the same place as **Position**. Set the amount of **Skew** to **–10**. **Fifteen** frames later, once again lining up with the **Position** keyframe, set the **Skew** to **0**.

6 **Done**-To continue lining up the **Skew** effect with the **Position** move, set a keyframe at **4:15** that keeps the **Skew** at **0** and at **5:15** return it to **–10**.

The Suspense-Style Glowing Back Light

This look has appeared in countless suspense films. It's an easy, attractive effect. Here's how to create this very popular look.

Tutorial: Creating the Suspense-Style Glowing Back Light

1 We'll begin this effect by duplicating the text layer.

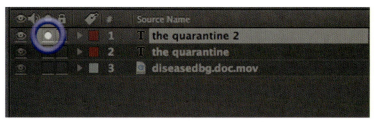

2 Turn on the duplicate layer's solo switch. This makes it so that we only see the copied layer; the rest are hidden.

3 Change the color to a bright green. Turn off the **Solo** switch.

4 Apply **Effects | Blur and Sharpen | Directional Blur** to the duplicate type layer. Move the duplicate to the layer below the original. Start the **stopwatch** for **Blur Length**.

5 **Done**-At the **1** second mark, increase **Blur Length** to **70**. Now a streaked glow will grow behind the type in the same shape as the original layer.

The *Star Wars* Backward Crawl

This lesson will demonstrate how to recreate the famous *Star Wars*-style backward crawl. As geeky as this might sound, this infamous effect is quite admirable for its economical value. It's a very simple but signature effect, and it's rather edifying to recreate it, or so I hope.

Tutorial: Creating the *Star Wars* Backward Crawl

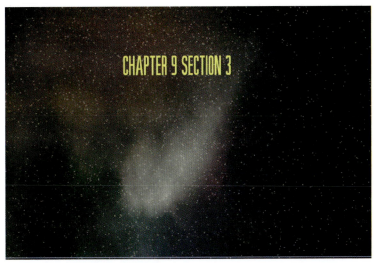

1 First we will have to do some arranging to get our type correctly formatted. The typeface for this effect in the original movie consisted of variations on Franklin Gothic. To create your body type, since this is a large body of text, arrange your type in a word processing software package and copy it.

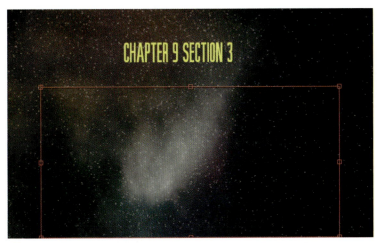

2 With the **Text** tool selected, click and drag to make a text box layer.

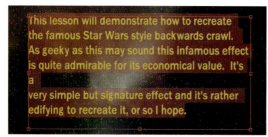

3 Paste your text within the text box. It's not correctly formatted yet, but we are getting there.

4 Open the **Paragraph panel**. With your type highlighted, switch to **Justify All**. Now it will much more closely resemble the *Star Wars* back-crawl.

5 Highlight your type layers and put them into **3D mode**. Create a new **Null Object** layer and put that into **3D mode**. Parent the type layers to the **Null Object**.

6 Adjust the **Orientation** on the X axis until it matches the tilt of the original. I found that around **300** degrees is where it matched up correctly.

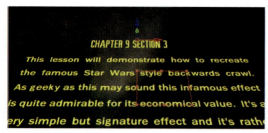

7 **Done**-Now it is time to move the crawl. The best way to move it is to control its center by animating our Null layer's **Anchor Point**. Test it out a few times to adjust the speed; set keyframes to take it off the screen at the bottom and over the course of time have it rise the top of the frame.

The Horror-Jittery Type in the Style of *Se7en* and *Saw*

Since 1995's **Se7en**, title sequences have received much more notice. The title sequence from **Se7en** also set the standard for what people want to see in a horror film's design package. The dark imagery, matched with skittering flashes of dirty, grimy images, have been a hallmark of the horror genre, and in this lesson I'll demonstrate how you can achieve that look.

Tutorial: Creating the Horror-Jittery Type in the Style of *Se7en* and *Saw*

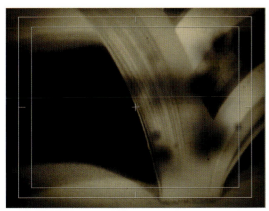

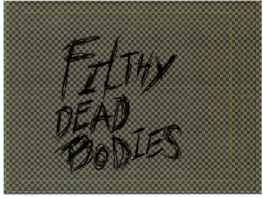

1 To match the look and feel of the background footage, you will need to process it pretty heavily. I used a close-up shot of the pages turning in a book and duplicated it with the **Multiply** blend mode. I also gave it some burned film effects with **CC Burn**. Finally, I added a color treatment to get that sepia look.

2 In Adobe Illustrator use a Wacom tablet to draw the letter forms. Since we want a hand-scrawled, rough look, use a thin, rough pencil brush and draw the lines over each other until you build up a texture that works. Make a second copy of the letters in white. Save your Illustrator file.

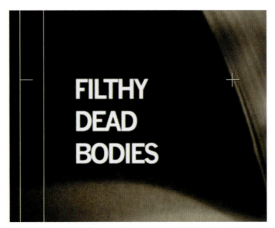

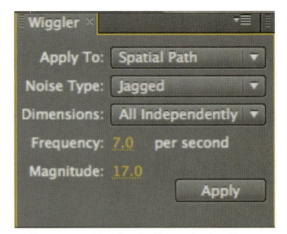

3 One issue that frequently comes up with dealing with a rough, hand-scrawled effect like this is that it becomes difficult to read, and it is very important that the type look cool **and** be legible. Make a new type layer and, using a tough, bold font, write the name of the movie.

4 Now we can add our jumping/jittery animation. After Effects has the **Wiggler** panel, which helps us deal with randomized effects. On the type layer, set two keyframes for **Position**. Make a small move with your title; we really just need two keyframes for the Wiggler to create random keyframes between them. Highlight the two keyframes. In the **Wiggler**, set it to apply to **Spatial Path** so that the random values affect the actual position of the layer. The **Noise Type** should be set to **Jagged** so it is nice and rough. Under **Dimensions**, set it to **All Independently**, so that the random values appear on both the X and Y axes. Adjust the **Frequency** (how often a random value is created) and **Magnitude** (how large the randomization of the range will be) according to what makes the type appropriately jumpy without making it too difficult to read. Click **Apply**. Try it a few times before you settle on something.

5 Put the white version of our scrawled type from Illustrator in the document above the typeface layer. Set its blend mode to **Difference** and lower its **Opacity** to **20%** . Now **parent** the white scrawled layer to the type, and it will follow the **Position** animation. Start the **stopwatch** for **Scale**. Set two keyframes in sync with the first and last keyframes for **Position** on the type layer.

6 Highlight the two keyframes for **Scale**, and use the settings above on the **Scale**. This will give it a great jump effect that complements the original type nicely.

7 **Done**-Bring in the black version of the scrawled type. Set its **blend mode** to **Opacity**. Then add **Scale** and **Opacity** and, just as we did previously, use the **Wiggler** on them.

The *Superman*-Style Explosive Type

This memorable effect can lead to numerous uses in a modern context. Here's how to do a digital recreation of the **Superman** title sequence.

Tutorial: Creating the *Superman*-Style Explosive Type

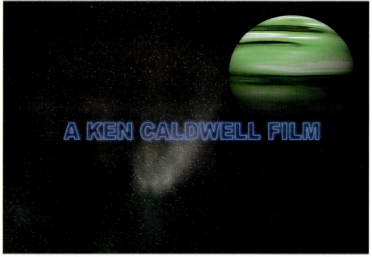

1 Create a new type layer with a blue stroke and no fill. Use a large bold font, such as Ariel Black. Duplicate it, and **parent** the duplicate to the original. Highlight both layers and put them into **3D mode**.

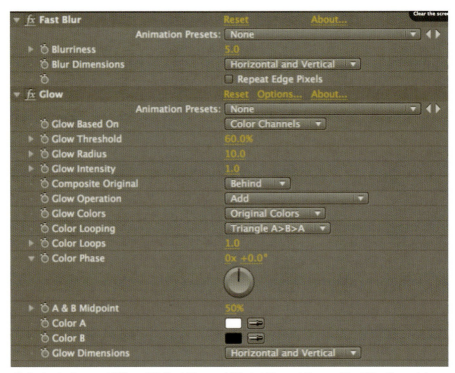

2 On the duplicate, add **Effects | Stylize | Glow** and **Effects | Blur and Sharpen | Fast Blur**. Try applying the settings shown above.

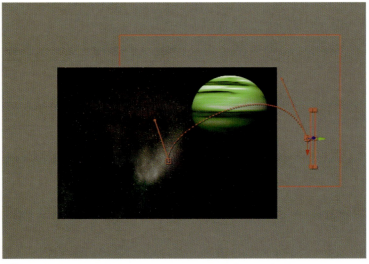

3 Using the **Position** and **Rotation** tools, animate the title flying in. Set the **Z Rotation** to start at **90** degrees, and **2** seconds later return it to **0**. Set **Position** keyframes for **Y** to have it come in from off the screen and **Z** to send it further back in space.

4 Duplicate the text layer again, removing the **Position** and **Rotation** animations. At the **2** second mark, add keyframes to **Scale** it from **100%** to **200%** at the **4** second mark, and reduce the **Opacity** from **100%** to **0%**. Apply Motion Blur.

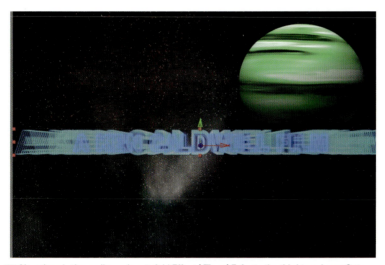

5 Now, here's the really cool part: Add **Effect | Time | Echo** to the third type layer. Set a keyframe for **Number of Echoes** to go from **0** to **45** starting at the **2** second mark and ending at the **4** second mark.

6 **Done**-Now, to complete the effect, in the original **Superman** title sequence the base text flies forward and fades off. So, add keyframes for **Position** on our first type layer starting at the **3** second mark, and bring the type toward the camera. Use **Opacity** to fade off the type. Do the same thing for our second copy of the text, since **Opacity** is not affected by **parenting** settings.

The *Matrix* Raining Characters

By now *The Matrix* (1999) number rain has been everywhere, but I think knowing how this effect is achieved is a handy skill to have in your repertoire. Here's one version of it that is pretty simple and effective.

Tutorial: The *Matrix* Raining Characters

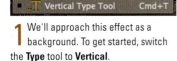

1 We'll approach this effect as a background. To get started, switch the **Type** tool to **Vertical**.

2 Use a green, futuristic font, and type out whatever text you'd like to use. Don't worry too much about what it actually says, since we will be changing it a lot.

3 Open the **Effects and Presets** panel. Go to **Animation Presets | Text | Animate In | Raining Characters In**.

4 Next, let's add an expression to loop the characters raining in. **Option-click** the **Offset stopwatch**, and add **loopOutDuration(type = "cycle", duration = 0)**. This will loop the animation.

5 Duplicate the type layer about eight times, distribute the copies across the screen, and change the type for each one. Also, move the keyframes for **Offset** around so that the loops won't sync up.

6 **Done**-To complete this effect, let's duplicate all the type layers and switch them into **3D mode**. Move them back in **Z Position**. Add **Effects | Blur and Sharpen | Directional Blur**. Turn up the **Blur Amount** to **17**. Finally, add **Motion Blur**, and there you have a *Matrix*-style raining character background.

The *Dawn of the Dead* Blood-Splatter Type

Some of the best recent visual effects come from a combination of old school techniques aided by digital manipulation. One of my favorite recent title sequences is **Dawn of the Dead** (2004), which uses a very cool mix of old and new.

Tutorial: Creating the *Dawn of the Dead* Blood-Splatter Type

1 Begin by setting the type in After Effects and go to **Save Frame As | Photoshop Layers**. Call it **dead1. psd**. Open the exported file in Photoshop.

2 Use the **Smudge** tool in **Finger Painting** mode, and drag the red out in a smearing motion. After you've done that a little, save the file as **dead2.psd**.

3 Repeat this process a number of times. As you spread the red out, turn off **Finger Painting** so that you stop adding red to the screen. Every time you've made a few changes hit Save As, and give each file a name that is one numerical value higher as in dead3.psd, dead4.psd. dead5.psd. As many as you feel are necessary.

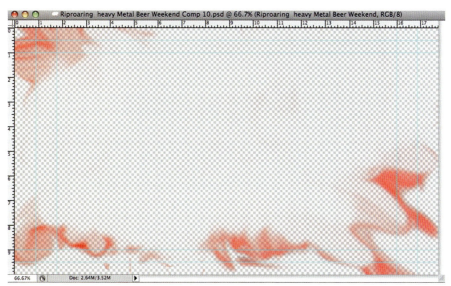

4 As you get it spread out to the outer edges, switch to the **Eraser** tool and start removing the middle.

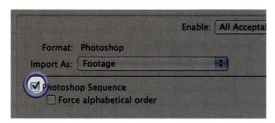

5 After you have done about 15 or 20 frames, you'll have as many as you'll need, so go back to After Effects. Import the **dead1.psd** file as **Footage** and turn on **Photoshop Sequence**.

6 Set the text layer to be **4** seconds long, and add the frame movie at the end of the text layer. **Right/Control-click** the frame movie and choose **Time | Enable Time Remapping**. Make the frame movie **1** second long.

7 **Done**-On the frame movie layer, add **Effects | Blur and Sharpen | CC Vector Blur**, and set keyframes for the **Amount** to go from **0–350** in the course of that last second. And there you have it—smearing blood type.

The *Lost*-Style Basic 3D Title

The opening to the TV series **Lost** has a famous animation that includes a very basic 3D effect. In this lesson we will recreate that look using a famous After Effects work-around. One of the things that After Effects desperately needs is the ability to extrude text into volumetric 3D. Until that becomes available, we can use this technique.

Tutorial: Creating the *Lost*-Style Basic 3D Title

FOUND

1 I've written this out in the famously out-of-the-box **Lost** typeface Century Gothic. Now flip on the **3D** switch.

1	T	Found 10
2	T	Found 9
3	T	Found 8
4	T	Found 7
5	T	Found 6
6	T	Found 5
7	T	Found 4
8	T	Found 3
9	T	Found 2
10	T	Found

2 Duplicate the type layer **10** times. Make sure all duplicates are in **3D** mode.

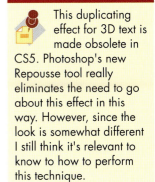

This duplicating effect for 3D text is made obsolete in CS5. Photoshop's new Repousse tool really eliminates the need to go about this effect in this way. However, since the look is somewhat different I still think it's relevant to know to how to perform this technique.

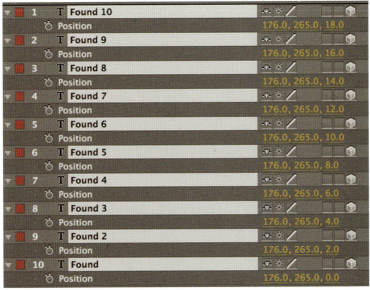

3 Open **Position** for all the text layers. The third number value is the **Z Position**. Increase the number values there in increments of **2**. This is going to create two pixel gaps in Z space between each copy of the layer.

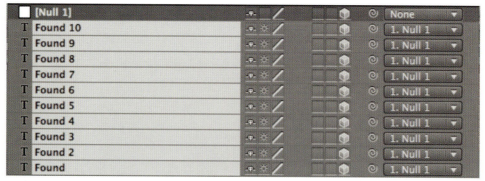

4 Go to **Layer | New | Null Object**. Put the new **Null** layer into **3D** mode. **Parent** all the type layers to the **Null** layer.

5 **Done**-Now we can use all the typical 3D effects and transformations, controlling it from the **Null** object layer, in what closely resembles true volumetric 3D.

The *Spider-Man*-Style Full-3D Text Animation

In this lesson we will utilize Cinema 4D and create full-3D animated text along the lines of big superhero movies like **Spider-Man** (2002). We will also look at the easy workflow between Cinema 4D and After Effects.

Tutorial: Creating the *Spider-Man*-Style Full-3D Text Animation

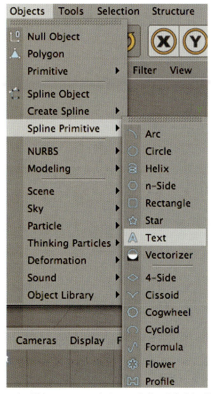

1 In Cinema 4D, go to the **Object** menu and choose **Spline Primitive | Text** to create our type object.

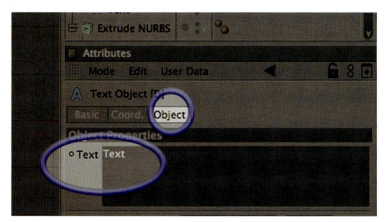

2 In the **Attributes** window, select **Object**, and then you'll see a **Text** heading. Right next to it you can type your title. For our superhero movie we will create an effect in which each letter flies out on its own, so I'm creating a separate object for each letter: *C, A, P, T, .,* *W, I, N,* and *D*.

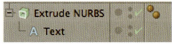

3 From the **Add HyperNURBS** tool, select **Extrude NURBS**, and make an **Extrude** for each letter.

4 Drag the text objects into the **Extrude NURBS** to make the letters 3D. Once again, do this for each letter.

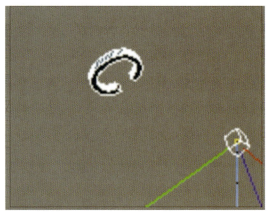

5 In the timeline, place the playhead at the **20** frame mark. Push the **Record Position** button (key icon) to make your first keyframe.

6 At the **30** frame mark, highlight the **Extrude NURBS** for the letter *C*, drag it up high above the rest of the text (with the **Move tool**), and spin it a few times (with the **Rotate tool**). Set another **keyframe**.

7 Repeat this process for each letter.

8 Now we will set this up to go over to After Effects. Go to the **Render Settings** tool. The **Render Settings** dialog will open. Under **General**, change the **Filter** to **PAL/NTSC**.

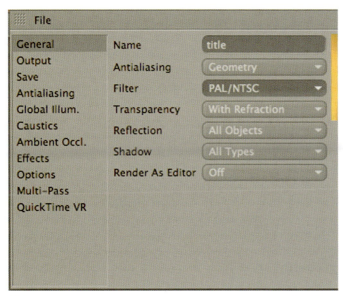

9 Under **Output**, match it to the settings you plan to use for your After Effects project. Select the appropriate size and format from **Resolution**. In this example I am using **720 × 480 D1 NTSC**.

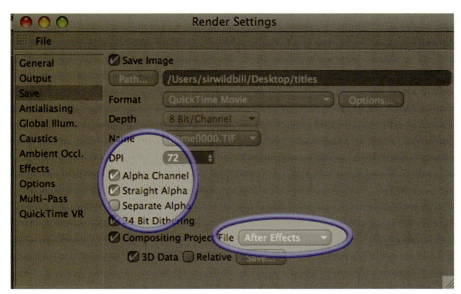

10 So we can use After Effects to animate our background, turn on **Alpha Channel** and **Straight Alpha**. Since AE and C4D are very friendly (seriously, C4D can almost be considered an honorary member of the Adobe Creative Suite; wouldn't that be the best), we can take our C4D project right into an AE comp by turning on **Compositing Project File** and choosing **After Effects** from the menu.

It's important that you install the Cinema 4D plug-in for After Effects. In the Maxon folder you'll find an **Exchange Plugins** folder. You might need to get the most recent version of the plug-in from Maxon's site; it should match the version of After Effects you are running, Figure 9.1.

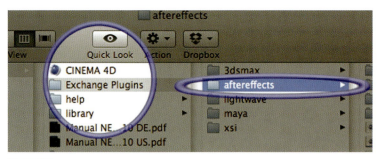

Figure 9.1

11 Now we can go ahead and render.

12 You will now have an .aec file that will open in After Effects, like a project file. However, make sure you have the After Effects plug-in installed or it will give you an error message.

13 **Done**-In After Effects I added some animated shape layers in 3D mode, to give it that superhero title sequence background feel. C4D and AE are a powerful combination, as demonstrated here.

10

COMPLETING THE CREATIVE PROCESS

Studios/Designers Clients: How Does It All Work?

Movie titles began strictly as a necessity, a means of displaying important information about a movie. However, in today's age, the title sequence is in many ways a method for setting the mood and tone of a film. The title sequence can transport the audience into the world of the film by taking the visuals associated with the film and using music and design to introduce the audience to this new place that they will occupy for about 90 minutes.

But how does a producer or director determine who should design the titles for a film? There are, of course, numerous factors. First, there is what the director wants creatively. Does the director want something that can be achieved within the existing production team, or will she need to reach out and find someone or an entire team? Next, there is the budget; directors can't always get what they want. Sure, that depends on the director and budget, but every film is highly dependent on the budget and the needs for the title sequence and what kind of reality can be expected.

So, again depending on the budget and the needs of the title sequence, the designer may be an individual or a full design team. For something large and expansive, a team will be needed to make the production deadline. Companies such as Imaginary Forces, A52, and many others focus on motion graphics work such as film titles.

In 2005 I created the opening titles for the film **Red Doors**, which was an independent film. I, not being a design team, worked directly with the producer, director, and editor. Typically, title sequences are done during postproduction, but that can be quite varied based on what is needed for the film.

In a recent interview on artofthetitle.com, designer Gareth Smith of Shadowplay Studio said that when he was working on the title sequence for the film **Up in the Air**, director Jason Reitman brought him in on the process quite early. Smith was sent screenplays before the film was shot, to give him

doi: 10.1016/B978-0-240-81419-3.00010-6

and his team time to develop concepts. Not only that, what if Smith noticed in the script an opportunity to request that the production team get a specific shot? Advanced planning like this might not be the norm, but it can create amazing opportunities for the title designer.

Title designers are often chosen based on some established relationship with the creative side of the film. The great Saul Bass started his career as a graphic designer, making film posters in Hollywood, when he had the opportunity to work with Otto Preminger on a poster for the film **Carmen Jones** (1954). Preminger was so impressed with the Brooklyn College graduate that he contacted Bass to create opening titles for **The Man With the Golden Arm**. Bass was able to convince Preminger to allow him to create this extremely famous sequence, and the rest is history.

Given the way the title sequence greets the audience and transports them into the world of the film, directors usually pick a title designer that they have some kind of relationship with. You never get another chance to make a first impression on an audience, so title designers are relied on to make it count.

Depending upon the designer's relationship to the production, budgetary concerns, and numerous other factors, the amount of time the designer spends working directly with the creative team will vary. Some directors will sit and supervise much of the creation of the title sequence. Sometimes the director is otherwise occupied, and the producer will be the point of contact for the designer. In my experience the relationship between the title designer and the editor is also important, and we will address that further a little later.

Planning a Movie Title Sequence

Everything in a movie is dependent on planning. Planning is absolutely essential to keep a movie on schedule and for the production to get the most out of the budget. Title sequences are often approached as an entire film or short film on their own. In the planning stage of the production, the concept of the title sequence should be decided. What will this title sequence do? What story should it tell?

Sometimes, as in the case of 2008's **The Incredible Hulk**, the title sequence tells the film's backstory, setting up narrative elements to clarify things that happen later in the film. It's a very good idea to create storyboards for the title sequence. Since it reduces the amount of production time, directors and producers don't want title designers searching for ideas when they are supposed to be making something, so a clear decision on what the title sequence is there for is crucial.

Sometimes, as in the case of big names such as Kyle Cooper, the lead designer on a title sequence is acting as a director of the short film that the title sequence will end up being. In the end, the film's director will be making all the final creative decisions, but exactly how much influence the title designer has is completely based on the designer's relationship with the director. In the case of Cooper, many directors refuse to work with him because his title sequences are often better than the film itself. Although that's nice, no one really wants to be shown up by the opening act.

Title sequences, in an ideal world, are subject to the same amount of preproduction and planning as the rest of the film. The sooner a designer is involved and making decisions, the better to get the ideal title sequence. As designer Gareth Smith stated, being involved early in the process helps immensely, and he was able to request shots from the production team. However, requests from the title designer are not always possible for the production team to accommodate due to budgetary concerns. Sometimes designers will be limited to working with the elements provided by the production. In other cases, designers need to assemble their own shoots, or order stock footage, or integrate computer-generated elements into the footage or in place of footage.

Project Element Preparation

When it comes time to prepare elements for a title sequence, it can be a messy situation. Title designers often deal with the design team from the graphic design department as well as elements from the production itself and elements that they generate on their own. Bringing it all together can be quite challenging but also rewarding.

When the clients give you the credit list, request that it be as close to the final list as possible. In designing titles and end crawls, something that can easily be fixed in a word processing software package will set you back a while fixing it with design software such as After Effects and the Adobe Suite. Clients might not immediately understand this, so do your best to explain it, but they are going to send you fixes and adjustments to the credit list anyway, so try to avoid setting things up in a way that causes you problems if it needs to be fixed later.

One thing that must decided early is what the title designer will be responsible for delivering. How long should it be? What format will match what the editor's working on, and what format will the production need for the final presentation? Going back to the very beginning of this book, remember that if for some reason it is unavoidable that you have to use raster-based type, having to resize later will be a true chore. So, one recommendation is that if you are working with raster-based type, you should set up the original resolution to match the final output size or higher. If the type can remain vector in format, this is less of a concern since the size can be changed later without losing image quality.

In the early stages of production, the title designer should meet with and urge the director, producer, and editor to make a decision as to what the final output is going to be. Now, if that is determined to be a 2K or higher film format, the title designer might be best off working at a lower resolution until the final title sequence is approved and then generate the higher resolution version.

Typical Order of Credits in an Opening Title Sequence

Here is the typical credit order in an opening title sequence:
1. Name of the studio that is distributing the film.
2. Name of the production company responsible for making the film. If an investor financed a substantial portion of the movie, they will usually be credited alongside the production company with "In Association with."
3. A (Producer's Name) Production.
4. A Film by (Director's Name).
5. Starring (this is optional or can be paired with the first cast member's name), followed by the names of all principal actors.
6. Film title.
7. Featured cast members. A card that states "Featuring" used to be fairly commonplace but now appears to be falling out of fashion; in some cases, to speed up a title sequence, featured players are held off for the end crawl.
8. Casting by.
9. Music, composer, or original score.
10. Production designer.
11. At this point it can vary; you might see makeup, costume, or visual effects credits here or skip to the next few credits. At this point it should vary based on what is most important to the movie. If the movie's a high budget sci-fi bonanza, it's appropriate to credit the VFX team or supervising visual effects artist here; if it's an historical epic, costume and makeup should probably get some notice here.
12. Edited by (the editor is the first of the people whose "thumbprint" is on the movie creatively; the other two are the writer and director).
13. Director of photography.

14. Producer, produced by, and executive producers. This is a sticky one. If there is one place in an opening movie title sequence where it is likely to change, it is here. Let's say you are working on an independent feature that gets picked up by a larger distributer; that means you have more executive producers to add to the title sequence. Also, you may run into the need to add "Also Produced By." Much of what this ends up being is controlled by the contracts of the various players involved at the studio, production company, and distributor.

15. Based on the (media name or title) by (Author's Name). This is highly dependent on the project; if the movie is based on an existing work, this credit is necessary.

16. Story by. This credit is employed either when a script has gone through a number of changes or someone wrote a story that the film's script is based on.

17. Writer or written by. The writing credits are highly regulated by the Writers Guild of America, so check to be sure that the credits are done correctly. A maximum of three writers can be credited on a feature, although teams of two can count as one if separated by an ampersand. However, if they worked on the script separately, they will be separated by the word *and*. Writers, like editors, are said to put their thumbprint on the movie.

18. Director or Directed by. The last credit belongs to the director, and the Directors Guild of America only allows one director to be credited as director on the film unless their was a death during production.

Timing/Deliverables

In the case of the sequence I made for **Red Doors**, a low-budget indie feature, the original plan was to finish at DV resolution. But as production progressed and the film was accepted into more festivals, an online HD version was needed and I had to up-res my titles. For the main title sequence, I had to move the animation into a larger document that matched the HD settings, but I had to render the titles by themselves without the background footage so that when the color-corrected final footage was ready, the titles could be placed over the footage.

Which leads to a concern about time. In 2005, I had been working on an older Mac G4 with a meager 2 GB of RAM. I believe I was running After Effects 7 at the time. Renders of the complete title sequence took about eight hours. Now, my little Macbook Pro with 4 GB of RAM and a dual 2.5 gHz Intel processor could run circles around that, but at the time it caused me to raise some concern. I warned my clients that any major changes that forced me to render the complete sequence again meant that we'd lose an entire business day waiting for the old Mac to putt-putt along.

3 **Cont'd** When you're choosing the duration of your title sequence, ask the editor how long the title sequence should be. Set your timeline to be a little longer than that. Title sequences are typically somewhere between 3 and 7 minutes. The thing that you want to avoid is a overlong title sequence that bores the audience. Though it is an important title sequence in the history of filmmaking and to this day a favorite of mine, 1978's **Superman: The Movie's** title sequence goes on **forever**. To the point at which the soundtrack seems like it's getting tired. Title sequences that lose narrative importance will start to wear on an audience.

If it becomes the case that you must show your progress via Web posts, be careful. Why? Well, there's no better way to look like you don't know what you are doing than to have the director ready to view and comment on your work but then discover he can't play the video you've posted on your site for him. Here's the real snag: There are many ways for videos to be unplayable in other formats. So, say you both are on Macs; you might not have all the same codecs, and that can be difficult to diagnose remotely. Do your best to find out whether your client is going to view the video on a Mac or a PC, what OS they are running—basically as much information as possible. Don't get fancy and try an untested format you aren't comfortable with. Also, if you know that the director or producer will be watching on a different format, try your piece on that format yourself. I have on many occasions taken videos to public PCs just so that I could make sure the files would work if the client happened to view them on a PC.

If I am able, I like to meet with the director personally, bring my laptop and present the material in the best possible light. Communication with clients via emails can lead to misunderstandings. I can't tell you how many times a vague comment in an email set me on a course that led to major confusion.

4 **Project-manage your work**. Project management can save you so much time. The best method I have found for project management is pictured here. Make five folders inside a main folder for your project. Use **Original Art** to store all provided elements from the client, so you have a path back to what you were given at the beginning of a project. When you have prepped your files, use the **Save As** feature to save them to your **Photoshop** folder. If a file will be imported into AE, you should save it to this **Photoshop** folder. Save your .aep After Effects project to the **AE Project** folder. Render all your output to the **AE Renders** folder, and after you encode a file to be posted online, save it in the **Posts** folder. Set up this folder system before you do any work on your project.

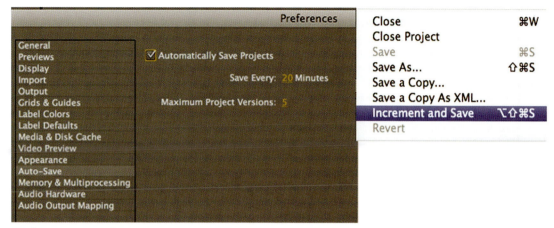

5 **Protect your work**. Two features that are sometimes overlooked can be absolute life-savers when it comes to protecting yourself and your work. These are AE's **Auto-Save** and **Increment and Save**. Auto-Save can be found in the **Preferences**; it has its own heading, and all you have to do is turn it on, choose a time period for Auto-Save to kick in, and choose the max versions of the same project you want. So, the default is 20 minutes, but that might be too long (with powerful software like AE, you can change the world in 20 minutes), while 2 minutes will probably get on your nerves and interrupt your workflow. I usually use somewhere between 4 and 8 minutes.

Increment and Save will do a **Save As** for you and add a number to the end of the filename. I like to do this every time I begin a project in which I'll be making changes from the last version. Often I will do this at the beginning of each day on job (so, if the client wants to go back to where we were two days ago, I can call that version back up in no time). Get into the habit of using these two features; lost work can cost you entire days' worth of time.

6 **Decide on the basic movement of every title**. As we have seen earlier, we are going to want the same basic movements on every title, so the hardest one is the first one. Experiment with movements and animation and decide which is the best, and use this one as a template for every title that will follow. If your client wants to have creative say at this point, bring them in, but this is a very early stage, and some clients who aren't familiar with this process might not want to come in and discuss type animation and fonts with you at this point, so use some discretion here. When we've settled on the style of animation we want, we will duplicate from this one for every other title.

Another helpful decision at this stage is to trim your title to the length you need it. If your trim points are hard to read, you can use **Shift-Command-D** to split a layer.

7 Finish the bed. The *bed* is the background. That might be
animation, footage, photos, or many different things. If it
might change, don't render it out; use **Pre-Compose**. When I
worked on **Red Doors** the editor provided me with an edited
sequence over which the titles would be superimposed. Now,
the footage that was in my AE timeline was never going to be
in the final film, it was only there for me to get my timing.

8 Get approved, and complete the sequence. In this world, the job is over when the client is happy, not when the deadline arrives.
Meet your deadlines, of course, but remember that there will be back and forth between you and the client side, with changes
being made often in that period. Typically the director will back off once she is happy with the creative aspects of your work, and
then the producer will take a more active role in making sure everyone is happy with their credits and that everything looks right.
I know that sounds strange but the cast and crew are concerned about how long their names are up on-screen during the title
sequence, so do your best to give the audience time to read everything and give every important team member their due. Names
can be tough since spellcheck doesn't exactly work with names, so check with someone on the production side that everything is
correctly spelled and displayed.

9 Done-Render to client spec. Keep in mind that the title sequence will have to work with other ongoing aspects of
production. Keep in close contact with the producer and the editor as to exactly what they need from you to complete
the film.

Rendering Your Title Sequence

There are two main editors who work on a film. The **offline editor** is one you're most likely familiar with; this editor is responsible for the creative decision making for the film's final cut. The **online editor** is responsible for assembling the final footage, color-corrected and perfected to match the final editing decisions made by the offline editor.

If the title designer is having her title graphics superimposed over footage from the film, she does her work leaving areas of the screen largely blank, with the exception of the title animation. She will most likely be creating titles with an **alpha channel** so that the titles could be placed over the final footage on software being used to complete the online edit.

This will mean rendering with a format set to some kind of high-resolution image sequence. This can be with TIFFs or Targas or other image sequence style formats. When rendering out to image sequences, make sure that you do it to a folder, because you will be creating hundreds of files. An image sequence literally means one file per frame. At 24–30 frames per second, a 5-minute title sequence is around 1,800 files!

In After Effects, you'll find these settings in the **Output Module Settings**.

Figure 10.1

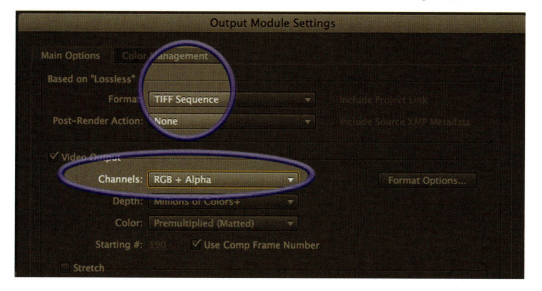

Case Study: Title Sequences by Ex'pression Graduates

College: Ex'pression College for Digital Arts
Instructor: Yael Braha
www.expression.edu

Title: *The Greatest Story Ever Told*
Genre: Drama
Title Designer: Justin Betham
Title Sequence: http://vimeo.com/7929995
Portfolio: www.justinbetham.com

Synopsis of Movie

The film is about a man struggling with schizophrenia and his ability to adapt his disorder into his daily regime. His home has a basement where he converses to inanimate objects, reasons with them, and also manages to receive advice from them about his daily life.

Description

The camera moves slowly into the pieced-otogether world, traveling through the front door of a dark house, down a lonely hallway, passing by spinning swirls that complement the feeling of confusion and chaos.

We travel down a spiral stairway and end in the basement, where a paper puppet resembling the main character is hung from the ceiling in a room filled with spirals spinning in the background. I chose to portray him as a puppet for his lack of control over changes in his personality. As the camera arrives at the puppet, the screen fades to black and a reveal of the title of the film fades in. After the title fades out, it transitions into the actual basement, where the film begins and where most of the film takes place.

The end title sequence starts exactly where the beginning titles finish, and the camera reverses out of the "handmade," isolated world. At the end of the film, the main character encounters a failed attempt to interact with a person from the outside world (a girl he met on a dating Web site). He ends up in the basement and experiences a mental breakdown. The film fades out and the camera reverses out of the room, away from the puppet, back out the stairway, and all the way out of the house.

Creative Justification

The title sequence was built to look like a fake, handmade set pieced together with a combination of heavy, thick paper and tape to resemble the main character's pieced-together thoughts.

As far as colors, I utilized a desaturated, minimal color palette. The mix of blue and gray hues give a cold, dark feeling of a calm emptiness. The choice of lack of color resembles the emptiness the main character feels. The lack of saturation also resembles his feelings of loneliness and confusion from his long hours spent in his basement.

The choice of typeface is Goudy Old Style. This typeface is a mix of gently curved, rounded serifs and hard diamond-shaped dots in the *i* and *j*. The mix of rounded curves and harsh diamond edges resembles the main character's mix of personalities. In the film, his mood shifts from being polite, level-headed, and pleasant to suddenly being overwhelmed with sadness, frustration, loneliness, and confusion.

Software and Techniques

The scene was created and rendered in Cinema 4D and assembled in After Effects, where typography, color adjustments, and music were applied.

Music: *Hajnal (dawn)*, by Venetian Snares.

Figure 10.2a Still Frames from "Greatest Story Ever Told", designed by Justin Betham.

Figure 10.2b

Figure 10.2c

Figure 10.2d

Figure 10.2e

Figure 10.2f

Figure 10.2g

Figure 10.2h

Figure 10.2i

Figure 10.2j

Figure 10.2k

Figure 10.2l

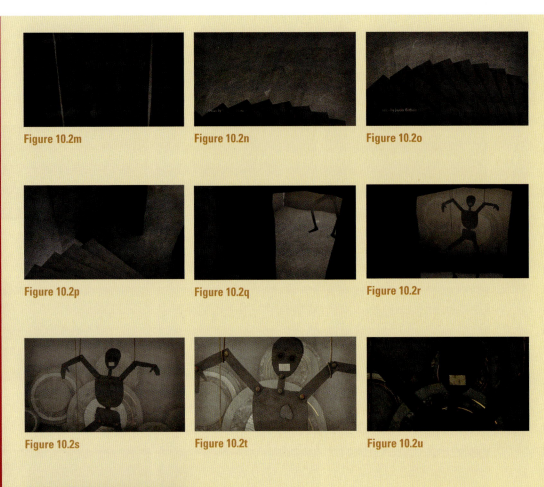

Figure 10.2m

Figure 10.2n

Figure 10.2o

Figure 10.2p

Figure 10.2q

Figure 10.2r

Figure 10.2s

Figure 10.2t

Figure 10.2u

Figure 10.2v

Title: *Seen and Not Heard*
Genre: Drama/Dark Comedy
Title Designer: Ame Garrucho

Synopsis of Movie

A deaf man surrounds himself with a world of imaginary sounds. He later decides to get a cochlear implant to really hear the world. Now, being able to hear, the man is not sure if that's what he really wants.

Description

All of the credits are handwritten and jittery to add to the organic/handmade feel of the textures in the background and masking tape borders. The credits also animate on in American Sign Language, to incorporate the theme of deafness from the film. Since the film did not have any background story behind the main character, the title sequence was meant to show a little bit of his life.

The entire sequence is based on the main character's daily routine before he goes to work in the first scene, but with a twist. There are imaginary sounds that the man creates in his mind throughout the piece as he proceeds with his routine of getting out of bed, walking to the restroom, washing his hands, putting his clothes on, etc. All the sounds don't match exactly with the objects, to show what the man "thinks" he is hearing.

Creative Justification

The title sequence is inspired by Shadowplay Studio's **Juno** title sequence. The look and feel were developed to incorporate the unusual sound effects with organic images. Since the sounds are jarring, the visuals needed to match that and give off the same feeling. A stop-motion and handmade feel seemed to be a good way to merge the two together.

Software and Techniques

Green Screen Production, Final Cut Pro 7, Adobe Illustrator, Adobe Photoshop, and After Effects.

Technical Challenges

Creating a jarring sound design with found sounds and handwriting credits several times to create a loop.

Figure 10.3a Still Frames from "Seen and Not Heard", designed by Ame Garrucho.

Figure 10.3b

Figure 10.3c

Figure 10.3d

Figure 10.3e

Figure 10.3f

Figure 10.3g

Figure 10.3h

Figure 10.3i

Figure 10.3j

Figure 10.3k

Figure 10.3l

Title: *The Better Angels*
Genre: Drama
Title Designer: Tina Chen
Title Sequence: http://vimeo.com/1202760
Portfolio: www.tina-chen.com

Synopsis of Movie

A retired history professor escapes from his son's home carrying a .38 revolver and the unflinching belief that he is Abraham Lincoln. He roams through parks and encounters various people along the way. It turns out that he is suffering from Alzheimer's disease and dementia.

Description

Main titles: The background is a historic letter written by Abraham Lincoln that slowly moves across the screen. The production company name fades in and out, followed by the name of the film and a single falling leaf. As the leaf falls, the letters of the title fall with it.

End titles: The background is a historic letter written by Abraham Lincoln that slowly moves across the screen. Groups of leaves blow on screen from the left and continue to move across the screen, then blow off screen to the right. The cast names fade in and blow off screen with the leaves. The leaves stop blowing as the crew names fade in and out.

Creative Justification

On one side, the historic letter gives depth and texture to the background while still having some relation to the film's storyline. On the other, falling leaves were used to represent the ephemeral nature of life and to tie the titles to the main setting of the film; the majority of the film takes place in park settings. Using the leaves without any photos or footage gives the audience a feeling of fantasy or an altered reality. The slow falling movement of the leaves and the minimal colors of browns, reds, and golds represent the somber, dramatic pace of the film.

Software and Techniques

Adobe Illustrator, Photoshop, After Effects, Maxon Cinema 4D.

Technical Challenges

Creating a realistic falling movement for the leaves.

Figure 10.4a Still Frames from "The Better Angels", designed by Tina Chen.

Figure 10.4b

Figure 10.4c

Figure 10.4d

Figure 10.4e

Figure 10.4f

Figure 10.42g

Figure 10.4h

Figure 10.4i

Figure 10.4j

Figure 10.4k

Figure 10.4l

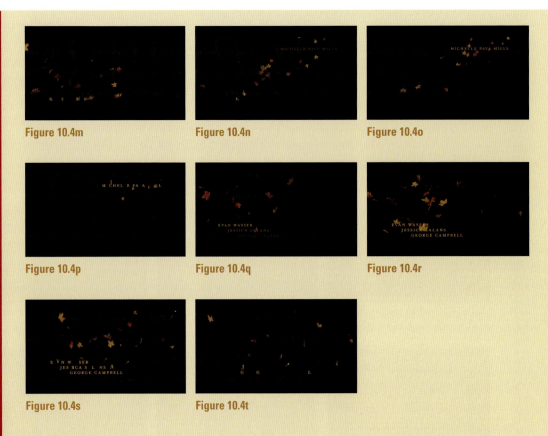

Figure 10.4m   Figure 10.4n   Figure 10.4o

Figure 10.4p   Figure 10.4q   Figure 10.4r

Figure 10.4s   Figure 10.4t

Title: *Number 24*
Genre: Suspenseful Drama/Horror
Title Designer: Iris Azadi
Title Sequence: http://irisazadi.com/number.html
Portfolio: www.IrisAzadi.com

Synopsis of Movie

A serial killer, who claims the charms and keepsakes of his victims, is about to take his 24th woman when the tables are turned.

Description

The style of the title design was minimal but detail oriented. I left much of the screen's real estate empty but used textures and subtle blemishes to set the mood. The font choice was Baskerville Old Face, a strong serif font with character. The color palette overall was muted and desaturated, giving the titles a drowned and dark feeling (without being a typical horror movie title sequence).

Creative Justification

The objective was to set the tone and mood of the movie without giving away its plot. I used information that is implied in the movie but never shown, using it to tell a backstory. By using ambiguous items, such as the silver and gold chain, Polaroids, and news clippings, I set up the beginning of the movie as though these items belonged to the 23 other women who were not shown in the movie. The end title credits are very similar to the opening titles except they are now covered in drops of blood. I did this only in the end, to keep the ambiguous tone in the opening titles.

Software and Techniques

C4D, AE, Video.

Music

IX, by Gregg Kowalsky; stock photo of woman, by razee81.

Figure 10.5a Still Frames from "Number 24", designed by Iris Azad.

Figure 10.5b

Figure 10.5c

Figure 10.5d

Figure 10.5e

Figure 10.5f

Figure 10.5g

Figure 10.5h

Figure 10.5i

Figure 10.5j

Figure 10.5k

Figure 10.5l

Title: *The Better Angels*
Genre: Drama
Title Designer: Conrad McLeod
Portfolio: www.conradmcleod.com

Synopsis of Movie

A retired history professor wanders into a public park with a pistol, all the while believing that he is Abraham Lincoln.

Creative Description/Treatment

Initially, I had incorporated other elements into the titles to foreshadow the main character's belief that he is Abraham Lincoln, but I decided on a more simple and ambiguous approach.

In this final version, a shattered clock represents the main character's fragmented perception of reality and failing memory. The gears and letterforms are scattered throughout an empty space, and as the camera slowly pushes in, the letterforms tumble into place and pass by and out of the shallow depth of field. The use of a sepia color palette and serif font reflects the historical aspect of the film as well as a solo piano piece to help set the dramatic tone.

Software and Techniques

Cinema 4D, After Effects, and Photoshop.

Figure 10.6a Still Frames from "The Better Angels", designed by Conrad McLeod.

Figure 10.6b

Figure 10.6c

Figure 10.6d

Figure 10.6e

Figure 10.6f

Figure 10.6g

Figure 10.6h

Figure 10.6i

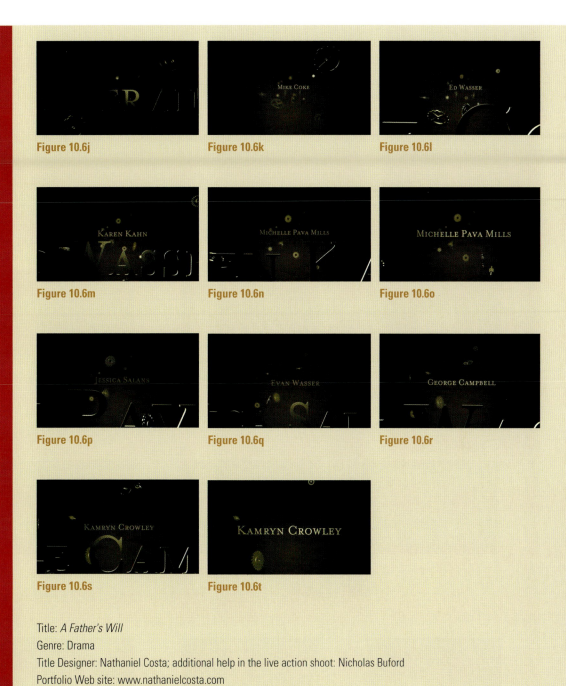

Figure 10.6j

Figure 10.6k

Figure 10.6l

Figure 10.6m

Figure 10.6n

Figure 10.6o

Figure 10.6p

Figure 10.6q

Figure 10.6r

Figure 10.6s

Figure 10.6t

Title: *A Father's Will*
Genre: Drama
Title Designer: Nathaniel Costa; additional help in the live action shoot: Nicholas Buford
Portfolio Web site: www.nathanielcosta.com

Synopsis of Movie

Richard, a soon-to-be father struggling with a fatal case of cancer, begins an experimental treatment, keeping him in a suspended state of hibernation, and awakens unaged 70 years into the future.

Description

The title sequences for this film are meant to simulate the main character's experience of his experimental medical treatment from a first-person point of view.

Creative Justification

The title sequence for *A Father's Will* explores undefined aspects of the plot, making the titles an essential part of the storytelling process.

Software and Techniques

AE, C4D, Live Action, Still Pictures.

Figure 10.7a Still Frames from "A Father's Will", designed by Nathaniel Costa.

Figure 10.7b

Figure 10.7c

Figure 10.7d

Figure 10.7e

Figure 10.7f

Figure 10.7g

Figure 10.7h

Figure 10.7i

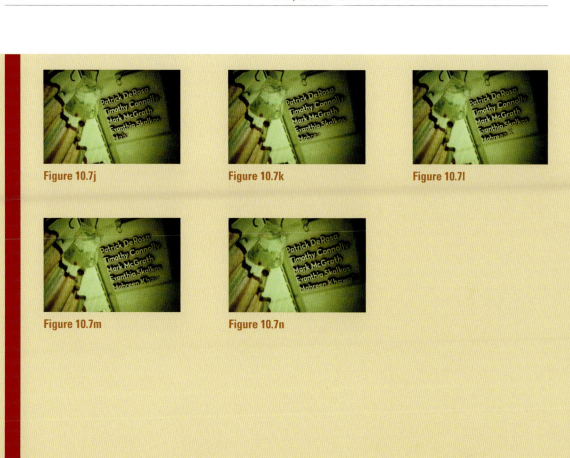

Figure 10.7j

Figure 10.7k

Figure 10.7l

Figure 10.7m

Figure 10.7n

RESOURCES

Websites

AIGA Design Archives: http://designarchives.aiga.org/
Art Directors Guild & Scenic, Title and Graphic Artists: www.artdirectors.org
Beck, Jerry, Cartoon Research–Original Titles: www.cartoonresearch.com/titles.html
Daily Motion: www.dailymotion.com
Forget the Film, Watch the Titles: www.watchthetitles.com
Hill, Steven, Movie Title Screens Page: www.shillpages.com/movies/index2.shtml
The Art of the Title Sequence: www.artofthetitle.com
Internet Movie Database: www.imdb.com
Motionographer: www.motionographer.com
Movie Title Stills Collection: www.annyas.com/screenshots/
Title Design Project: www.titledesignproject.com/
Titulos De Credito: http://tituloscredito.blogspot.com
Tylski, Alexandre, Generique & Cinema: www.generique-cinema.net/

Title Design Studios

21Boom: www.21boom.com
Big Film Design: www.bigfilmdesign.com
Blind: www.blind.com
Blur: www.blur.com
Digital Kitchen: www.d-kitchen.com
DR Film Design: www.drfilmdesign.com
Energi Design: www.clickenergi.com
Gunshop: http://gunshop.tv/
Kompost: www.kompostnyc.com
Imaginary Forces: www.imaginaryforces.com
Jamie Caliri: www.jamiecaliri.com
Mk12: http://mk12.com/
Momoco: www.momoco.co.uk
Pic Agency: www.picagency.com
Picture Mill: www.picturemill.com
Prologue: www.prologue.com
Reel Fx Entertainment: www.reelfx.com
River Road Films: www.riverroadfilms.com
Shadowplay: www.shadowplaystudio.com
Susan Bradley Film Design: www.susan-bradley.com
Trollbäck+Company: www.trollback.com
Voodoodog: www.voodoodog.com
yU+co: www.yuco.com

doi: 10.1016/B978-0-240-81419-3.00016-7

BIBLIOGRAPHY

Albers, J. (1975). *Interaction of Color*. Yale University Press.

Arditi, A., & Cho, J. (2007). *Letter Case and Text Legibility in Normal and Low Vision*. Arlene R. Gordon Research Institute, Lighthouse International.

Aynsley, J. (2005). *Pioneers of Modern Graphic Design*. London: Michael Beazley.

Bass, S. (1960). Film titles: a new field for the graphic designer. *Graphis, 16*(89), 208–216.

Bass, S. (1966). Movement, Film, Communication. In G. Kepes (Ed.), *Sign, image, symbol* (pp. 200–205). New York: G. Braziller.

Bass, S. (1969). Film titles: a new field for the graphic designer. In L. Jacobs (Ed.), *The emergence of film art: the evolution and development of the motion picture as an art. From 1900 to the present* (pp. 382–383). New York: Hopkinson and Blake.

Bass Instinct (1995). *Creative Review, 48*.

Bellantoni, J. & Woolman, M. (1999). *Type in Motion: Innovations in Digital Graphics*. New York: Rizzoli.

Bankston, D. (2005). The Color-Space Conundrum. *American Cinematographer*.

Benson, J. L. (2000). *Greek Color Theory and The Four Elements*. Amherst: University of Massachusetts.

Benson, J., Olewiler, K., & Broden, N. (2004). *Typography for Mobile Phone Devices: The Design of the QUALCOMM Sans Font Family*. Punchcut.

Birren, F. (2006). *Color Psychology and Color Therapy: A Factual Study of the Influence of Color on Human Life*. Kessinger Publishing.

Bornstein, M. (1975). *The Influence on Visual Perception on Culture*. Max-Planck-Institut für Psychiatric and Yael University.

Borsatti, C. (2007). *I grandi incipit del cinema. La chiave d'ingresso del film*. DeAgostini Editore, Collana scuola golden.

Box, H. C. (2003). *Set Lighting Technician's Handbook* (3rd ed.). Focal Press.

Boxer, S. (2000). Making a Fuss Over Opening Credits; Film Titles Offer a Peek at the Future in More Ways Than One. *The New York Times*.

Brown, B. (2007). *Motion Picture and Video Lighting* (2nd ed.). Focal Press.

Carlson, V., & Carlson, S. (1991). *Professional Lighting Handbook* (2nd ed.). Focal Press.

Chris, M., & Meyer, T. (2007). *Creating Motion Graphics with After Effects* (4th ed.). Focal Press.

Codrington, A., & Poyner, R. (2003). *Kyle Cooper*. London: Laurence King Publishing.

Cook, P. (2008). *The Cinema Book* (3rd ed.). London: British Film Institute.

Credit to the opening titles. (2003). *Design Week*.

Curran, S. (2001). *Motion Graphics: Graphic Design for Broadcast and Film*. Rockport Publishers, Inc.

Design Museum London. (2005). Saul Bass, Graphic Designer (1920–1996). *Design at the Design Museum*. Retrieved from http://designmuseum.org/design/saul-bass.

Eastman Kodak Company. (1970). *Basic titling and animation for motion pictures*. New York: Eastman Kodak Company.

Foster, J. (2009). *Lights, Camera, Action*. Pro Video Coalition.

Geffner, D. (1997). First Things First: David Geffner on the Art of Film Titles. *Filmmaker Magazine*.

Griffith, D. W. (1915). *The Birth of a Nation*.

Guggenheim, D. (2006). *An Inconvenient Truth*.

Hess, J. (2004). *Napoleon Dynamite*.

Hitchcock, A. (1958). *Vertigo*.

Hitchcock, A. (1959). *North by Northwest*.

Hitchcock, A. (1960). *Psycho*.

Jonze, S. (2009). *Where the Wild Things Are*.

Kubrick, S. (1964). *Dr. Strangelove*.

Leterrier, L. (2008). *The Incredible Hulk*.

Lee, A. (2003). *Hulk*.

Lynch, D. (1997). *Lost Highway*.

Maddin, G. (1997). *Twilight of the Ice Nymphs*.

Milestone, L. (1960). *Ocean's Eleven*.

Nair, M. (2001). *Monsoon Wedding*.

Niccol, A. (2005). *Lord of War*.

Noé, G. (2002). *Irréversible*.

Park, C. (2005). *Sympathy for Lady Vengeance*.

Pasolini, P. P. (1966). *Uccellacci e Uccellini*.

Polanski, R. (1965). *Repulsion*.

Reitman, J. (2007). *Juno*.

Reitman, J. (2009). *Up in the Air*.

Ritchie, G. (2000). *Snatch*.

Ritchie, G. (2008). *Rocknrolla*.

Schnabel, J. (2007). *The Diving Bell and the Butterfly*.

Silberling, B. (2004). *Lemony Snicket's A Series of Unfortunate Events*.

Slade, B. (1979). *The Partridge Family*.

Snider, Z. (2004). *Dawn of the Dead*.

Snider, Z. (2009). *Watchmen*.

Spielberg, S. (2002). *Catch Me If You Can*.

Truffault, F. (1966). *Fahrenheit 451*.

Tykwer, T. (1998). *Run Lola Run*.

Wegener, P. (1920). *Der Golem*.

Weitz, P. (2009). *Cirque du Freak: The Vampire's Assistant*.

INDEX

Note: Page numbers followed by *b* indicates boxes, *f* indicates figures and *t* indicates tables.

Tone, 124, 124*f*, 267, 268
  defined, 268
  harmonics, 268
  overtones, 268
  see also Sound
Tracking
  defined, 78–79
  fonts and, 79
  typefaces and, 79
Tracking animation, 295
  After Effects tutorial, 295*b*
  defined, 295
Tracking option (After Effects),
    296*f*
Transitions
  alternative, 27–28
  decision-making factors for, 9
  match frame, 10–11
  Nimmo, Stacy on, 107
  Radatz, Ben on, 217, 218
  title sequence, 9–30
Treatment, as pre-production
    step, 5
Triadic color harmony, 125, 125*f*
Triple title cards, 30
Trollbäck, Jacob
  Pop!Tech 2008 case study, 260
  TED 2009 case study, 171, 171*f*
TrueType, 80
Tungsten light fixtures, 131
Two-dimensional motion
    tracking, 12–13
Type 1 (PostScript), 80
Type
  animation, moving from After
      Effects to Flash, 98–99
  animation (Flash), 96–97, 97*b*
  editing from Illustrator
      document, 193*b*
  horror-jittery, 333
  importing Photoshop
      documents and, 193
  large blocks of, 207*b*
  Matrix raining, 338
  Photoshop layer styles with,
      147–155
  size, 76
  Superman-style explosive, 335
  synching with sound, 279*b*
Type tool (After Effects), 200*f*,
    321*f*, 338*f*

Typefaces
  The Alphabet Conspiracy case
      study, 102
  bitmap, 75
  color combinations for, 127–129
  custom, creating, 91–93
  display, 75
  do's and don'ts for, 76–77
  emotional qualities, 74
  end scroll, 322
  kerning and, 78
  ligatures, 76
  lowercase, 76
  mixed case, 76
  monospaced, 75
  moving, for the Web, 93–98
  properties for, 75
  sans serif, 75
  script, 75
  serif, 74
  small caps, 76
  stroke weight, 76
  tracking and, 79
  type size, 76
  uppercase, 76
  x-heights, 75
  see also Fonts
Typographic narrative, 79*b*
Typography
  function of, 73
  Websites for, 80*b*
Typos, avoiding, 32*b*

U
Uccellacci e Uccellini (Pasolini),
    54–55
Uppercase
  defined, 76
  Legibility Index (LI), 85, 85*t*
Urbanicity case study, 282*b*
  color use, 283
  concept and inspiration, 282
  Holmes, Steve, 282
  influences, 287
  research, 287

V
Variable frame rates, 224, 224*b*
Vector images, 157
  defined, 157
  resizing, 168

Video
  DI workflow, 37
  end scrolls with, 322
  frame size, 38, 218*t*
Video cameras
  ASA rating, 230
  color-balancing, 133–134
  default recording speed, 220
  defined, 215
  focus rings, 227
  frame format, 218
  framing, 239
  f-stops, 229
  white balance alteration, 134
  see also cameras
Video-based title sequence, 14
Virtual cameras
  creating title sequences with,
      256–259
  functioning of, 256
Von Goethe, Johann Wolfgang,
    115–116

W
Warm colors, 116, 116*t*, 119*t*
Waveform monitors, 247
Web
  titles, 87–89
  video displays, 93
  viewing considerations, 93–94
White balance
  defined, 133
  video camera alteration and, 134
White Noise option (Audacity), 275*f*
Wide shot (WS), 239
Wiggler panel (After Effects), 334*f*
The Women (Cukor), 47
Workflow, importing text/files,
    191–193
  composition, 191–192
  files into After Effects, 191
  footage, 191
Workflow, title sequence, 5–7,
    163–171
  bed completion, 358*f*
  building and creating, 354
  concept pitching, 355*f*
  concept planning, 354*f*
  getting approval, 358*f*
  with graphic design
      department, 165